TO BRAVE EVERY DANGER

Judith Cook has published books on a variety of subjects from current affairs to Elizabethan theatre as well as biographies of Daphne du Maurier, J. B. Priestly and that of Mary Bryant in **'To Brave Every Danger'**. She has just published her third in a series of historical thrillers set in Elizabethan England with more to come. She has also written extensively for the theatre and from 1990 to 1992 was Arts Council resident dramatist in Plymouth. Her association with Cornwall goes back to childhood and she now lives in Newlyn with her partner, Martin Green, and two cats.

'In my view, Judith Cook's book knocks spots off stories of Dick Turpin or Robin Hood and it's nothing short of scandalous that the story hasn't been published sooner'. *Mail on Sunday*

'Have many hankies ready, there's bound to be a film of this one'. *Evening Standard*

'An extraordinary book ..it makes you wonder what else we don't know about women's history'. *Glasgow Herald*

'Every bit as much an organiser as Flora MacDonald, as tough as Boadicea and quite as brave as Grace Darling. **A haunting book**' *Literary Review*

The Epic life of Highwaywoman

Mary Bryant

TO BRAVE EVERY DANGER

Judith Cook

TRURAN

First published in 1993 by Macmillan London Ltd

This edition published in 1999 by
Truran
Croft Prince, Mount Hawke, Truro, Cornwall TR4 8EE
www.truranbooks.co.uk

Truran is an imprint of Truran Books Ltd

Reprinted 2001
Reprinted 2003

Cover illustration 'A Fishergirl, Newlyn' (oil on canvas) by
Edwin Harris (1855-1906)
Private collection/Courtesy of Simon Gillespie
Studio/Bridgeman Art Library, London/New York

ISBN 1 85022 126 X

Printed and bound in Cornwall by R Booth Ltd
& Troutbeck Press, Antron Hill, Penryn TR10 9HH

Main text set in Bodoni

CONTENTS

ACKNOWLEDGEMENTS

Writing this book would not have been possible without all the assistance I received from libraries and records offices. I would, therefore, like to thank most sincerely the following: The Algemeen Rijksarchief, The Hague; the British Library; the British Newspaper Library; Cornwall County Archive; Cornwall County Record Office; the London Library; London University Library; the Mitchell Library of Sydney, New South Wales (home of the greatest collection of material on the early days of the penal settlement at Port Jackson) and the Public Record Office.

I am also very grateful indeed for the assistance I received from the Authors' Fund of the Society of Authors, which enabled research to be undertaken in Australia, and to Krissoulla Syrmis who tracked down so many papers for me in the Mitchell Library.

BOOK ONE

CORNWALL

CHAPTER ONE

Interesting Times

MARY BRYANT was a mariner's daughter from Cornwall who was, in turn, a highway robber, the mistress of an officer on a prison hulk, one of only a handful of convicts who escaped from Botany Bay, and the navigator of one of the world's most incredible voyages in an open boat. When, finally, she returned captive to England, she was defended by James Boswell. Yet she remains almost unknown in this country, while in Holland, although her life only briefly touched Dutch history, she is considered a 'national heroine'. Among Australians she has recently begun to take her rightful place in the early period of their history, even though she spent less than four years of her life in Botany Bay. In England, however, the country where she was born, grew up, and to which she finally returned, there is no such recognition.

A dark-haired, grey-eyed Cornish girl, she was never a beauty, yet those who met her seldom forgot her. She haunted the memories of those who came into contact with her, flitting like a bright wraith through the journals of the literate who made that first momentous voyage to New South Wales.

She was, indeed, a remarkable person but she also lived in a remarkable era. There is a well-known Chinese curse which says: 'May you live in interesting times,' and Mary certainly did, since she was born into an age of unprecedented economic and political change both in England and abroad. Not only were there revolutions in America and France, which the Establishment feared would 'infect' the population at home, but also the effects of the Industrial Revolution were sweeping the working people off the land to work in the mines, mills and factories. For those who grew up in the eighteenth century nothing would ever be the same again.

Mary was a child of those times and was, to a large extent, a victim of them, reaching her teens during the American War of Independence and its aftermath of economic bankruptcy. She grew up in a land where a fast-increasing underclass was kept down ruthlessly by a property-owning, increasingly brutal regime, employing a ferocious penal system. While this helped mould her character, and certainly set her on the path that would lead her in chains to the other side of the world, she was also greatly influenced by the remote county in which she spent her childhood.

For the modern-day traveller who spends hours on the train or battles with the roads in his car, Cornwall might seem a very long way from anywhere. In the middle of the eighteenth century it appeared incredibly remote, another world, cut off by its rivers and moorlands even from neighbouring Devon. It was a county of small towns, even smaller villages and tiny hamlets of grey stone houses, their walls three-foot thick to keep out the rain brought in by the prevailing westerly winds. Physically, of course, the county remains much as it was. On the north coast, the dark, savage cliffs rise hundreds of feet above a boiling sea, but in Mary's day it was a place of scattered hamlets and crofts and few people. Then, as now, the south was a different world, one of wide bays, wooded rivers and estuaries, the two great harbours of Fowey and Falmouth, and peaceful towns and villages. If we curse the roads of Devon and Cornwall today, spare a thought for the eighteenth-century traveller, rattling and bumping along in his coach if he were well-to-do, saddle-sore and weary if he had a horse, and limping along with blistered feet if on foot. When Mary's parents were newly-weds there was only one major road running down the spine of Cornwall and a single bridge, well inland. Travellers coming into the county from Exeter and Plymouth either faced the long inland route or took their chance on one of the numerous Tamar ferries, the roads down to which were notorious for highwaymen and footpads (highway robbers who couldn't afford a horse).

You are never far from the sea wherever you live in Cornwall, a sea which then provided food and livelihoods for a far larger proportion of the inhabitants than it does now, a sea which could, and often did, kill. The Broad family, into which Mary was born, were descendants of a people who had once had their own language, akin to Welsh and Breton, which had not long died out. Fiercely independent and deeply suspicious of anything outside their own borders, the Cornish had rebelled on a number of occasions, from the Peasants' Revolt onwards, marching out to fight against king and government. One such episode is still commemorated in Cornwall's 'anthem', 'And Shall Trelawney Die?'. Yet, unpredictable as ever, when the Civil War came, most fought for the Royalist cause, stubbornly hanging out long after the rest of the country had accepted Cromwell.

Before the 1750s, there were few signs of the changes which were about to take place. Indeed, Cornwall had hardly altered from the days when the medieval pirates, the 'Fowey Gallants', had sailed out of Mary's home town or when the Rashleighs had provided a ship to fight the Armada.

The most dramatic impact had been made by the Civil War, which had left behind a bitter legacy, still tangible a century later. Many savage battles had been fought in Cornwall, one right on Mary's doorstep. Here, Richard Grenville, the King's General in the West, had placed his army on the outskirts of Fowey on the iron-age hill fort of Castle Dor, legendary 'castle' of King Mark and the setting for the tragedy of Tristan and Iseult. Grenville had enticed the Parliamentary troops to do battle with him on the hill, then had forced the fleeing soldiers down to Par marshes where, caught between the incoming tide and a further battalion of the King's men, they were either put to the sword or drowned. The war had divided families and members of those families one from another. Even in Mary's day there was still no love lost between the big landowners in the Fowey area, the Rashleighs and Robartes, who had fought on opposite sides, while a member of the Treffry family had been one of those who had signed Charles I's death warrant.

In Mary's time, there were three major industries in Cornwall – mining, fishing and working on the land – and the Broads were related to people engaged in all three. Indeed in many instances men worked in more than one: a miner might well have a smallholding where he grew his own food, or would work in the mines in the winter and spring and on the boats in the summer and autumn. They were able to do this because the system of employment in the Cornish mines was unique. Most miners favoured the 'tribute' system, whereby a group would get together and arrange to work a specific 'pitch' at an agreed price (easily extractable ore fetching a lower one), sharing out the proceeds between them. These miners looked down on those prepared to work for weekly wages. It was, of course, a risky business, although before the arrival of the steam-pumping engine (which, as we shall see, was soon to change everything dramatically) there was a limit to how deep a mine could be worked, and mine owners could still lay off their workers whenever the price of copper or tin fluctuated. At this time most miners lived adjacent to their small local mines, their neat rows of cottages close to its boundary, each with a small patch of garden for growing 'tatties' and 'neaps' (turnips). The still unenclosed common land provided grazing for pigs and sometimes the odd cow.

Off shore, pilchards, the county's great glittering silver harvest, dominated the Cornish economy, providing not only a staple food, but also an extremely lucrative export. The largest shoals came with the summer, the secondary, smaller ones, in the autumn. Their arrival heralded frantic activity involving everyone living in or around ports such as Fowey, as well as the smaller harbours and coves. Women and children joined the men in offloading the fish, the women leaving their babies and toddlers to the older children as they worked at the pressing, to release the oil, before salting them down in barrels. Even the waste made a fertilizer for the land.

During the winter months, coastal families in Cornwall depended to a very large extent on salted pilchards for their survival, which is why the year 1786, when the 'harvest' failed was so significant for the county in general and for Mary in particular. The fish brought much needed money into the local economy, tens of thousands of hogsheads were exported annually to Mediterranean countries for Friday and Lenten eating, taken by local sailing ships over to France, across the Bay of Biscay to Santander, and down through the Straits of Gibraltar to Italy. Mariners like Mary's father, William Broad, made the journey time after time, bringing back, in place of the fish, oranges, lemons, spices and other exotic cargoes. The vital importance of the pilchard shoals to the people of Cornwall cannot be underestimated and Mary would have learned, as soon as she could talk, the old rhyme:

> Here's a health to the Pope may he live to repent,
> And add just six months to the term of his Lent,
> And tell all his vassals from Rome to the Poles,
> There's nothing like pilchards for saving their souls!

For women, outside the seasonal help on the harvest or with the pilchards, work was very limited and it was not until the end of the century that they were employed as surface workers in the mines. The only employment was service in the households of the gentry, merchants and businessmen or the larger farmers.

Low incomes, long distances from major centres of population, along with easy access to the coast with its hundreds of hidden coves, led, inevitably, to large-scale smuggling. By the mid-eighteenth century Cornwall's economy was highly dependent on the 'Free Trade'. Vast amounts of contraband were brought in over the Channel, losing the government hundreds of thousands of pounds in revenue every year. Brandy and tobacco were the two biggest money-spinners, but there was also a market for wine, silk, muslin and, during the period of a punitive salt tax, salt from France. By the mid-1750s it was both so accepted and so prevalent that cargoes were regularly being run ashore even in broad daylight, before being carried openly through the streets. Everyone had a hand in it, from the landed gentry, through the local squirarchy and the Church, down to the humblest family living in a tiny cottage. Persuading a local jury to convict a free-trader, even when caught redhanded, was extremely difficult, leading to the old joke about the smuggler who was told by the judge, 'You will leave this Court with no stain upon your character except that you have been acquitted by a Bodmin jury.'

This attitude to smuggling, a trade which hardly diminished even during the Napoleonic Wars, perhaps helps to explain Mary's own attitude to authority. Cornishmen saw no wrong whatsoever in participating whole-heartedly in a practice which drove the government to impotent fury. Wrecking, however, is more of a legend than a reality. For people living hand-to-mouth, a wreck might well have been a godsend – in fact in St Just parish they would pray not that there 'would be wrecks, O Lord, but that if they be, then that they be sent ashore here to the benefit of the poor inhabitants'. Making use of the goods which came ashore was one thing, taking human life another and there is no proof that ships were ever lured on to the shore by false lights, whatever romantic novelists might say. There was no need, the savage coast provided wrecks a-plenty.

Indeed, life in eighteenth-century Cornwall bore precious little resemblance to that portrayed in most popular novels, being anything but romantic. Marriages between dashing land-owners and beautiful country girls were pretty thin on the ground. The classes kept to themselves – the rich in their vast estates, the rest in their small neat houses built of stone or lath-and-plaster. A typical cottage, such as that in which Mary grew up, had a kitchen dominated by a big open fireplace, where the food was cooked either over a turf fire or in the 'cloam' (clay) oven in which furze was burned to heat it before the bread or pasties were put inside to bake. Water was carried in from the streams or a local well. Sanitation was at best an earth closet, at worst a hole in the ground.

Most ordinary folk never travelled more than a few miles from their homes, and for those that did it was often easier to go by sea or river, even though by 1754 a new toll road was under construction. The wealthy had their carriages, local carriers their carts, but most goods were carried by pack animals. Anyone contemplating, say, a trip to London, would face a long and gruelling journey, particularly if on horseback, subject to the endless delays of wind and weather and the growing danger of highway robbery.

> Ride to Lunnon on a hoss? See what money it do cost!
> Rubs us raw and rubs us bare, afore we do get half way theer.

In London, that remote seat of government, wits described Cornwall as being 'rich only in Members of Parliament', for the county was entirely composed of rotten boroughs. This was another reason for the cynicism of the population towards 'Lunnon' politics, for this small county, which in 1754 had a population of only 135,000, returned no fewer than forty-four MPs drawn, as one might expect, from the landed gentry – the Rashleighs and Treffrys of Fowey, the Edgecumbes of Mount Edgecumbe and Cothele, the Carews of Antony and the Boscawens of Falmouth. Only during election time were the handful of people eligible to vote courted by their so-called representatives.

Fowey even had a direct link with the great Pitt family, for in 1740 Thomas and William, eager that Thomas should also get into politics, privately surveyed all the rotten boroughs most ripe for buying and came up with some twenty-one, all in Cornwall. This suited them very well, for they had already bought the ancient estate of Boconnoc, near Fowey, from Lady Mohun, who had been forced to sell following the death of her extravagant husband in a duel. Tiny Fowey returned two MPs, voted in by forty-five worthies. One was usually a Rashleigh, the other a Treffry of Place House, the mansion which still stands in the centre of the town. If it was not a Treffry, then it was an Edgecumbe. In 1746, when Thomas was trying for Parliament, Fowey was represented by a Jonathan Rashleigh and a George Edgecumbe and although the Pitts spent over two thousands pounds, a vast sum then, on trying to 'buy' the two seats, the voters of Fowey took the money but returned their own men. At least they were wined and dined. Further west in Hayle, the local MP did not bother with bribes – as he owned most of the property in the town he simply told his voters that if they did not vote for him he would turn them out on to the street.

Nepotism ruled, not only in the handing out of Parliamentary seats, but also in the lucrative church livings, as these too were the gift of the gentry, whose younger sons often went into Holy Orders, whether they had a vocation or not. If they had more than one living, these would be farmed out, usually to ill-paid, ill-educated curates. Cornish people were naturally devout, but the openly comfortable lifestyles of so many wealthy parsons, with their grand vicarages, servants and worldly social lives, drove thousands of them to listen eagerly to the words of John Wesley and embrace Methodism. Methodism brought losses as well as gains, however, for it offered the people justice in the next world, something which would prove exceptionally useful to a government terrified that the populace would follow the example of the Americans and the French and start asking for it in this.

The first hurdle for any eighteenth-century child was surviving to adulthood. Families were large, but infant mortality was high and all too often babies appearing under 'Baptisms' in the parish register are noted under 'Deaths' a few years, or even days, later. Epidemics of the childhood diseases, such as smallpox, typhoid, measles, whooping cough or the most feared scourge of all, diphtheria, killed rich and poor alike, as the sad memorials in Fowey parish church show – like that erected by William Toller, who had eight children, four of whom died before they reached the age of three, and of another family, the Stephens, which reads:

Four babes, two brothers and two sisters, we,
Were lovelie branches of one fruitful tree,
Our parents present joy and future hope,
But deathes rude hand did us in budding crop.

An earlier prolific Treffry, John, who died in August 1590, is noted as 'having by Jane, ye daughter of Reinald Mohun,

Esquyer, one daughter; and by Emlyn, his second wife, daughter of John Tresithey Esq., nine sons and seven daughters – for whose Godley End ye Lord be Praysed.' One can only assume that poor Jane died in childbirth, leaving her successor to ensure the line with a massive brood.

News of events in the outside world reached most of Cornwall only fitfully. The main source for what was happening in foreign parts and elsewhere was the *Western Flyer and Sherborne Mercury*, published by Messrs Goadby of Sherborne. It was packed with information for those who could read and find their way around it – there being no such thing as headlines then. The front page was devoted to advertisements, for everything from house sales to patent medicines (especially patent medicines!). The inside was a wonderful mixture of news, gossip, the court circular, Parliamentary reports, lurid details of public hangings in London and elsewhere, along with details of local court proceedings, both Magistrates and Assizes.

The *Sherborner*, as it was known, was brought down to Cornwall by special messengers on horseback, known as 'Sherborne Riders'. Crowds would gather to fight for copies, pressing money on the tired and dusty riders and giving orders for future editions. More people than might be assumed were literate in Cornwall, so each copy was read eagerly, then passed from hand to hand until it fell to pieces. According to the Cornish historian, Hamilton Jenkin, as late as the mid-nineteenth century Cornish gossips were known as 'regular Sherborners'.

The picture of Cornwall as the century rolled into its second half is, therefore, a relatively peaceful one; its scattered population endured a hard life, but usually had enough to eat – and drink, too, for there were numerous 'kiddlies' (small ale-houses mostly brewing their own beer) which were always busy. Income from the Free Trade, both direct and indirect, helped out many families when times were hard, and an abundance of local festivals, saints' day feasts, especially May Day, provided enjoyment and an opportunity to let off steam.

★

TOWARDS THE end of the 1750s, when the young mariner William Broad was sailing regularly out of Fowey, signs of impending change were all around him. The most obvious was that in the mining industry. For the last twenty years the price of copper had fluctuated wildly but, with the coming of the steam-pumping engine, it was now possible to keep the mines free of water at almost any depth. It was no longer economic for the big mine owners to invest in small scattered mines and so they now sank deep central shafts leading down, level upon level, to as much as 2000 feet. Instead of the miners being able to live close to their work, surrounded by land which helped to support them, many were now sucked into the new, fast-growing mining towns to live in the rows of mean back-to-back houses which are the hallmark of the Industrial Revolution. Without the means to grow much of their own food or the freedom to diversify their labour, they became dependent on their employers for their livelihood, which could be terminated at any time.

Indeed there were layoffs and closures, resulting in grinding poverty. As John Rowe writes in *Cornwall in the Age of the Industrial Revolution*: 'Any check in the progress of the mines threw on the parochial rates not the infirm young, the impotent aged, and the hapless sick envisaged and provided for by the framers of the Elizabethan Poor Law, but many able-bodied persons, destitute from sheer inability to find employment.' Diseases, especially typhus and cholera, raged through the mining towns in the summer, while diphtheria decimated the children in the winter. Not surprisingly, there were growing signs of unrest.

From now on control over the lives of many people passed into the hands of unknown masters. Whatever the vices of the landed gentry and merchant bankers who had funded the mines previously, at least most, if not all, were Cornish born and lived locally. But the new steam-pumping engines, which encouraged hopes of vastly increased profits, led to the arrival of the 'mine adventurers', speculative capitalists from outside Cornwall who knew little or nothing about mining except that it might make them a fortune. Midland industrialists soon cornered the market in smelting the ore, forming cartels in order to take the maximum profit. James Watt, inventor of the first widely used steam-pumping engine, insisted he be paid a 'royalty' on every ton of ore raised from a mine where one was installed.

Underneath it all, propping up the massive edifice of owners, adventurers, speculators, smelters, bankers and businessmen, all vying with each other for their cut, were the miners, working in appalling conditions, often up to their knees in water, in spite of the pumping engines, breathing in the lethal dust which would lay them in their graves before they reached the age of thirty-five. For too many families there was now no slack which could be taken up when times were hard, nothing to which they could turn their hands if the fishing failed or if there was conflict abroad.

Much of this, however, lay in the future. William Broad would have had friends and relatives who had left the small mining villages around Fowey for the bigger mines inland and would have heard tales of the conditions in which they lived, but the changes would not have affected him yet. Some time around the year 1760, unaware of what was in store, William Broad got married.

CHAPTER TWO

Fowey Haven

THE MOST likely year for the marriage of William and Grace Broad is 1761. We do not know when and where it took place because it seems that she was not a Fowey woman, and it was customary for the wedding to be celebrated in the bride's own home parish. Had Grace been living in Fowey at the time, then the marriage would have been noted in the parish register, known locally as 'the Church Book'. It also does not appear either in the Methodist records of the parish or in any of the registers of nearby parishes such as Lanteglos, St Veep, Par, St Blazey or Lostwithiel.

As William was a sailor it is possible that he met Grace in one of the ports he visited regularly – perhaps Penzance or Falmouth further south, or St Ives or Padstow on the north coast. Plymouth, with its busy Sutton harbour, was also only just over the border. It might even be that she hailed from much further afield, Lowestoft or Great Yarmouth, say, in the east, or Bristol in the west, even London, since all of them were regular ports of call for coastal traffic out of Cornwall. But on the whole the Cornish were very clannish, preferring to marry their own kind rather than 'foreigners', a term still used to denote anyone born east of the river Tamar.

Wherever she came from, William would almost certainly have taken his new wife home to one of the small cottages which still climb up out of the town along the steep street now called Lostwithiel Street, but which was then the High Street. Or they might have lived in the warren of little houses which stood alongside the church of St Fimbarrus, a church dedicated to one of that standing army of obscure Celtic saints. These houses were pulled down during the last century after various vicars complained that the constant traffic between them and the town turned the churchyard into a public thoroughfare; once they had gone the Treffrys of Place House swiftly incorporated the land they had been built upon into their own grounds and gardens.

In the 1760s the entry to Fowey Harbour was guarded by two forts (each with guns) of which the remains can still be seen. Every evening a huge chain, linking the two forts, was hauled up to prevent unwanted shipping from entering the port. The main part of the town ran alongside the river Fowey, way down from the high hill behind, with its windmill clearly visible to shipping. Along the waterfront and raised above it, where the bed-and-breakfast houses stand today, there were good-sized town houses, the properties of merchants and ship-owners. A small stone stairway led down at one point to the old St Catherine's chapel. The main street of the town was as narrow as it is today, but exit and entry was made more difficult by archways at each end, with living accommodation above them.

The shipbuilding yard at Caffa Mill, just downriver from the important Bodinnick ferry, was a busy place with three quays and a slipway, building good-sized fast cutters and sloops, while nearby were the workshops of all the ancillary trades which provided employment in the town – ropemakers, sail-makers, blockmakers, cordwainers, coopers, and victuallers.

The main Town Quay was always busy because of the number of shipowners whose vessels sailed out of Fowey, or 'Foye' as it used to be spelt and is still pronounced. Fowey Haven had been well known to mariners from earliest times, offering as it does a safe harbour to shipping. An old record notes that it was

> esteemed to be the best outlet westward of any in the west of England, as all vessels sailing in this direction can leave it, in the prosecution of their voyages, with wind South East by South; and all coasting vessels, whether bound up or down the Channel, that may be embayed between Rame Head and the Deadman Point, in a heavy southerly gale, can always find

safety by running for this port without cable or anchor. As many as thirty large vessels may be anchored safely in the inner side of the sand bar off Polruan.

All sailing ships dreaded the possibility of being 'embayed', of finding themselves driven inexorably towards the shore, enclosed by the arms of the bay, unable to go about and tack out of danger. The result would be wreck on a lee shore.

Small boats would ferry the hundreds of barrels of pilchards out to the ships waiting to take them to the Continent, while others, offloading from incoming vessels, would bring to the Town Quay salt, oranges, lemons, silks and spices or, more mundanely, seacole or slate. At night time, the little coves and beaches outside the big chain would be busy with other sorts of cargo – brandy, wine and tobacco.

The parish records of the time show a good cross-section of trades and professions in the town. The two major occupations of ordinary working people were mariners or labourers. The term 'labourer' was often used to describe those miners who were paid weekly wages, and although the nearest mines were only three or four miles outside the town many were becoming used to a long walk to work. Mariners could be deep-sea sailors – sailors who sailed regularly between Cornwall and the Continent – or, more usually, those who provided the crews for the coastal trade, although some might well have taken berths on any ship wanting a hand. At this stage the dreaded press gang had not begun to take away every able-bodied man it could lay its hands on for service in the Royal Navy. Although there was a steady amount of fishing out of Fowey, especially for pilchards, few men registered themselves solely as fishermen.

Along with the trades already described, there were also carpenters, local boatmen, masons, a wheelwright, peruke (wig) makers, barbers, a hatter, a scrivener, a parish clerk, an attorney-at-law, a Revenue Officer and the Salt Officer for the south coast, a local man named Thomas Lanyon. His task was to collect the tax due on salt, a commodity vital to the pilchard industry. The tax was not yet punitive and Fowey folk paid it, if not happily, at least without serious trouble.

The register shows that shipping was in the hands of the Goodalls, Stephenses, Tollers, Majors and Williamses, and that the town shipwrights were William Nicholls and John Willcocks; that William Beare was a ropemaker and William Collins and John Bone were cordwainers. The large Puckey family followed a variety of trades from smiths and carpentry to labourers in the mines. The local inhabitants seem to have needed a good many wigs for the town boasted no less than three peruquiers – Richard Willington, John Hawkins and Alexander Hoskings. Those wanting a smart hat went to Henry Lukey, the hatter, and letters and correspondence were seen to, for a price, by Thomas Courts, scrivener. Literacy was patchy but William Broad could, at the very least, sign his own name in the parish register. Coats for Sunday best would have been made by Thomas White, tailor; building work undertaken by the firm of Thomas Jago, who prided themselves on being related to old Cornish landed gentry.

Another offshoot of the gentrified Jagos was the vicar of Fowey, Nicholas Cory. He lived in a large, handsome, double-fronted vicarage next to the church. It needed to be large as Mrs Jago, according to the births register, was presenting her husband with a baby every year. His was a fine pluralistic living, which took in other parishes at Landrake and Torpoint, livings he was later able to hand on to two of his sons.

There were no shortages of places for refreshment in Fowey for, as well as the little 'kiddlies', it was well off for inns and taverns. The Rashleighs had moved from their beautiful house just off the Town Quay and this had become the Ship Inn. It is still there, along with at least two other taverns the Broads would have known: the Lugger, which has kept its name, and the King of Prussia, possibly then called something different, which takes its name not from the Prussian Empire, but from the nickname of Cornwall's most notorious and successful smuggler, John Carter, of Prussia Cove near Penzance. He had cannons mounted at the mouth of the Cove to dissuade Revenue cutters, and boasted that he had never let anyone down on an order, even if it had meant having to retrieve his cargoes after they had been seized by the Excisemen.

A very popular public house, the Rose and Crown, then stood at the corner of the churchyard; it later became notorious after its landlord, a 'foreigner' from Devonport called Wyatt, murdered a wealthy Jew who had put up there for a week. At the trial it was revealed that Wyatt and the Jew, whose name was Valentine, had run an illicit trade in counterfeit money, known as 'coining', but had fallen out prior to Wyatt leaving Devonport. Valentine had come calling for a share of the profits. Wyatt was hanged outside Bodmin gaol, a gruesome business as the execution was botched and it took twenty minutes for him to die. His body was then hanged in chains, possibly on the gibbet at the Four Turnings outside Fowey, which was specially erected for the exhibition of local felons as a warning and an example to all.

Fowey was isolated both from the rest of England, although Devon was only just over thirty miles away, and from the Cornish towns, because of the difficulty of reaching it by road. In the 1760s the only route into the town was a winding lane, which still exists but which is now only used as an alternative route to the Bodinnick ferry. Most people who wished to travel inland used the river Fowey, rowing or sailing to the town of Lostwithiel where they could reach a main road.

There were plenty of Broad relatives to help Grace settle into her new home. William had a brother, John, who was a carpenter and there was at least one other married brother, described as a 'labourer', as well as a number of other Broads. The women would have shown her where to draw her water (there was, as yet, no Town Tap), and where to wash the household linen. Furze to start fires could be cut from the hills above the town, turf was purchased from those selling it from carts in the streets.

We can picture the young couple one Sunday morning shortly after they were married and before William went back to sea. They would have made their way to the church in their Sunday best, William in a suit he might well have had made for his wedding, Grace in a pretty muslin bonnet and one of the scarlet wool cloaks so prized by smart young Cornish girls. They would have sat at the back of the church, the front pews being reserved for the Rashleigh and Treffry families and, almost more important, the Mayor and Alderman.

Just as the representation of the electors had virtually become a hereditary office, the town Corporation was also tightly controlled by a small coterie of Fowey families. It was almost impossible to break into that magic circle, the same handful of names – the Lambes, Stephenses, Pomeroys and Grahams, along with the ubiquitous Rashleighs – provided the incumbents for the office of Mayor, while the Kimber family handed on the post of Town Clerk from father to son from the 1740s to the 1780s.

The arrival of the Corporation at church for Sunday morning service was one of the sights of the town and what William and Grace would have seen is described in detail by Susan Sibbalds, a young woman living in Fowey at that time.

Well do I remember our thinking the Mayor and Alderman above all superior and their dresses so imposing – cloth cloaks, trimmed with fur, Winter or Summer, their hair fully powdered; large stiff sausage curls, one row on another above their ears, the hair behind in a black silk bag with a large rosette of black ribbon; small cocked hats stuck on the tops of their heads and large buckles on the shoes completed the visible part of the costume of these Dignitaries. Nor must Ralph Paine, the Mace-bearer, who walked before them be forgotten, for in his own opinion, as well as ours, no doubt, he was a great character in his large brown cloak with a cape and cocked hat trimmed with gold lace – who could be greater in his own estimation? And what an air of authority it gave to the whole Corporate body when Ralph placed the large Mace at the head of their Pew as a terror to all evil doers!

The description of the elaborate hairstyles of the Corporation suggest the peruquiers had been busy the previous Saturday.

Following church, if the weather was fine and if there was time after the Reverend Nicholas Cory's lengthy sermon, William might well have taken his wife for a walk along the lane which ran from the town centre to Readymoney Cove just below the fort guarding the harbour entrance, its strange name said to date from the Armada when gold pieces were washed ashore there from a wrecked Spanish galleon. From the raised walk they would have seen over the river to the villages of Bodinnick and Polruan, smelt the fresh smell of the incoming tide, pointed out the ships anchored in the middle of the river.

Then it would have been home to Sunday dinner, most likely with William's parents. If times were good there might have been a small piece of pork or even a cut of beef, served with potatoes, turnips and cabbage. If Grace was a Cornish girl then she would have already known how to make the county's most famous fare, the Cornish pasty (which would have borne little resemblance to the poor relations now sold throughout the country), along with such delicacies as Heavy Cake (a rich fruit cake) and Saffron Cake, which is more like a currant-filled bread, coloured and heavily seasoned with the spice which comes from the crocus. If she were not Cornish, then her mother-in-law or sisters-in-law would soon have taught her.

In April 1762 Grace became pregnant and, nine months later, was safely delivered of a daughter. The exact date is not known, as the birth dates of children were seldom recorded at the time. On January 22 1763 the baby was christened Grace, after her mother, by the Reverend Nicholas Cory. William proudly signed his name in the Church Book as 'William Broad, Mariner'. The little girl soon became known as 'Dolly' to avoid confusing her with her mother.

It was only a few minutes' walk from the cottages to the church to which Grace, accompanied by William, would have proudly carried her new baby, followed by the godparents, William's relations, and their friends, one of whom would have brought, in a clean white napkin, a thick round of currant cake, about eight inches across. After the ceremony, the party would have returned home, but anyone they met between church and house would have been offered a piece of the 'crib' or 'kimbly' cake. As each person took some they would have been asked to pray that the baby 'may have the Good God's grace and grow up a good woman'. Centuries later, Sir Arthur Quiller-Couch wrote that he thought the custom referred to the evil eye and its influence, which might fall on the young couple or on the child and which could be averted by the taking of this unexpected gift.

So Grace settled down in her little cottage with her new baby. It looks as if William then went off to sea, for at a time when it was commonplace for the young women of the town to have a baby every year, there was a gap before a second child was born to the young Broads.

CHAPTER THREE

'The Merry Morning of May'

Unite and unite and let us all unite,
For summer is acome unto day,
And whither we are going we will all unite
In the merry morning of May.

I warn you young men every one
For summer is acome unto day,
To go to the greenwood and fetch your May home
In the merry morning of May.

All out of all your beds,
For summer is acome unto day,
Your chamber shall be strewn with the white rose and the red,

In the merry morning of May.

Popular Ballad

THE FIRST of May marked the dawn of Cornwall's great festival, and followed a night during which few folk would have had a full night's sleep. On the north coast in the fishing port of Padstow, where they held the most elaborate May Day celebrations, and where some of William Broad's relatives were living, only the very old, the infirm and the smallest babies would have gone to bed at all.

At midnight the drummer would have begun to beat his big drum below the huge, decorated maypole in Padstow's town square, summoning the townspeople to the start of the May ceremony. There they would have gathered to sing all the verses of 'In the Merry Morning of May', before marching down to the Golden Lion Inn to rouse the landlord. As is still the tradition, they would have chanted questions to which he had to sing the correct responses. The young people would then have raced off to the woods with whoops and shouts to pick the May blossom, bluebells and branches of greenery, to decorate, by the time morning came, every house and cottage in the town.

At first light the children, dressed in their best and decked with ribbons and flowers, went from house to house throughout the town singing in the May, for a reward of little cakes or small coins. Then followed the major dramatic event – the emergence of the Hobby Horse, that strange capering creature with a head like an African ritual mask, a pagan symbol whose roots go back to well before records began, some say at least four thousand years, to the ancient bronze-age settlements at the mouth of the river Camel. The right to play the horse was, and still is, jealously guarded by selected families, with the right to dance in the horse passed on from father to son.

As it pranced around the town with its attendants, its 'teaser', a fantastically dressed figure with a staff crowned with flowers, preceded by the fiddlers and the drummers, the townspeople danced with it and shouted ''oss!, 'oss!', girls screaming as the 'oss' pulled them under its skirts, while barren wives pressed forward to touch it for luck. Whether it was due to the potency of the horse or a night spent in close proximity to a young man in the woods above the town, every February produced its crop of ''obby 'oss babbies', regarded with indulgence so long as the couples concerned finally wed.

All the towns and villages of England had their own May Day celebrations. Upriver from Fowey the young men of the villages of Lerryn and St Veep spent the night jealously guarding their maypoles since it was the custom for one village to try to steal that of the other, a tradition which often led to broken heads. Bringing in May and other greenery to decorate houses was almost universal, as was the maypole dancing, the early morning singing, the feasting and revelry and the drinking of vast quantities of ale and cider. It was a true celebration of the end of winter, a festival which drew in young and old in a joyous welcome to the coming of summer.

So Grace Broad, feeding her new baby daughter on 1 May 1765, would have been greeted as she woke to the sound of children singing, under her window, their celebration to the start of May Day, a day that could hardly have been more propitious for a christening, a day guaranteed to give a child an auspicious start. It was already apparent that this second daughter was different both in temperament and appearance from the first, being a thinner, restless baby with a voracious appetite. Dolly, now two years old, was a placid, good-natured little soul, no trouble at all.

By mid-morning the christening party had assembled at the house, all of them in their best clothes with May Day posies pinned to their cloaks, shawls or jackets, some of the girls wearing new bonnets also trimmed with spring flowers, the growing number of children born to various family members, including Dolly, washed and scrubbed and told to sit still and not get dirty. It was likely to have been a noisy party which arrived at the church door for all the town ale-houses would have been doing brisk business since dawn.

So the Broads' second daughter was christened, quite simply, Mary. It was noted in the Church Book under 'Christenings' – 'Mary, daughter of William Broad, mariner, and Grace, his wife' – duly signed by William. There would have been no shortage of takers afterwards for the christening cake with all the town out on the streets, no lack of well-wishers to call out, 'May Mary have the Good God's grace and grow up a good woman!' before going back into the taverns to wet the baby's head. There was no reason to believe anything other than that she would indeed grow up to be a good woman, a credit to her respectable parents.

Two years and two months later, on 19 July 1767, Grace gave birth to another daughter, but this time there was no festivity, no family procession to the church, no christening cake. The baby is unlikely even to have been taken to the church. It is far more probable that an urgent message was sent to the Reverend Nicholas Cory, or William may even have gone in haste himself, to beg him to come out to the cottage at once to christen the child and welcome it into God's family, for the obviously weak baby, given the name of Jane, lived for only a few hours and was buried in the churchyard two days later. It is likely that the tiny coffin was attended only by the men of the family, the women staying home to comfort the bitterly disappointed, exhausted Grace and to look after the two other children, now aged four and two.

Only one further child was born to William and Grace. Some time in the New Year of 1769, Grace had a son, christened William after his father on 15 January, amid relief that he appeared strong and healthy. But he lived for only six months, his name listed under 'Burials' for the following 4 June. He might have been born with some physical problem but it is far more likely that he succumbed to one of the many childhood epidemics which swept eighteenth-century England, town and country alike. Certainly the number of burials increased sharply that year.

Whether Grace was unable to conceive another child or whether, perhaps from complications arising from delivery, she was thereafter unable to carry a child to full term, we do not know. Even though William must have spent a good deal of his time away from home, the wives of other young sailors continued having children throughout their childbearing lives, but Grace did not. At least she had two healthy growing girls.

WHERE IN Cornwall William Bryant, later to become Mary Broad's husband, grew up is unknown. No existing published source material has been able to throw any light on where he came from, although one semi-fictional account makes him Mary's childhood sweetheart, growing up with her in Fowey. However that is unlikely as there is no family of that name recorded in the town in the Church Book, the Methodist registers or the tax rolls. The first mention of Bryants in the Fowey area is under 'Marriages' in the parish register of

Lanteglos, in the 1790s, and the first child christened William was not born until the early nineteenth century, his place of birth being listed as Bodinnick.

There is, however, one clue, and that is Will's age. From his records we know that he must have been born in either 1762 or 1763. The fact that he subsequently came to trial in Launceston does not necessarily mean that he came from the north end of Cornwall, he could have been caught fifty miles away from home, but it does make it a possibility that he was living not too far away. A careful search through the parish records from Launceston itself, down to the south coast, does show that in 1761 a Thomas Bryant of Boconnoc married an Anne Gilbert of the same parish and that in July 1762 their son, William, was christened in the local church. Boconnoc, the large estate owned by the Pitts, as already noted, was about nine miles upriver from Fowey so it is feasible that Mary and William might have met when they were children, possibly when the Bryants came downriver to Fowey to buy necessities.

Watkin Tench, the other Cornish boy to feature prominently in Mary's life, was born between May 1758 and May 1759 though, again, nobody seems to know where. It was not obligatory to register births officially so the only means of tracing the unknown, or relatively unknown, people of the time, as distinct from the landed gentry, is to search through the parish records. Tench's mother was Welsh and his father, we are told, Cornish, and it seems he grew up in Penzance, but paid frequent visits to North Wales. His background is quite different to that of the Broads and Bryants as he obviously had middle-class parents. Nobody knows what his father did, but as Watkin was a protégé of the landowning Wynn family of North Wales, it is possible he was either related to them or that his father was connected with them professionally. The young Watkin received a first-rate classical education in England and was then sent to Paris for further study, where he learned to speak fluent French, before entering the marines as a commissioned officer.

★

APART FROM the bare facts in the parish register we know nothing of Mary Broad's early life until she reached the age of twenty: thereafter it is well documented. It is reasonable to assume, however, that she and Dolly grew up much as any other girls of their background in the Cornwall of the latter half of the eighteenth century. Had little William lived, then William and Grace might well have scraped up the money to send him to the Dame School at the top of the hill so that he could learn to read, write and number, but for most ordinary families there seemed little point in educating daughters. The best they could look forward to was to go into 'good service' before settling down as wives and mothers.

Good service was what Dolly was destined for, since she showed an immediate aptitude for domestic tasks, and was the kind of girl who happily helped her mother about the house, wanted to learn to cook and was naturally adept at sewing and mending. No doubt Mary also learned basic household skills, for it is unlikely that she would have been excused her fair share of the household chores. A woman like Grace would have considered that she had not done her duty had she not ensured, so far as she was able, that by the time her daughters were ready to marry they could run their own households and look after their husbands. What is known is that some time during those early years, Mary Broad learned to handle and steer a small sailing boat with considerable skill.

All her subsequent history points to a girl who was a tomboy by nature, who paid scant heed to convention and preferred the company of boys and men to that of women. It might well be that William Broad, realizing there would be no son to whom he could teach such skills, took his small daughter on the river when he was home from sea, teaching her how to row and handle a sailing boat. He might even have taught her some navigation, based on the positioning of the stars, as well as how to fish, watching her struggle with childish fingers as she baited the hooks with pieces of spider crab, stale bread or lug worms with which to catch mackerel. If this was indeed the case, then by the time she was nine or ten Mary would have been quite capable, her skirts tucked up, of rowing a small dinghy across the river, taking due note of the tides, especially the strong outgoing springs.

As the two girls grew up it became apparent, even to them in their backwater, that times were changing and not for the better. In 1776, when Mary was eleven, America declared its independence and for the next six years England was at war with her own colony. The immediate result was the disappearance of noticeable numbers of young men. Some volunteered for the Army and, after only basic training, were shipped off at once to fight; some enlisted in the Navy or the company of marines based in Plymouth. Watkin Tench, who had just joined the marines with the rank of lieutenant, was sent off to America within weeks. Others were forced into the ships of the Royal Navy as the press gangs turned their attention to the West Country ports. On one occasion the women of Newlyn, in west Cornwall, pelted the press gang with rotten fish, while their menfolk took to the woods and moors, resulting in that particular gang leaving empty-handed.

The war soon put paid to any trading by sea, for within eighteen months the French had come in on the side of the Americans. Their privateers lay off the coast between Brittany and Cornwall, preying on Cornish merchantmen on their way to London, who were left defenceless as most of the British Navy was thousands of miles away. A year later, Spain joined forces with France and there followed a prolonged siege of Gibraltar which entirely cut off all trade in pilchards and tin to the Mediterranean. The winter of 1778/9 was one of the worst ever known to Cornish fishermen and led, in May 1779, to an Act being rushed through Parliament in three weeks, temporarily lifting the tax on salt. It was hoped that this would encourage the sale of pilchards at home, but by this time even the fishing boats were not putting out to sea for a large Franco-Spanish fleet was cruising up and down the western Channel (even on some days anchoring inside Plymouth Sound) leaving English shipping effectively under siege in its own ports. That a poor diet, coupled with disease, took its toll on the people of

Fowey is shown in the records, burials almost doubling from what they had averaged in preceding years.

But however hard and dangerous the times, life goes on and in the summer of 1779 Elizabeth Broad, the daughter of John Broad and niece to William and Grace, married a young lad called Edward, one of the prolific family of Puckeys in the town. Elizabeth, a little older than Dolly, was like a sister to her two cousins and they must have attended her wedding, were possibly even her bridesmaids. Dolly was then sixteen and Mary fourteen.

Even though making ends meet was now difficult, the women of the family would have done everything they could to see there was a good spread of food and plenty of drink to ensure the wedding went off 'fitty'. There might well have been rabbit, officially from common land but more likely from one or other of the estates belonging to the big landowners (even though the penalty for poaching was several years in the notorious Bodmin gaol). Flour was now extremely expensive, but enough had been put by to bake a Heavy Cake and to make pastry for pies to go with the different kinds of cheese and cold meats. 'Tatties' and 'neaps' were piled in earthenware dishes, gallons of ale and cider standing ready in barrels.

The night before the wedding Elizabeth's hair would have been washed and set in rags to ensure it curled the next day and her dress ironed and laid by. Even had it not been wartime, it was unlikely she would have had a new one; it was more usual for the bride to wear her Sunday best or to borrow one off a friend. Since, in this case, the first child followed five or six months after the wedding, Elizabeth, being some months 'forward', might well have cast around to find a suitable gown belonging to a larger friend, over which she could pin a new shawl across her expanding figure. In eighteenth-century Cornwall, pregnant brides were commonplace, illegitimate children less so, for family and friends could exert heavy pressure on young men to ensure they recognized their obligations. A few names of those having to cope alone are noted by the Parish Clerk – William, bastard child of Sarah Andrews, Eliza, bastard child of Elizabeth Vanson, and, a sad note, 'John, a bastard infant, found drowned.'

But the bride almost certainly did have a new muslin bonnet and a posy of garden flowers to carry, as she led the wedding party on foot to the church. Outside the gentry and the professions, only a farmer's girl would expect to be driven and in this case the church was only a few minutes' walk away. So off she went, arm in arm with her father, while her mother, brothers and sisters, cousins and as many of her friends and relations as could take the day off followed behind. All the girls would have been dressed in their best (lifting their skirts when possible to show the new white cotton stockings bought for the occasion), most with posies pinned to their shawls. The procession would have halted at the church gate, decorated with love-knots of white ribbons and nosegays of flowers.

Outside, the groom, his family and friends would have been waiting and there was likely to have been much joking and laughing between the two parties with exchanges such as 'Here's the maid come at last, us reckoned her'd thought better of it and called it off,' and, 'Ned here was deciding which of the rest of you maids he'd have instead.' To which the bride might respond, 'You be lucky to get me, Ned Puckey, and you knows it!'

Wedding ceremonies for ordinary folk were brief, for music and bells cost money. As soon as it was over Ned and Elizabeth went to the vestry to sign their names (unusually, both could write), and then the whole party set off back to the bride's home for the wedding feast, very possibly calling in at several hostelries on the way to drink the health of the happy couple and accept the good wishes of the clientele. Weddings were always the subject of much good-natured banter and a bridegroom wearing a new pair of 'duck' trousers (made of strong cotton) was likely to have a popular verse sung to him, after suitable adaptation:

> His ma she bought a yard o'duck a trousers for to make,
> And Jinny Puckey cut 'un out but made a grand mistake,

> Then Tailor Vine he took a 'and and thought to do it fine,
> But when the trousers was put on, the forepart were behind!

With such few opportunities for having a good time, a spread of food and a party was much appreciated. If bride and groom were moving immediately into their own cottage then very basic furniture – a board bed, table and chairs and maybe a dresser since in this case the bride's father was a carpenter, some cooking pots and earthenware crockery – would already have been installed. Any small wedding presents, such as pots and pans or a small ornament, would have been proudly displayed along with the linen which had possibly been spun, and certainly made, by Elizabeth for her linen chest.

Then, after an afternoon of feasting, the furniture would be pushed back and the floor cleared for dancing and games. A guest who could play the fiddle was extremely popular and the first dances involved everyone who was capable of standing, whatever their ages. When the older members of the party had tired and sat down to discuss local gossip or other weddings or the progress of the war, the games would begin. Kissing games were always popular at weddings. One involved all the girls having to stand in a circle facing inwards, while a selected young man crept around the outside of them with a handkerchief. When he reached the girl of his choice he would drop it quietly, then continue on his way, singing:

> Fire, fire, in my glove!
> I sent a letter to my love
> And by the way I drop't it, drop't it, drop't it

If he reached it again before the girl saw it then he was entitled to a kiss or a number of kisses. Needless to say, there was soon a good deal of cheating on the part of the girls, who remained stock-still if they particularly fancied a young man or who kept looking behind them if they thought they were the target of one they did not.

As the night drew on, older members of the party and those with small children, would drift off home to bed, leaving the floor to the young people. Bride and groom were expected to take to their bed before the guests left and eventually had to do so, only too well aware of what might be in store for them. As it was, they would have left to a barrage of remarks such as, 'If you'd a-waited a piece longer, you'd've saved money for parson and 'ad weddin' an' chris'nin' at one go!' Cautiously opening the door of their new home, they would then have crept up the ladder to the floor above before carefully inspecting the bed. Very often their friends would have been there before them and put a variety of objects in it. If the guests were particularly boisterous the newlyweds might also have been subjected to a 'shallal', particularly popular if it was known the bride was already 'forward'. In the darkest part of the night the young men would creep up under the bedroom window, carrying objects wrapped in cloths. At a given signal they would remove the covering to reveal an array of pots, pans and chamber pots, pieces of metal and tin plates, and at a whispered, 'One, two, three, NOW!' they would beat on them with spoons and forks until the town rang with a sound loud enough to wake the dead. This was kept up until the groom stuck his head out of the window, which was the signal for further ribald exchanges until neighbours, who had had more than enough of it, opened their doors and told them to get off home and be quick about it.

CHAPTER FOUR

Death Sentence

> When in countries that are called civilised, we see age going to
> the workhouse and youth to the gallows, something must be
> wrong in the system of government . . . Civil Government does
> not consist in executions . . . Why is it that scarcely any are
> executed but the poor?
>
> Tom Paine, *The Rights of Man*

SOME TIME during the year 1785 Mary Broad made a disastrous choice – one which led to a series of extraordinary adventures. Like the protagonist in a Greek tragedy, once she had embarked on a course of action, the result was inevitable given the times in which she lived.

Seventeen eighty-two saw the end of the war into which Lord North had blundered, with victory to the Americans. Mad King George III still sat on the English throne and occasionally the odd paragraph would appear in the newsheets to the effect that he was 'worse', 'better' or no longer under restraint. The war had bankrupted the country, so the obvious answer, as it always is, was to raise taxes, and in the five years following the war they rose by over 20 per cent. Land, houses, windows, candles and salt all carried increasing levies, but these were often hard to collect and in 1785 Parliament was told that new measures to improve collection needed to be implemented for although the window tax had been collected from some 714,911 houses and cottages, it was still owed from an estimated 284,450. The population responded by blocking up the windows of their already dark homes.

Poor summers led to bad harvests and rocketing prices for corn, which were an open invitation to profiteering, and while the nation's attention had been on the War of Independence, the landowners had accelerated their enclosure of common land. 'A Country Farmer', author of an anonymous pamphlet published in 1786, writes that this practice was being pursued with unremitting ardour under the specious pretence of improvement, 'but in fact to the great injury of the public in general and the utter ruin of thousands of individuals in particular and an advantage to none except a few landowners . . .' All that was required for an Act of Parliament to be obtained so that common land could be enclosed was for the person to find two witnesses who would swear that the land was of no use to anyone, even 'if it be of the best soil in the kingdom, and produce corn in the greatest abundance and of the best quality'.

Small farmers, who had relied on the land to supplement their own crofts, were no longer able to make a living and so were driven out. Whole villages were deserted as the population took to the roads, the land on which they had grown their food or grazed their few animals swallowed up by greedy landowners. The old, the sick, the infirm and the very young had no recourse but to throw themselves on the mercy of the parish, while the dispossessed young, with no work, no prospects and no homes, turned not surprisingly to crime. Yet others fled overseas 'to supply that deficiency and to free themselves from a country where Hunger, the work of human misfortunes, stared them in the face, and all means of satisfying that craving appetite, even in a land of plenty, totally obliterated,' continues the pamphleteer. Meanwhile, troops of the 'most abandoned thieves that ever disgraced a civilised country, roam the highways and glut the gallows with food.'

In the towns and cities there was now a vast underclass, the urban poor supplemented by those driven in from the countryside, a poverty-stricken, half-starved population living cheek-by-jowl with conspicuous wealth. The criminal class had its own hierarchy, its aristocrats the smart highwaymen who took to the 'High Toby', at the lower end the little street girls, the wily elves who sold their bodies from the age of nine or ten to supplement their thieving, the boys living in the eighteenth-century equivalent of Fagin's Den, the Thieves' Kitchens of London's Seven Dials, Covent Garden and the backstreets of Southwark. They had their own language, the thieves' cant, and their own rules. On the fringes were the amateurs, forced into crime by necessity – the badly treated servant girl who stole from her mistress, the errand boy who filched a handkerchief hanging from a pocket, the young woman who turned to prostitution after being thrown out of her workplace on a whim.

The country seethed under a wave of injustice. The Government, terrified by what had happened in America, and uneasily aware of unrest across the Channel, reacted predictably, denying that it was the enclosing of land, high food prices, and taxation that was at the root of it. As the Speaker told the House of Commons on 13 January 1786: 'Great as these taxes are, they are liberally and cheerfully given, in the most firm and full confidence that they will be found effectually to answer the end proposed, of supplying the whole of the public expense and preventing any further debt' – a true example of the triumph of hope over experience.

No, it could not possibly be the system that was wrong. What were needed were harsher punishments, to combat the wave of sheer evil and inherent wickedness that was sweeping the land. The result was that more and more crimes became capital offences, *pour encourager les autres*, in the words of Voltaire, and soon the number rose to nearly two hundred. The most heinous crimes were treason, mutiny, murder, arson and highway robbery, followed by sodomy, criminal bankruptcy, burglary, forgery, shooting at a Revenue Officer, stealing sheep, cattle or horses, picking pockets of sums above a shilling, shoplifting above five shillings, stealing more than two pounds from a house, cutting down landowners' trees, breaking fishponds, counterfeiting, smuggling by persons armed for the purpose, mail robbery, sacrilege, destroying turnpikes, being at large in the kingdom after the passing of a sentence and return from transportation. Transportation was something of a problem as, hitherto, felons had been sent to America, but this was obviously no longer possible. Many had become free men by willingly fighting on the side of the colony.

After hanging came a raft of punishments for a whole range of other offences such as keeping a bawdy house, petty larceny, bigamy, overloading a boat if you were a waterman, making and selling fireworks, watering beer and fighting in the street. They included imprisonment of various kinds (rapidly becoming a desperate problem in itself as the gaols were overflowing), transportation, the stocks and flogging. Flogging was a popular form of punishment with high entertainment value, since thieves, whores, vagabonds and brawlers were publicly whipped either at the whipping post or the cart's tail. Those carrying out the task were paid four pence a time: sometimes, to give a real frisson, women were employed to flog women.

An example of the kind of people who ended up on the gallows is given in a report in the *London Evening Post* of 9 October 1782:

> Yesterday morning about 9 o'clock the following malefactors were brought out of Newgate and carried to Tyburn in three carts where they were executed according to their sentences, viz: Henry Berthand, for feloniously impersonating one, Micháel Groves; . . . William Jones, for stealing from a warehouse in Aldersgate Street a deal box containing a quantity of haberdashery goods; Peter Verrier, accomplice with Charles Kelly, already executed, for burglary in the house of Mrs Pollard in Great Queen Street; William Odern, of robbing two women in Spittlefields; Charles Woolett, for robbing Bernard Cheale on the highway of a metal watch; John Graham for feloniously altering a bank note with intent to defraud; Charlotte Goodall and John Edmonds, for stealing from the house of Mrs Fortescue at Tottenham where Goodall lived as a servant, a quantity of linen; Thomas Cladenbole for assaulting Robert Chiton on the highway and robbing him of a gold watch; and John Weatherley and John Lafee for feloniously coining and counterfeiting the silver money of the realm called shillings and sixpences. They all behaved very penitent.

The newspapers of the day were full of executions, which were ostensibly there to act as a dreadful warning, but in reality were read with avidity by all those capable of doing so. Readers liked to know who the victims were, exactly what they had done, what they wore for their executions, their behaviour on the scaffold, what they said – if anything – and how they were 'turned off'. Pride of place was given to the Tyburn executions, after which the reader would turn to the local criminal news.

The Cornish people were overwhelmed by the tide of new taxes and there is still evidence today of the blocked windows resulting from that particular tax. Homes were made dark by day and darker by night as candles became a luxury. Worst of all for the coastal people was the restored punitive tax on salt imported from France. It took a bushel of salt to cure a thousand pilchards, an amount which barely provided sufficient food to see a moderately sized family through the winter. It is little wonder, therefore, that the free-traders reverted to adding French salt to their cargoes as well as French wine and brandy. Women salting pilchards on the quays often smuggled little packets home, pinned to their petticoats, with which to cure their own fish, risking a gaol sentence if they were caught.

The fishing was poor but even had it been good there were no longer enough fishermen to take advantage of it as so many good men had fallen victim to the press gangs and were still serving in the Navy, their boats and nets rotting on the beaches. Nor was there work to be had easily in the mines. The ring of smelters had used the war to tighten their grip on the industry, forcing mine owners to pay any price they asked to have their ore smelted. On top of this cheaper copper from Anglesey was flooding on to the market. At first the mine owners had tried to maintain their profits by increasing production but inevitably the price of copper and tin reached rock bottom in a falling market, resulting, by the mid-1780s, in miners being laid off by the hundred.

No longer able to turn back to the land, with fishing at a standstill and a series of cool, wet summers resulting in insufficient corn to meet the needs of the county, unemployed mobs of miners invaded the towns with increasing violence, on several occasions marching into Truro and smashing everything in their path. Highly priced corn had to be imported into Cornwall, its price rising with every pair of hands through which it passed. One convoy of corn was hijacked outside Bodmin by angry women who chased away the drivers and then took it back to their own villages for distribution to the needy.

IT WAS against this background, both national and local, that the keen reader of the *Western Flyer and Sherborne Mercury* would have learned that among those coming up for trial at the Launceston Assizes was one William Bryant, 'for feloniously and knowingly receiving contraband cargo and using the name of Timothy Cary'. All published sources on Bryant say the same thing – that he was transported for smuggling and for assaulting a Revenue Officer, although a moment's consideration should make that appear unlikely. Given the climate of the times, had he really 'half-killed' a Revenue Officer, he would certainly have swung for it.

The court record of his trial shows that he was sentenced at the Launceston Assizes, commencing 20 March 1784, by one or other of the presiding judges, Sir Beaumont Hotham or Sir James Eyre, Knight, and Baron of the Court of Exchequer. He was acquitted on the first indictment – which certainly lends credence to those stories that a Cornish jury would never convict a free-trader – but guilty on the second, that of 'forgery', presumably of saying he was 'Timothy Cary' and signing himself as such. Having failed to convict him for receiving contraband, it had obviously been decided he should go down for something and William Bryant was sentenced to seven years' transportation – when a place had been found to which felons could be sent.

He was fortunate. Sentenced to death at the same assizes were Anne Thomas, hanged for the murder of her male bastard infant, and John Tout, for stealing one lemon, one handkerchief (value twelve pence) and other goods to the value of 5s 4d.

The first part of William Bryant's sentence was served either in Launceston or Bodmin gaol, the former described in an official report as being at that time 'in a most filthy and dilapidated state'. There was no water, no privy, and no courtyard in which prisoners could take exercise. The author of the report, James Nield, noted: 'Upon asking the keeper when the place had been cleaned and white-washed, I well remember his telling me that he had frequently applied to the Mayor to have this done, but the answer had always been "the blacker it is the better; it has more the appearance of a gaol."' The doors in some cells were just four foot high, in others the only light came through a heavily barred, two-foot by nine-inch window. Prisoners slept on straw.

Conditions in Bodmin gaol were allegedly better but it had a bad reputation because of its regular epidemics of typhus or 'gaol fever', which decimated the prisoners. Both Launceston and Bodmin gaols suffered from the chronic problem affecting gaols throughout the nation – desperate overcrowding.

ACCORDING TO the records kept of all convicted felons, Mary Broad at nineteen was a slim girl, five feet four inches in height (quite tall for a Cornish woman), with long dark hair, grey eyes and a good complexion. Her eyes and mouth were large and she had no disfiguring marks in the way of pockmarks or scars. From what came after we also know that she was tough, extremely independent, resourceful and highly intelligent, but there is no point evading the fact that what she did would be considered a serious crime even today.

Her story remained almost unknown until the 1930s when a short book appeared which purported to tell her story, followed by two academic monographs. The book, *The Strange Case of Mary Bryant* is a real curiosity. It was written by a military gentleman named Rawson, and in it factual information is interspersed with fictional chapters in most of which Mary somehow manages to have her gown ripped from her shoulders, thus revealing her 'magnificent bosom', a forerunner to the genre known today as the 'bodice-ripper'. Although Rawson obviously had access to court records, he embarks on a history of which the early part is wildly inaccurate. Mary is a 'Devon lass' and she and Will were lovers when both were living in Devon. For some unexplained reason Will is put in Winchester gaol after being caught smuggling and half-killing a Revenue Officer, whence Mary, disguised as a boy, gallantly organizes his escape. He is recaptured, she is then gaoled herself for stealing a silver teaspoon and later, during the voyage to Botany Bay, gives birth to their lovechild – something of a feat as its father had already been in prison for two years when Mary was arrested, and her child was not born until eighteen months after that.

Although two academic monographs (see Bibliography) put some of the record straight, much of the early myth is repeated each time the story is told. Mary is said to have been sentenced either for stealing the spoon or a cloak. Indeed, many of the women who were transported on the early convict fleets were guilty of offences just as trivial. But Mary was not one of them – whether she had always been a wild girl or whether it was a sudden decision, highway robbery is no minor aberration and there is far more of the Moll Flanders or Jenny Diver in Mary than the helpless victim of circumstance.

Having said that, in Cornwall the winter of 1785/6 was bad beyond anything hitherto experienced. What fishing there was had failed as the shoals of fish simply did not come. The plight of Fowey was especially singled out by W. G. Maton in Volume II of his *Observations of the Western Counties of England*, published in 1797, in which he states that during that winter of 1786 the people of Fowey were in such dire straits that in their extremity they had been reduced to 'feeding their families on limpets'.

So why did Mary make the choice to do what she did? We can only conjecture. If she was given the chance to state her case at her trial, then her reasons are not recorded. The most appealing excuse is that she was so appalled at the suffering in Fowey as friends and family sickened and died around her, so angry at the injustice of it all, that she threw caution to the winds and embarked on a bold and dangerous venture to provide herself with funds with which to buy food to keep her family from starving. The whereabouts of William Broad during this time are unknown. He might well have been at sea, since it is known that he had neither died nor left his family.

Mary was nineteen during that winter, well of an age either to have married and settled down or to be making progress somewhere in good service, as Dolly was certainly doing. It is possible that she was still living locally when she first took to the road, perhaps employed by the Treffrys at Place House or working as a barmaid in one of the taverns, but there was little money about locally to pay even low wages. Perhaps she went into service in Plymouth only to later lose her place. Young servant girls could easily be turned out by master or mistress – because they were considered to have loose morals; because their morals were not loose enough (if they refused to go to bed either with the master or his son); or because they were considered lazy or impertinent. When a servant girl was sacked in this way it was almost impossible for her to get the reference she would need for employment anywhere else and after days, even weeks, of fruitless searching the only alternatives were likely to be thieving or prostitution or both.

It might even be that some 'bad lot' visiting Fowey took a fancy to Mary and she to him and they ran away together to live rough in the woods of the Tamar valley – when caught Mary gave her place of origin as 'forest dweller', the equivalent of today's No Fixed Address. If this was what happened then she might not even have been operating on her own initiative, but on the orders of her ponce.

Highway robbery was considered one of the gravest of crimes. A 1785 copy of the *Sherborne Mercury* notes: 'Highway robberies threaten the traveller, whether by night or day – the lurking footpad lies, like a dangerous adder on our roads and streets . . . the horrid burglar, like an evil spirit, haunts our dwellings, making night hideous.' It is unlikely that Mary donned the caped coat, tricorne hat and mask so often portrayed in popular fiction, galloping up to her prey and holding them up at pistol point while demanding 'Your money or your life,' although she might well have found breeches more practical than a skirt, both as a disguise and for greater freedom of movement. She is far more likely to have been one of those 'lurking footpads', and as two accomplices were found guilty with her they most likely operated as a team, one or both of the other girls sitting by the roadside until a likely pedestrian or farmer's cart appeared, whereupon they would cry or show symptoms of distress. If the driver or pedestrian stopped then Mary would appear – with or without a pistol – and demand their valuables.

The first time Mary held someone up she was probably as frightened as her victim and as she counted her booty she very likely shook with relief. But with practice came confidence: too much confidence. Some time in January 1786 Mary and her two accomplices, Catherine Fryer and Mary Haydon (also known as Mary Shepherd), held up a woman on a main road into Plymouth, the most likely being the one which entered the town through Plymouth Dock (now Devonport) since it was much used by foot passengers from the ferries. The woman, Agnes Lakeman, obviously decided to put up a fight because Mary attacked and beat her before taking away her silk bonnet and valuables to the tune of some £11 11s. Whether Agnes's screams attracted passers-by, or whether she struggled to her feet and chased her attackers into the streets of Plymouth, raising a hue and cry, we are not told. Certainly all three were caught, taken before a local magistrate, gaoled and remanded to come up at the next Exeter Assizes.

Between Mary's arrest and her trial, the *Sherborne Mercury* continued with its reports of executions. Alongside advertisements for Dr Norris's remarkable drops (which cured anything) was a report on 7 February of 'a miserable spectacle at Tyburn when no less than twenty miserable wretches were, at one moment plunged into eternity.' All the offences were extremely petty. 'The oldest of these poor creatures was not more than thirty. Three of them were Roman Catholics and had their priest in attendance. They were all turned off in ten minutes, just before nine o'clock. So great a number have not been executed at one time since the year 1740 when Jenny Diver and twenty others were executed.'

In the same issue much space is given to the execution in Winchester of Robert Carpenter, a Navy agent based in Portsmouth, found guilty of forging seamen's 'Wills and Powers', documents that all serving sailors had to leave behind them before going to sea. Carpenter went out in style, conveyed to the gallows in a mourning coach, 'very neatly dressed', in a fashionable mourning suit. He waved cheerily to the crowd, marched up the steps of the scaffold in a spritely fashion, shook hands with the hangman and then, as the writer of the previous report had expressed it, 'plunged into eternity'.

From a lifetime of fresh air and freedom in Fowey, followed by the rough outdoor living in the 'forest', Mary would have felt for the first time all the horrors of close confinement. She could have been under no illusion as to what was in store. There would be no mercy shown to a highway robber; very often it depended upon the whim of the judge as to whether those committing lesser offences were hanged or not, but this was not a minor offence.

The week before the commencement of the Exeter Lenten Assizes which began on 20 March 1786, she, her accomplices and other felons so committed, were loaded into an open cart, their legs in irons and all of them shackled together. By this time they would have been dirty, flea-bitten and very hungry. As the cart creaked slowly through the streets of Plymouth, those inside were subjected to the insults and catcalls of passers-by, supplemented by a hail of rotten fruit. It is forty-five miles from Plymouth to Exeter along a road which winds its painful way up and down the steep edge of Dartmoor. The journey would have been uncomfortable and slow, taking two days. When prisoners needed to relieve themselves, sadistic cart drivers and gaolers would refuse to unlock the individual from the main chain, insisting that all the rest got down from the cart too, a practice ensuring maximum humiliation. The most likely place they stopped for the night would have been Ashburton, which is roughly halfway and had a number of posting inns. Here the driver would have been able to find lodgings, while the gaoler, or gaolers, kept watch over the prisoners still chained in the open cart. They may have been given something to eat.

Eventually the prisoners were delivered to Exeter Castle, part of which was used as the gaol. On 20 March the Lenten Assizes opened with traditional ceremony. The same two judges who had presided over the assize when Will Bryant was sentenced, were still on the western circuit, so the stately procession through the town was again led by Sir Beaumont Hotham and Sir James Eyre, holding to their noses, as was the custom, posies of scented flowers.

The first and most important case was not that of Mary Broad, or 'Braund', as it is spelled in the court records, but that of Thomas Ruffel, a steward tried for the murder of his master and mistress, John and Catherine Breale. The trial was exceptionally long for those days, as Ruffel put up a spirited defence. Indeed, he fought for his life every step of the way, his trial lasting over three hours, a long time for a provincial assize at that time. The end result, however, was never really in doubt and he was duly found guilty and sentenced to be 'hanged, dismembered and then anatomized'.

Next came the case of Susannah Handford who, finding herself to be with child by the blacksmith of Chudleigh, 'took powders' to produce an abortion, given to her by one Christopher Kingdon. 'She was soon took ill and suffered excruciating pain for several days but without the intended effect. A surgeon was sent for and the woman confessed her condition.' A warrant for the arrest of Mr Kingdon had been issued but unfortunately, the judges were told, he had absconded and so could not be brought before the court. Neither could the unfortunate Susannah who had bled to death.

Either on 20 March or on the next day, Mary was finally brought into court. Almost certainly Miss Agnes Lakeman, and possibly other witnesses, gave evidence against her. The record in the Trial Book of the western circuit gives only the basic details – that she had been caught redhanded and Agnes Lakeman had injuries to prove it.

So, in a routine fashion, one of the two judges placed the black cap on top of his formidable curled wig and sentenced Mary Broad to be taken from that place back to gaol and 'from thence to a place of execution and there hanged by the neck until you are dead', for 'feloniously assaulting Agnes Lakeman, spinster, on the King's Highway, putting her in corporeal fear and danger of her life on this said highway and violently taking from her person and against her will in the said highway of one silk bonnet (value 12d) and other goods to the value of £11 11s (her property),' and, as the judge added, 'may God have mercy on your soul!' In the margin of the list which notes 'Mary Braund – to be Hanged', there is a faint scribble which is either 'High Roby' or 'High Toby'.

She was then hustled from the court, taken back to Exeter gaol and told to go to her prayers. Would she be executed in Exeter or taken nearer home to Bodmin, her body to hang in chains at the Four Turnings as a terrible example to passers-by and to the eternal shame of William and Grace Broad?

CHAPTER FIVE

Prison Ship

A<small>T THE END</small> of the Exeter Lent Assizes the judges, as was their practice, considered the lists of those condemned to death and made their choice as to who should live and who should die. It is difficult to discern in some cases how they arrived at their decision, why one should hang for an offence for which another was reprieved. While there was no sentiment over hanging women, unless they were pregnant and could 'plead their bellies', it is certain that in some cases women had their death sentences commuted to transportation for a very basic reason: they could service the male convicts and so keep them quiet. From young teenagers without any sexual experience to middle-aged women, all were classed as whores once they became convicted felons.

On 24 March, after four days spent contemplating her imminent death, Mary was informed that she was not to hang and that her sentence had been commuted to seven years' transportation. Her accomplices, Catherine Fryer and Mary Haydon, were also to be transported.

But transported where? The gaols were now overflowing with putative transportees. Various parts of the African coast had been considered, not least on the grounds of economy for the same ships could be used for transporting the convicts out as for bringing slaves back; but the only experiment tried so far had been little short of a disaster as most of those sent there had died almost immediately. Government and Parliament were now much exercised as to where to send the large numbers of human beings that society did not want. The new territory discovered by Captain Cook was under consideration and emerging as first choice but, as yet, no final decision had been made.

Mary, once over the initial shock and relief that she was not to die at twenty, was left to contemplate what the future might hold. At the end of the last week in March, those prisoners whose death sentences had been so commuted were lined up and the Order of the Judges read to them:

> At assizes and general delivery of the gaol of our Lord the King, holden at the Castle of Exeter on the Twentieth Day of March 1786, before Sir James Eyre, Knight, Baron of the Court of Exchequer, Sir Beaumont Hotham, and others, their fellow Justices.
>
> WHEREAS Thomas Watson, Anthony Mayne, James Martyn, William Coombe, otherwise Kneebone, Samuel Barsby, Samuel Piggott, James Horton, William Cheaf, John Ball, William Brower, Mary Braund, Catherine Fryer, Mary Haydon (otherwise Shepherd), were, at this Assizes, convicted of Felony for which they were excluded benefit of Clergy, his Majesty hath been graciously pleased to extend the Royal Mercy to them, on condition of their being transported beyond the seas for and during the term of Seven Years, each, and such Intention of Mercy hath been signified by the Right Honourable Thomas, Lord Sydney – one of His Majesty's Principal Secretaries of State.
>
> It is therefore ordered and adjudged by the Court that the said above-named convicts be transported beyond the seas accordingly, as soon as conveniently may be, for and during the term of seven years respectively.
>
> By the Court

Once again the prisoners were loaded into carts, shackled together. Mary was by this time only too used to being permanently 'ironed'. Each felon had to wear heavy anklets of iron, from which a chain was then attached and fastened either to a band around the waist or even to an iron collar. The effect of these irons, worn for such long periods of time, can easily be imagined: skin was rubbed raw, festering sores appeared and there were cases noted where such damage occurred that gangrene set in and limbs had to be amputated.

Among those reprieved from death was James Martin, a lively Irishman, whose crime was 'stealing eleven iron screw bolts, value 2s 6d, and other goods, value 2s, the property of William, Viscount Courteney'. The main family of Courteneys lived just outside Exeter in Powderham Castle and Martin had been a labourer on the estate. He, too, is destined to play a significant role in this story. Among those for whom transportation had been the original sentence were two women who would become Mary's friends in adversity – Elizabeth Cole, sentenced to seven years' transportation for 'stealing pottery ware' and Elizabeth Baker, sentenced likewise for 'stealing a calf skin'.

Before setting off back to Plymouth it is most likely that the felons had the edifying experience of seeing Thomas Ruffel hanged. This public event took place in the Heavitree area of Exeter and it was very nasty indeed. Ruffel was hauled to the scaffold, cursing and swearing, fighting every step of the way and refusing any expressions of penitence. When he reached the gallows he tried to assault the hangman and was finally 'turned off' in such a way that he jerked and struggled on the end of the rope, taking several minutes to slowly strangle to death.

Once again the cart rumbled off on its way, but this time it was bound not for Plymouth gaol but for Devonport and the prison hulk *Dunkirk*; for in spite of having been informed repeatedly that the gaols could hold no more, the justices continued to sentence people to seven, fourteen or twenty-one years' transportation. The government was therefore under considerable pressure to quickly find somewhere to store the convicts until a final decision was taken as to where they should go.

Enter one Duncan Campbell, an entrepreneur with a bright idea. He had previously carried hundreds of felons to the Americas and knew the business well. He suggested that he be allowed to buy, cheaply, old warships for which the country no longer had any use and that they be anchored at various suitable places and used as prison ships. The convicts could then be used for a variety of heavy labouring tasks under the supervision of overseers. The Home Office thought it a brilliant idea and were so delighted with Campbell that they happily gave him the contract for providing food and clothing for the prisoners as well.

The first hulks were stationed in the Thames between Gallions Reach and Barking and those incarcerated on them had to earn their 'keep' by raising sand, soil and gravel from the river and building new hards and quays along the foreshore. In no time at all they, too, were full to bursting point. At first the men had been able to sleep in hammocks, but as more and more were sent aboard, platforms were erected below deck along the sides of the ship, which were used as tables in the day and beds, each sleeping six men, at night. Each sleeper was allotted a space six foot in length by twenty inches in width. Every morning those prisoners chosen randomly for the working parties were rowed ashore, some raising ballast while others wheeled it away and spread it to make the 'hards' along the Embankment. Others worked as pile drivers. It was slow work because the men were fettered, having to manage as best they could with the irons around their ankles and the chains connected to their waists. Overseers moved among them continually, cutlasses drawn.

So 'successful' was this novel way of dealing with the prison population that Campbell was allowed to buy more old ships and anchor them elsewhere, some off Portsmouth and one, the *Dunkirk*, in the Hamoaze waterway off Devonport. This latter was the first that would also take women.

As the hulks filled to over-capacity, so disciplinary problems grew. There were numerous attempts at escape, which were routinely followed by floggings and even closer incarceration. The most successful escape was that of twenty-one men, which ended in running battles with sailors from the Woolwich Arsenal and some runaways taking to Epping Forest where they managed to get clean away. The worst incident so far occurred during the week Mary had lain in Exeter prison – on 24 March 1786, according to the Annual Register of Events, the prisoners on board one of the prison hulks off Portsmouth 'rose on their keepers and were not subdued until eight were shot dead and thirty-six wounded.' Those guarding the *Dunkirk* had been warned of the Portsmouth incident and the prisoners on board were left in no doubt that any similar uprising would be put down without mercy.

The days in the cart on the road back from Exeter were the last Mary and her companions would spend in the open air for a long time. As they were hauled out on to the foreshore they had a clear view of the *Dunkirk*, a deeply depressing sight. A typical prison hulk of the day, she was bulky and cumbersome-looking. Most of her original superstructure had been cut away, her masts reduced to stumps, her decks cluttered with a ramshackle collection of huts, cabins and platforms. All portholes and hatches facing the shore were firmly shut. This was because every time the wind blew the stench from the hulk had drifted ashore, leading to many complaints from local residents.

The number of escapes, revolts and deaths on the hulks had led to the setting up of a Committee of Inquiry which at first reported there were no real problems regarding the standard of accommodation, rather the reverse, 'the said Hulks are at present convenient, airy and healthy . . .' However others who visited the hulks, including the *Dunkirk*, took the view that they had become centres of infection and that all those incarcerated therein looked very unhealthy. Male prisoners were supposed to undertake ten hours of hard labour in the summer and seven in the winter, but there was no proof, said the more liberal visitors, that they were being reformed by what they were doing, they could not even work efficiently, fettered as they were.

In groups of half a dozen or so at a time, Mary and her companions were rowed out to the hulk where she swayed at anchor with the tide. As they reached their prison, her sides towered above them, dirty and encrusted with weed. They struggled up the gangway as best they could, slipping on the mud and slime, to be lined up on deck and counted. Their names, crimes and descriptions were written in the Gaol Book, a note made of the provisions allocated to them. As these details were being read out they had a brief time in which to look at their surroundings and catch the foul smells emanating from the hatchways on deck.

The *Dunkirk* was guarded by a smart detachment of marines from the nearby barracks and a number of them stood sentry duty. Officers chatted to each other and looked the prisoners over with some care, especially the women, discussing the more attractive young felons. Over the water, as the sun sank behind the tower of Maker Church, Mary could see once again the green fields and woods of Cornwall, some trees just beginning to show the first signs of spring. The water was busy with small boats plying between ships at anchor and the naval port and growing dockyard, or taking travellers downriver to Plymouth harbour. Ferries carried boatloads of passengers from Torpoint to Devonport, Cremyll to Stonehouse, fishing boats put out to sea from coves and beaches. Some forty miles away her parents would now be facing, as best they could, the terrible shame which had befallen them, as her case and its conclusion had been duly reported in the 2 April edition of the *Western Flyer and Sherborne Mercury*. It would have been a field day for the village gossips.

In no time male and female prisoners were separated and then hustled below to their quarters, the hulk 'stink' hitting them in the face like a physical blow, the stench made up of closely packed, unwashed bodies, rotting food, stagnant bilge-water and 'the necessaries', the buckets in which they had to urinate and defecate and which were only emptied once a day. There was noise too – quarrelling, cursing, whining, weeping, shouting, along with the sounds of the ship's timbers creaking with every movement of the tide as it slapped beneath the hull.

After the open cart and the time on deck, it would have taken Mary's eyes a while to adjust to the small amount of light filtering in from the hatches on the seaward side of the vessel. The most noticeable feature of the prison was the strong screen of iron bars which separated the men from the women; only the *Dunkirk* took both. The headroom was hardly enough to allow a moderately sized person to stand upright. A sea of pale, dirty faces regarded the new arrivals with only minimum interest, sullenly making room for them in a space in which they had to live, eat and sleep among the dirt and vermin. The hulks were never cleaned out. Each morning the prisoners were allowed a little water with which to wash, while on Sundays the men were given a clean shirt and permitted to shave. No proper clothing provision had been made for the women who were soon reduced to wearing rags.

It would not have been surprising if some women, on first surveying the nightmare scene, might have considered hanging preferable to an unspecified period spent in such conditions. But Mary, once over her initial shock, set about seeing how best she might survive.

ALSO ON board the *Dunkirk*, in very different circumstances, were both William Bryant and Watkin Tench. Will had been taken from his Cornish gaol to the hulk to await transportation. Watkin Tench was there as part of the marine detachment guarding the prisoners. He was also bored, dispirited and on half-pay, as were many officers now the American War of Independence was over.

He had had a fascinating war. In March 1778, while on sea service off the American coast, he had been promoted to First Lieutenant and in the July of that year had been serving on the *Mermaid* when she was driven ashore on Cape Henlopen in Delaware Bay by ships of a French squadron. The officers and crew of the *Mermaid* then surrendered to an American ship and became prisoners-of-war in Maryland for some months.

During his time in Paris, Tench had become fascinated by the works of Rousseau and Voltaire and he was – and remained – astonishingly liberal in his attitudes for the age in which he lived, so there is little doubt that he had a good deal of sympathy for the American cause and the ideals of liberty and citizenship. He had been repatriated at the end of 1778 in an exchange of prisoners and, after returning to active service, was promoted to Captain-Lieutenant in 1782, in Plymouth, by Major General Collins, whose son David would be the Judge-Advocate of the first penal settlement in New South Wales. In the March of

1786, when Mary was put aboard the *Dunkirk*, Watkin Tench was wondering if there was still a real future for him in the marines.

By the early summer of 1786 the prison system had reached near breakdown. Two years later Lord Beauchamp had reported from the Committee on the Working of the Transportation Acts that some prisoners had already been 'confined Three Years, or Three Years and a Half, since they were sentenced to Transportation, that there is no stated County Allowance, that they are maintained under discretionary Orders from Magistrates when they visit the Prisons, and that if the Law remains as it is, the Evil will be greatly increased.' There were prisoners on the *Dunkirk* who had already spent five years in one gaol or another and Will Bryant had already served over two years of his original sentence.

Nervous Members of Parliament pointed out that the hulks had become such pits of infection that there was every chance that a variety of diseases would spread from them, causing nationwide epidemics. It was against this background that, Africa finally being dismissed as unsuitable, a decision was taken to establish a penal colony at Botany Bay, 'situated on the coast of New South Wales, the latitude at about 33 degrees south which, according to the accounts given by the late Captain Cook, as well as the representatives of persons who accompanied him during his last voyage, and who have been consulted upon the subject, is looked upon as a place likely to answer the aforesaid purpose.'

So, continued Lord Sydney, announcing this decision to the Treasury, 'I am therefore commanded to signify to your Lordships his Majesty's pleasure that you do forthwith take such measures as may be necessary for providing a proper number of vessels for the conveyance of 750 convicts to Botany Bay, together with such provisions, necessaries, and implements for agriculture as may be necessary for their use after their arrival . . .' Provisions equal to two years' consumption were considered necessary and their Lordships were asked to use 'every possible expedition in preparing the ships for the reception of the convicts, and for transporting the supplies of provisions and necessaries for their use to the place of their destination.'

From the government's point of view, Botany Bay was not only an appropriate dumping ground for undesirables but also, just as important, it would establish a substantial British presence on the Australian continent, where, it was considered, the Dutch already had undue influence because of their base in the East Indies. In other words it would be both a penal settlement and a strategic base on the other side of the world. In spite of some objections that sending convicts to Botany Bay would encourage rather than deter wrongdoing, for the felons would not be undergoing 'servitude for the benefit of others as was the Case in America . . .', a new Order for Transportation was put in hand and a Captain Arthur Phillip was appointed Governor of the new colony.

Week after slow week passed for Mary in her filthy prison. At least the men had the chance to get out of the ship to work on shore, even though they were often picked at random to do so. Not so the women, virtually all of whom came from the West Country; most were due to be transported for theft. Among these local girls, Mary's crime of highway robbery gave her a considerable status, for unlike the 'she lags' awaiting transportation in up-country gaols like Newgate, these were not sharp, streetwise women, they were wretched, poor country girls, lacking even a basic education. They grew thinner and paler on the appalling food supplied by Duncan Campbell, their hair crawled with nits, their bodies with lice. No thought was given to basic female hygiene, not even sufficient cloths for menstrual blood. Women fought, went mad, miscarried, gave birth and died battened down below decks on the *Dunkirk*. They had little to take their minds off their misery.

The news, when it finally came, that they were to be shipped out to Botany Bay could hardly be assimilated by women whose longest previous journeys had been from gaol to the Assize Court and who, before that, had rarely travelled more than ten miles from home. To such as these Botany Bay might as well have been on the moon.

MALE AND female convicts were kept apart effectively by the iron grille, although they were able, of course, to talk (or shout) to each other through the bars. Whether or not Mary had met Will Bryant before her imprisonment, she certainly had plenty of opportunity to get to know him on the *Dunkirk*. He always had an eye for the women, however, and she was one of many from which he was later able to take his choice. While there are legends of convict orgies on prison hulks, in reality this was highly unlikely; what with the gaolers and overseers below, the marine sentries on deck and the officers in charge in their cabins, there was precious little chance for any real contact between the sexes, even if they had been able to get through the bars.

Mary soon saw that not all the young female convicts had to fight for every scrap of stale bread, smelt like latrines or were clothed only in filthy rags. A small number were clean, regularly spent time out of both irons and the prison decks, and looked comparatively well nourished. It did not take her long to discover the reason for their apparent good fortune: these girls were the mistresses of either their gaolers or the marine officers.

Choices were few for young bachelor marine officers and many, like Watkin Tench, struggling along on half-pay, were unable to contemplate marriage. There were plenty of cheap whores to be had in what is still Plymouth's red-light district, along Union Street, which ran from the city to Stonehouse and Devonport, or in the brothels which stood side by side along Castle Street, off the old port. These women, however, were notorious for passing on venereal disease. A young, country felon, on the other hand, who could be cleaned up, who had no access to anyone else and who was always available, became a tempting proposition.

Mary chose to do what many other women would have done in her circumstances – she opted for the chance, at least now and then, of being able to wash, eat a decent meal and sleep in a comfortable bunk, even if there was also a marine officer in it. So Mary made her decision and accepted the offer of – who? We do not know and she never said, although most of those around her must have known. One source suggests her lover was Watkin Tench but although he writes of her a number of times with tremendous sympathy and admiration, it is the writing of someone who seems curiously distanced, if Mary had, indeed, been his mistress.

The attitudes of the women to those who chose to sleep with the officers was probably mixed: hostility from the ones who would never have demeaned themselves in this way, envy and jealousy from those who were never given the chance, and understanding and acceptance of reality from others who were either doing the same or were only waiting for the opportunity.

As she washed herself properly for the first time in weeks, combed what lice she could out of her hair, put on a clean dress and, unfettered for the first time in weeks or months, ate food off a plate and had someone speak kindly to her – or at least did not continually bawl and shout – Mary knew she had made the choice which would help ensure her survival over the next few months. From the cabin on the deck she could see the sky again and the stars, smell the familiar salt smell of the incoming tide instead of the stench of the overflowing lavatory buckets, see the ships at anchor in the river and berthed at the dockside, the grey bulk of the barracks on the Devon shore, and the trees, now in full leaf, of the woods across the water in Cornwall. She would have been aware, however, that she was unlikely ever to walk freely in those woods again, for any sentence of transportation almost always meant 'life' for women. No provision was made by the State to bring convicts home after their term had expired. Men were often able to find berths as hands on the ships of various nations which put in to New South Wales – there were always berths to be had owing to the accidents, deaths and diseases of long voyages – but there were no such opportunities for women.

By the autumn of 1786 Watkin Tench knew he would

probably be acompanying the convicts to Botany Bay for when the Admiralty called for volunteers for the First Fleet now being assembled, he signed up for a three-year tour of service, thus returning to full pay again. He agreed to go 'for the protection of the settlement intended to be made there, as well as for preserving good order and regularity among the convicts.' On 12 December Watkin Tench records that it had been confirmed to him that he would definitely be going to Botany Bay. At about the same time, Mary must have discovered she was pregnant.

Did she fall in love with her officer, an affection doomed from the start by her status, or did it remain a purely business transaction? Convict records show that it was expected, and sometimes enforced, that the father of a child born to a convict woman while in custody had to register himself as the father, whoever he might be and whatever position he might hold. Later, in New South Wales, even the married Judge-Advocate, David Collins, would give his name to a child born to a young convict woman. The only clue to Mary's possible feelings for her lover, and to his identity, is that she gave the child the second name of 'Spence', a name not found among the branches of the Broad family. Mary was almost alone in not revealing the father's name and her child was, therefore, registered merely as 'a bastard'.

CHAPTER SIX

The First Fleet

WHILE MARY was making the best of life on the hulks by seeing to the sexual needs of her officer, Arthur Phillip, the man chosen to be Governor of the new British territory of New South Wales, was trying, with increasing desperation, to get the whole enterprise off the ground.

He was just forty-eight when appointed on 12 October 1786, a slight man, thin-faced, already balding and not, from his portrait, a typical example of a robust eighteenth-century naval officer. He was second-generation English, his father, Jakob Phillip, having emigrated from Frankfurt and then taken a London-born wife. He had seen his first action at sea at the age of only sixteen, during the Seven Years War against France. At twenty-five he found himself retired on half-pay, at which age he married. However the marriage was not a success and, as divorce was next to impossible to those without money and influence (it required a Bill in Parliament), in 1769 the couple amicably agreed to separate as there were no children. In 1774 he sailed with the Portuguese Navy in their war against Spain, during which time he captained a ship commissioned to transport four hundred Portuguese convicts to a penal colony in Brazil. They had all arrived in comparatively good shape, which seems to have been the obvious reason for his new appointment.

Phillip rejoined the British Navy in 1778 and soon rose to be master of a Ship of the Line, *The Europe*, during the War of Independence; but by 1784 he was, once more, on half-pay and farming in Hampshire. He appears to have been an eminently practical man and, by the standards of his day, fairly enlightened in his views.

His commission, signed by Lord Sydney, states that the government reposed 'especial trust and confidence in your loyalty, courage and experience in military affairs' and thus appointed him Governor of the territory called New South Wales:

> extending from the northern cape or extremity of the coast called Cape York, in the latitude 10°39 South, to the southern extremity of the same territory of New South Wales or South Cape, in the latitude 43°49 south, and of all towns, garrisons, castles, fortifications or other military works, which are now, or may be hereafter erected, upon this said territory. You are therefore carefully and diligently to discharge the duty of Governor in and over our said territory by doing and performing all and all manner of things there unto belonging and we do strictly charge and command all our officers and soldiers who shall be employed within our said territory, and all others whom it may concern, to obey you as our Governor thereof; and you are to observe and follow such orders and direction from time to time as you shall receive from us, or any other of your superior officers according to the rules and discipline of war, and likewise such orders and directions as we shall send you . . .
>
> Given at our Court of St James, the twelfth day of October 1786, in the twenty-sixth day of our reign. By his Majesty's command, SYDNEY.

New South Wales, Phillip was informed, was a country which 'by the fertility and salubrity of the climate, connected with the remoteness of its situation (from whence it is hardly possible for any persons to return without permission) seems peculiarly adapted to answer the views of Government with respect to providing a remedy for the evils likely to result from the late, alarming and numerous increase of felons in this country, and, more particularly, in the metropolis.'

A fleet therefore was being assembled. In addition to the crews necessary for the ships allotted for the task there would be two companies of marines to form a military establishment on shore, both to protect the settlement against natives and to preserve order. The vessels would also carry a cargo of stores, utensils and 'implements necessary for erecting habitations and agriculture,' along with sufficient provisions for the voyage, and for up to two years afterwards, by which time, it was optimistically assumed, the colony would be self-supporting in foodstuffs such as grain and livestock raised by 'the common industry of the new settlers'. It was hoped, continued the order, that marines could 'if possible' be found with other skills, men who in civilian life had been carpenters, blacksmiths, woodmen, farm labourers and potters.

The fleet would put in at various destinations *en route* to take on board seed for planting food crops, such livestock as was possible and limes against the scurvy. Seven to eight hundred convicts would leave with the First Fleet and one vessel was to be properly fitted with accommodation for women 'to prevent any intercourse with the men.'

It would be necessary to provide at least one surgeon, preferably more, and a chaplain. Law and order would be dispensed by a Judge-Advocate. This was a grand title and one might therefore assume that a good lawyer would be despatched with the fleet, possibly even one of His Majesty's judges, but this was not the case. The Judge-Advocate appointed to preside over the Courts of Civil and Criminal Jurisdiction was a captain of marines, David Collins, who had no training or experience. He was expected to administer justice according to the Laws of England, although he had no qualifications for the post. This meant that Phillip would be left without any legal advice on which he could rely and the law would be administered on strictly military principles.

Finally, Phillip was informed, there was the problem of servicing the sexual needs of the men – the marines, sailors and male convicts – as there would obviously be insufficient convict women to go round. So it was suggested that after the ships had arrived in Australia, 'a tender [a type of barge which could be attached to a vessel to carry cargo] might be employed in obtaining livestock from the Cape [of Good Hope] or from the Molucca Isles . . . and, if it be thought advisable, may also be employed in conveying to the new settlement, a further number of women from the Friendly Isles, New Caledonia, etc. which are contiguous thereto and may be procured without difficulty; for without a sufficient proportion of that sex it is well-known that it would be impossible to preserve the settlement from gross irregularities and disorders.' 'Gross irregularities' being a euphemism for homosexuality.

Nowadays it almost beggars belief that white males, sitting in London, could decide that predatory bands of sailors might comb the Pacific islands and take, by force, any native women with whom they might come into contact, abduct them from the place where they had lived all their lives and then dump them down, like meat, to take their chance among men who had had no outlet for their sexual feelings for months, even years. But to the average eighteenth-century mind it appeared an eminently sensible solution to the problem. It is to Phillip's credit that, from the beginning, he would have no part in it, feeling it quite wrong to snatch young native women from their homes 'to pine away in misery' in a penal colony.

All Phillip had to do now, it appeared, was to find sufficient ships to put a fleet together, ensure that they were properly victualled and carried the requisite stores and then arrange for some seven to eight hundred convicts to be loaded on to them; a responsible but manageable task. However, not for the first time, the attitude of the government was that once it had set a scheme in motion – to tumultuous applause in the House of Commons – it was as good as done and such small matters as resources and organization were not its concern.

From the very beginning Phillip gave a good deal of consideration as to how he would run the new colony. Early on he informed Lord Sydney that the convicts needed to be isolated from the rest of the colony during their process of reform, or even longer if it was felt that they were not the right kind of people to become founding fathers, but, he emphasized, 'there can be no slavery in a free land and consequently no slaves'.

Time passed and nothing much seemed to be happening. Finally, after pressure, Lord Sydney ordered the Admiralty to commission sufficient ships. This was done by the simple expedient of posting up advertisements in coffee houses frequented by the owners of ships, ship-brokers and merchants. From the answers received, the Navy Board commissioned five vessels as convict transports – the *Alexander, Friendship, Charlotte, Lady Penrhyn* and the *Scarborough* – but Phillip considered this was not enough and so a sixth ship, the *Prince of Wales*, was added to the number. There were also three supply ships, the *Borrowdale, Fishburn* and *Golden Grove* and two warships, the *Sirius* and the *Supply*.

The ships to be used as transports were, fortunately, comparatively new, three-masted and square-rigged, but none was very big, in fact the *Charlotte* was only registered as a barque. The largest, the *Alexander*, was 114 feet by 31 feet in the beam.

During the winter of 1786/7 Phillip wrestled with the practicalities of carrying 1500 people – officers, marines, plus, in some cases, their wives and children, sailors, seamen, and all the convicts – in so small a space. (As Robert Hughes remarks in *The Fatal Shore*, the ration of tonnage per person on a modern passenger liner is 250, on the First Fleet it was well under 3 tons.) However, as Phillip wrote to the Admiralty, even this was too generous for, after taking on sufficient stores, 'we will have not one ton and a half per man'.

None of the ships was initially adapted for carrying large cargoes of human beings and the voyage would be uncomfortable for everyone. However, compared with the conditions experienced by those unfortunate enough to travel on the convict fleets which followed immediately afterwards, those transported on the First Fleet – even the convicts – could count themselves fortunate. By the time the Second Fleet set sail, everything had been put out to private contract, not just the provision of clothing and food as was the case with the First Fleet.

As it was, the quarters for the marines and seamen were cramped and uncomfortable enough, those for the convicts much worse. The headroom below decks was so low that even small women would have been unable to stand upright. There was no fresh air or light at all as there were no portholes or sidelights and candles were banned for fear of fire. Convicts slept on racks, four to a 'bed', seven foot by six. The only air which could circulate to the closely packed men and women, once again sharing their space with unemptied lavatory buckets, was from a small sail rigged to direct air, when possible, down to the prison decks, but in the event of a storm then all hatches were battened down, irrespective of the effect on those travelling below.

To ensure there was no trouble from the convicts throughout such a long voyage they were penned in and separated by specially built bulkheads, studded with nails, running from side to side of each ship. Each one had a number of 'loopholes' so that, if necessary, muskets could be fired through them. Hatches between the decks were nailed down with oak stanchions, and on the top deck there was a barricade of planks, some three feet high, topped with iron spikes to prevent, as Philip Gidley King, second lieutenant on the *Sirius*, put it, 'any connection between the Marines and Ships Company, with the Convicts'. Sentinels were posted continually on each hatchway and a guard, always under arms, on the quarter deck.

It is not surprising, given his ability to pare the cost of keeping convicts to the bone, that the government gave the task of providing all the supplies to the fleet to the ubiquitous Duncan Campbell, who was fresh from his success of half-starving the prisoners held on the hulks. He was determined to maximize his profits, but in Arthur Phillip he seems, for once, to have met his match. Phillip was a meticulous man who checked everything himself and he soon discovered that what Campbell inventoried as 'a pound of flour' was very often only half a pound of rice, that there were no anti-scorbutics for the first part of the voyage, and that all Campbell was providing for a new colony breaking ground in an unknown land was six scythes. Only five dozen razors were provided, 200 pounds of buckshot (Phillip estimated he would need at least 560), there was no wine for the sick, hardly any medicine, no cloth to replace worn-out clothing or needles nor thread with which to sew it.

After a fruitless (and largely unanswered) correspondence

with Lord Sydney, Phillip turned in exasperation to his under-secretary, the far more intelligent and hard-working Evan Nepean, who had at least understood the situation. Phillip wrote to him that the lack of food would be very severely felt 'supplying only enough bread to give each prisoner the pitiful ration of six ounces [about two slices] a day'. The lack of anti-scorbutics would be even more serious as it would lead quickly and inevitably to disease. 'The contracts,' he wrote, 'were made before I ever saw the Navy Board on this business. I have repeatedly pointed out the consequences that must be expected of the men's [sic] being crowded on board such small ships, and from victualling the marines according to the contract which allows no flour – this must be fatal to many, and the more so as no anti-scorbutics are allowed on board . . . in fact, the garrison and the convicts are sent to the extremity of the globe as they would be sent to America, a six-weeks passage.' He added that he feared he would go down in history as the officer who knew 'that it was more than probable that he lost half the garrison and convicts, crowded and victualled in such a manner, for so long a voyage,' and that the public would impute his ignorance and inattention 'to what I have never been consulted in and which never coincided with my ideas'. If the government and Navy Board had considered Phillip to be a 'safe' appointment, some-one unlikely to question what he was told to do, then they were now to be firmly disabused of that notion.

CHAPTER SEVEN

Transportation

All you that's in England, and live at home in ease,
Be warned by us poor lads, forc'd to cross the seas,
That are forc'd to cross the seas among the savages to go,
To leave friends and relations, to work at the hoe.

Anon.

SHORTLY AFTER Mary discovered she was to have a child, word got round the convicts on the *Dunkirk* that those felons selected for the First Fleet were soon to be put on board the transports. After the ships had been fitted out and converted at Deptford, the *Friendship* and *Charlotte* set sail for Plymouth, the *Prince of Wales* and *Scarborough* for Portsmouth, while the *Lady Penrhyn* and *Alexander* anchored off Woolwich. The first prisoners were loaded from Portsmouth on 6 January 1787, those from Plymouth on the seventh of the month. What the convicts were not to know was that it would be another four months before they would actually set sail for New South Wales.

From the end of December onwards, carts and coaches made their way to Woolwich, Portsmouth and Plymouth from all over the country laden, as Robert Hughes describes, with: 'Pale, ragged, lousy prisoners, thin as wading birds from their jail diet.' Many had festering sores from the 14-pound irons they had worn for years (having had no money they had been unable to bribe their gaolers and thus ensure their removal). There are descriptions of men who, months later, once their irons were finally removed, found their right legs jerked uncontrollably when they tried to walk. Children as young as nine were ironed, or even double-ironed, since they had nothing to offer. Any items brought on board the hulks that had survived earlier imprisonment had long been exchanged for extra food or beer, relief from the irons, or had been stolen by other prisoners. The gaolers on the Thames hulks, noted for lacking any kind of feeling for their captives, welcomed Campbell's starvation rations as they resulted in many deaths, which were regarded as profitable for the corpses could be sold to dissecters for £5-6 each.

A chain of twenty prisoners was brought down from Newcastle to Plymouth shackled together throughout the entire journey and 'could not get up or down without the whole of them being dragged together'. Husbands were forcibly wrenched from wives and families, wives from their husbands and even from their children. One woman was forced to travel on top of a coach all the way from Carlisle, even though the weather was very bitter. She had only just given birth to her first child which she was obviously suckling. An onlooker quoted in a report to the Home Secretary wrote: 'The child was torn from her breast and deposited, probably to perish, in the parish poor-house: in this state of bodily pain and mental distraction, she was brought to Newgate . . . and then sent out to Botany Bay. I saw her on board, and she could not speak of her child without an agony of tears.' Female convicts from Lancaster arrived not merely handcuffed but with heavy irons on their legs, causing swellings and inflammation. Others wore iron hoops around their legs and arms and were chained to one another.

At last on the afternoon of 7 January 1787, all the prisoners on the *Dunkirk* were lined up and the names of those destined to sail with the First Fleet read out: 'Henry Branch, James Branchflower, Curtis Brand, Lucy Brand (alias Wood), James Branegan from Exeter, Patrick Brannegan from Dublin, Mary Broad . . .'

The prisoners tied anything they had left to take with them in bundles. For the last time they came up on the deck of the hulk to look over the river to the leafless trees. Those who had spent months, even years, down below had to close their eyes against the blinding light, nearly naked women wrapped their rags closer around themselves against the January cold. Take a good look around you, they were told, you'll not be likely to see England ever again. Once more they were shackled together and, a few at a time, were rowed over to the Devonport quays where the carts were waiting for them. They were the fortunate ones, for their journey was short, half an hour at most, to the warehouses below the Citadel on the crowded quayside of the old port, where they were to spend the night. Offloaded, they had a good view of the waiting transports on which they were to sail, themselves objects of interest to passers-by, harbour workers, customers of the many taverns and whores from the brothels which lined Castle Street.

In some cases the families of those bound for Australia came to bid them a tearful farewell. Whether the Broads made the forty-mile journey from Fowey to see Mary for what they and everyone else must have assumed would be the last time is unknown; they may not even have been aware that she was about to leave the country. Certainly there was no question of Dolly saying farewell to her sister for, by this time, she was in service in London.

The felons from the *Dunkirk* were then bundled into the warehouse. Here were row upon row of men and women, coughing, sobbing, crying out and cursing against a counterpoint of rattling irons and chains. Some talked fearfully of what they would find on the other side of the world – were there Indians with feathers in their hair such as those they had heard of in the New World? Were there cannibals? During that long night many must have exchanged their stories – where they were from and what they had done to bring them to this extremity.

Whether or not Mary had any strong affection for the father of her unborn child, he had at least ensured her relative comfort on board the *Dunkirk*. Now she was on her own with the prospect of giving birth on the voyage, God knew where.

Sources differ as to which convicts were boarded where, indeed even as to exactly how many convicts were shipped with the First Fleet. Some of those whose names appear on the registers did not go; some of those who went were not on the initial lists. The records of the Public Record Office differ from those based on Australian sources and both again from the records of some contemporary historians. Of those who did go, most, as was to be expected, were guilty of offences against property. Mary and Ann Davies from Shrewsbury had stolen a copper kettle, a cloak, a pair of shoe buckles and a silk hat worth two shillings. They had both been in service and were aged twenty-three and twenty-five respectively. Mary Dixon, tried at the Old Bailey in March 1786, had stolen two flat irons, two forks and two teaspoons. Ann Forbes, also brought up in the same court, had stolen two gowns, one petticoat and a silk cloak, the property of her mistress. In fact a substantial proportion of the young women were servants who had stolen clothing from their mistresses. Eliza Pulley (or Powley) broke into a house near Thetford in Norfolk and stole some cheese (value three shillings), bacon, butter, raisins and flour. She was homeless and aged twenty-six. While all the women were treated as prostitutes there were only two actually described as such, Mary Allen and Ann Mather, both of whom had stolen goods from clients.

The oldest convict to be transported on the First Fleet was Dorothy Handland, described as an 'old clothes woman'. She was eighty-two and had been convicted of perjury. She was to make her mark on Australian history by being the first recorded suicide: she hanged herself from a tree shortly after arrival. Another convict, Elizabeth Beckford, was seventy when her mistress had her prosecuted for stealing cheese from the larder.

At the other end of the scale were John Hudson, a nine-year-old chimney sweep's boy whose master had sent him into a house to find what he could and who was caught with five silk stockings, two cloth aprons and an old pistol; James Grace (aged eleven) charged with stealing one pair of silk stockings (value 7 shillings) and 10 yards of ribbon (2 shillings); and Elizabeth Hayward (aged thirteen), who stole a gown, a bonnet and a cloak from the wife of the master to whom she had been apprenticed as a clogmaker. The court had wanted very much to hang fifteen-year-old Margaret Dawson, as she had stolen a large number of clothes – gowns, stockings, shoes, petticoats, a hat, a cloak, a garnet ring, some lace, six dollars and a silver moidore, along with some copper coins – but the prosecutor persuaded the judge to allow her to be transported and to show mercy because of her age and as it was her first offence.

Nor was it only country women and servant girls who were transported for such petty thefts. John Ball was sentenced at the same assize as Mary for stealing one sheep (value 10 shillings), as was William Brewer, while William Brannigan was convicted for the theft of a looking glass. Three other men also need to be mentioned, for they were all to become involved with Mary Bryant. Sam Bird of Croydon, and his brother John, were arrested on suspicion of breaking into a warehouse and stealing 1000 pounds of saltpetre (worth £30). Sam was duly found guilty of the crime. James Cox (otherwise known as 'Banbury Jack') was sentenced to transportation for life for stealing 13 yards of thread lace (value 5 shillings), while William Allen, brought to court in Ormskirk in Cheshire the following year, received a transportation sentence of only seven years for robbery with violence. There was no logic in the sentencing policies of the various courts, the fate of the prisoners depended entirely on the whim of the judge or magistrate.

However, while Mary's own crime might have set her apart from the majority of her fellow women felons on the *Dunkirk*, there were others waiting to board that night in Plymouth who were in a very different league. Apart from the London girls who had made their living from theft, there were those such as Margaret Stewart, described as a hawker and pedlar, who with her man Thomas Sadler had made her way down through the Midlands to the West Country, stealing washing put out to dry, and anything else she could lay hands on, for sale at the many fairs they visited. They were finally arrested in Exeter where, posing as a wealthy husband and wife, they had bought a few minor items and stolen many more. For several days they were successful until one of the traders whose shop they had visited recognized them and turned them over to the authorities. William Lane, an Essex labourer, had stolen from a storehouse 320 pounds of pickled pork, 80 pounds of butter, three casks of brandy, six gallons of shrub and some peppermint water, but even this paled beside the haul of Elizabeth Lee who somehow made off with 30 gallons of port, 12 of malmsey, 3 gallons each of white port, raisin wine, orange wine, claret, brandy, rum and gin, 424 bottles of beer, one hundredweight of candles and a garnet ring!

There were a number of highway robbers, all but one of whom used to attack on foot, the exception being a fully fledged highwayman, who had held up a coach on horseback and at pistol point but had become so flirtatious with one of the female passengers that the coach driver had been able to knock him over the head.

There were also some extremely tough women, such as Elizabeth Barber and Elizabeth Dudgeon. Barber, a twenty-seven-year-old book-stitcher, had attacked one John Price with a knife in his own house and stolen a silver watch and half a guinea which she had given to her man, William Woodley. Elizabeth Dudgeon, aged thirty-two, had stolen a sum of money. Both Elizabeths had been sentenced to transportation back in 1782 and, although the War of Independence was not yet over, it had been decided that a single ship, the *Mercury*, would sail for Nova Scotia in Canada with a small cargo of transportees. Due to bad weather, the *Mercury* had been forced to put into Tor Bay, off the south coast of Devon. Chained below as the ship tossed and turned with every likelihood of it being driven on to a lee shore, the convicts begged the master to release them from their irons. He told them curtly he would shoot them first. During the night they managed to release each other and then overpowered the crew. Many then escaped to the shore in the ship's boats, but most were later recaptured. The two women had taken a prominent part in the rebellion and had only narrowly escaped hanging. Now they cared nothing for anything or anyone.

As dawn finally broke on that cold January morning, the long task of ferrying out the felons to the two transports began. Even though it had been decided that all the women should travel on one vessel, the ships off Plymouth took on board both sexes of convicts; the two mutinous Elizabeths were on the *Friendship*, Mary Broad and William Bryant on the *Charlotte*, the only ship to have been properly adapted to separate the men from the women; for which Mary would be grateful. While her condition was not yet apparent, she must have discussed it with the other women, if only to try to discover if there was anyone aboard with basic midwifery skills. After ten months on the *Dunkirk*, she knew very well the likely fate of a baby born to a half-starved woman in filthy conditions. As she took her single blanket and made herself a place on the shelf-bed she would share with three other women, she could only look with foreboding at what lay in store for her.

As the men exchanged information about themselves, it soon became apparent that William Bryant was in an exceptionally fortunate position. If he reached Australia alive, he was one of the handful of convicts with a skill so vital that the whole colony might well have to depend on it for survival – he was the only professional fisherman. It is a mark of the total lack of forethought given by the authorities as to what would happen when this bizarre cargo hit shore that there were hardly any men on board with even the most basic practical skills. Although it was a matter of life or death that housing be provided as quickly as possible, there were only two brickmakers, two bricklayers and a mason. It was vital that ground be broken straightaway and seed planted for crops, yet there was only one professional gardener. There were virtually no other artisans, most of the male felons being unskilled labourers who had lived their whole lives either in towns or cities without the slightest idea of how to grow food, care for livestock or build a dwelling to protect themselves from the weather.

Will was loud-mouthed, confident, attractive and, most of all, a survivor, a quality Mary would have considered thoughtfully as she noted the ratio of men to women and what that would mean when they reached Australia, *if* they reached Australia.

For nearly two weeks the transports remained anchored off Plymouth due to heavy gales followed by fog. As orders had been given that prisoners were not to be allowed on deck until the fleet left home waters, they were forced to spend twenty-four hours a day confined below, as gale-force winds and rough seas lashed against the sides of their prisons. Finally, the two ships set off for their rendezvous at the Motherbank off Portsmouth. Watkin Tench sailed with the *Charlotte*, a lieutenant by the name of Ralph Clark on the *Friendship*. Tench continued to take everything in his stride, Clarke, however, was a young man consumed by sexual guilt, as we shall see.

Once off the Motherbank there were further delays, as Arthur Phillip was still wrestling with the authorities to make them respond to his request for more stores and victuals. He was soon to make another urgent request. It was mid-March before all the ships finally assembled off Portsmouth, one of the last to arrive being the *Lady Penrhyn* from Woolwich. She, too, carried female convicts. Phillip had seen many repellent sights during his naval service in the wars, and afterwards, but he was outraged and nauseated by the state of the women from London. In a letter to Evan Nepean, dated 18 March, he writes: 'The situation in which the magistrates sent the women on board the *Lady Penrhyn* stamps them with infamy – almost naked, and so very filthy, that nothing but clothing them could have prevented them from perishing and which could not be done in time to prevent a fever, which is still on board that ship, and where there are many venereal complaints that must spread in spite of every precaution taken hereafter.'

The descriptions of the condition of most of the convicts before they were even transported read like those of the victims of Belsen or the Gulags – skeletal, almost naked, figures covered in dirt and sores, unfortunates who were, ironically, sailing across the world to build gaols in which to incarcerate themselves.

The fever from the sick women aboard the *Lady Penrhyn* delayed the fleet still further as it spread to the *Alexander*, where, by April, eleven prisoners had died and the rest had to be rapidly disembarked if they were not to perish before the fleet even sailed. Sailors were put aboard to scrub the ship with creosote, fumigate her with smoke and swab out the convict quarters with quicklime. Even so five more convicts died after their return, along with a woman on the *Lady Penrhyn*.

For Mary, fastened down below in far worse conditions even than her first weeks on the *Dunkirk*, the waiting was interminable. At least the hulk had had hatches and portholes open on the seaward side. Here there was nothing but dark, not even a candle, the only light filtering down from open hatchways on the deck. The motion of the vessels, as they lay off shore, was nauseating for all, not just for a woman in the early stages of pregnancy. To the stench of the latrine buckets and unwashed bodies was added another that they would get to know well, the stink of sour vomit. More convicts died.

, The barrier between the sexes on the *Charlotte* precluded much intercourse – of any kind – between male convicts and sailors and the women; not so on the *Lady Penrhyn* and *Friendship*, where prostitution soon flourished. Four women on the *Lady Penrhyn* were found in the crew's quarters and were put in irons and the second mate dismissed. 'The women in general,' wrote Phillip, 'possess, I suppose, neither virtue nor honesty. But there may be some who still retain some degree of virtue and these should be permitted to keep together and I have given strict orders to the ships' masters that they are not abused or insulted by the ship's company as was often the case when they were sent to America.'

Most of Phillip's pleas fell on deaf ears. By April, he was seriously alarmed. Writing about the *Lady Penrhyn*, he says: 'Some of the men are too sick to move, and no kind of surgeon's instruments have been put aboard that or any other transport. It will be difficult to prevent most fatal sickness among men so closely confined, and aboard that ship, which is to hold 210 convicts, there is not sufficient space for them to move in sufficiently large numbers for more than forty to be in motion at the same time.' Phillip realized that it was now absolutely essential that the fleet left for New South Wales because 'the most fatal consequences may be expected if the full number is kept on board the vessels for any length of time before we sail.'

At the end of April Mary reached her twenty-second birthday. Home in Fowey, Grace must have remembered only too cruelly how she had carried her new daughter through the streets of the village to be christened, streets decorated with flowers and greenery to celebrate the first of May. During that first week of the month Phillip, who had spent a good deal of abortive time in London, finally admitted defeat and returned to Portsmouth to join his ship, the *Sirius*. There was still no clothing for the women, who would soon be experiencing extremes of cold and heat and Phillip had had to be content with a promise that it would be sent out to await their arrival at one of the ports the fleet would visit *en route*. Nor was there the small arms ammunition, for which he had asked continually, ever mindful of the possibility of mutiny at sea.

On 12 May he gave the signal to sail but the crews of the transports refused to man the yards until they had been given their wages and allowed on shore for one final night. One of the marine lieutenants, Philip Gidley King, felt there was some right on their side as they had been employed for seven months and noted in his journal that, 'during which time they had received no pay except their river pay and one month's advance'. The men needed money to provide themselves with necessaries for a long voyage. Withholding the wages was a deliberate policy of the masters, who would then sell them what they needed at exorbitant prices once they were at sea. The row left the fleet still in port over that night while the men were allowed ashore; some never returned.

Finally, on Sunday 13 May 1787, with a fresh breeze blowing from the south east, the fleet weighed anchor and sailed away from the Isle of Wight. Once again sources differ as to how many convicts actually sailed. Bateman, in *The Convict Ships*, gives the numbers as 568 men and 191 women; the women, in spite of all Phillip's requests, distributed between four vessels.

Back in London they were singing a new song:

> Let us drink a good health to our schemers above,
> Who at length have contrived from this land to remove,

Thieves, robbers and villains, they'll send 'em away,
To become a new people at Botany Bay.

Some men say they have talents and trades to get bread,
Yet they spunge on mankind to be clothed and fed,
They'll spend all they get and turn night into day,
Now I'll have all such sots sent to Botany Bay.

There's whores, pimps and bastards, a large costly crew,
Maintained by the sweat of a labouring few,
They should have no commission, place, pension or pay,
Such locusts should all go to Botany Bay . . .

There was much more in the same vein; sentiments towards those who committed crimes against property in an age of great poverty and high unemployment have changed little over the years, not least the popular belief that most convicted criminals have a luxurious time in jail and that most poor people are lazy and workshy. The edition of the *Western Flyer and Sherborne Mercury* for 19 May 1787 notes merely: 'Sunday last there sailed for Botany Bay, the *Sirius* of 24 guns, commanded by Capt. Phillip. Capt. Hunter, with the following supply and convict ships – *Friendship* (Capt. Walker), *Charlotte* (Capt. Gilbert), *Alexander* (Capt. Sinclair), *Prince of Wales* (Capt. Mason), *Lady Penrhyn* (Capt. Silver) and *Scarboro'* (Capt. Marshall).' There was no mention of the hundreds of wretched people, many from the West Country, setting out on such a momentous voyage.

As the ships laboured for three days up the Channel to rendezvous, once more, off the Scilly Isles, those below wept, prayed and groaned. When Mary Broad told her companions that she had every intention of coming back, nobody believed her.

BOOK TWO

THE FATAL
SHORE

CHAPTER EIGHT

The Long Voyage

They go to an island to take special charge,
Much warmer than Britain and ten times as large,
No custom-house duty, no freightage to pay,
And tax free they'll live when in Botany Bay.
Popular ballad

NOWADAYS THE route taken by the First Fleet to reach its destination seems very strange, but one must remember that there were no short-cuts – no canals – and the only motive power was the wind. In the eighteenth century, mariners venturing to the South Seas usually took the route chosen by Phillip, a triangular one from England to the Canaries, on to South America, then across to Cape Town and finally to Australia. The shorter route was around the notorious Cape Horn.

Shortly before leaving Portsmouth, Phillip had visited the transports and spoken to the convicts. Peering through the gloom at the rows of white faces, he told them he recognized how appalling the conditions had been while they were waiting in port. From now on they would be put in irons or shackled only as a punishment, if they behaved themselves they could walk free. Also, they would be allowed regular exercise on deck and, in good weather, would be able to spend a reasonable amount of further time in the fresh air: how much depended once again, on their good conduct. The new regime would start once out of sight of land.

The convicts had, so far as was possible, become used to the motion of the ships at anchor. Now they were thrown this way and that as the fleet tacked its way down the Channel, the sound of the water racing against the hull being magnified in their enclosed environment. Above they could hear the wind whistling in the rigging, the creak of the canvas, the voice of the captain shouting orders, the running feet of the crew as they obeyed them. Depending on which route they took to the Scillies rendezvous, they might well have passed within sight of the well-known landmark of Gribben Head, almost at the entrance to Fowey Haven.

As the last of England, Bishop Rock, fell away behind them, up on the decks of their respective ships, two young men regarded the sight with very different feelings. For Watkin Tench on the *Charlotte* the voyage was an adventure into the unknown. He had no wife and no serious sweetheart and was eager to see this new world. He would, he decided, keep a detailed journal which he might even consider publishing on his return. He had been told he wrote well. He remembered his captivity in America and wondered what was happening in France, a country ruled by a class apparently ·bent on self-destruction. He had made it his duty to talk to the convicts below before sailing. Most were, he considered, 'submissive and decent', many telling him they were prepared to make the best of it as nothing could be worse than prison, the hulks or the last two months spent in the dark. The dark Cornish girl was intriguing, intelligent, he thought, independent too; and unfortunately now, it seemed, pregnant.

Lieutenant Ralph Clark, on the other hand, aboard the *Friendship*, said he could hardly see through his tears at the thought of his wife and baby son at home in Yelverton. He never ceased to confide to his diary how he was the luckiest man in the world, for he had a *perfect* wife, quite, quite perfect – and pure. He had hoped to see her one last time, praying the ship might put again into Plymouth on its way down the Channel but it was not to be. 'Oh my God all my hoppes are over of seeing my beloved wife and son.' He is a figure more reminiscent of the Victorian era than the last quarter of the eighteenth century, a puritanical young man racked with sexual longings (it shows in his face in his portrait), a man who could see only two categories of women: pure idealized Madonnas like his own

Betsey Alicia and depraved immoral temptresses always out to entice. He reminded himself how he had only once been drunk in his life, on his wedding night before approaching the chaste, Betsey Alicia. He prided himself that he would always be faithful, not only in deed but also in thought, remembering how he had once visited a Plymouth family with a naval colleague who was attracted to the daughter of the house and how his colleague had taken 'liberties with her when I was in the room that he, as a married man, should not have done and more so on her side, as a virtuous young woman, ought not to have suffered – which I mentioned to my beloved Betsey the moment I came home!' The one existing portrait of Betsey shows an extremely pretty, very lively looking young woman with dark curls and big eyes who could easily pass for a Jane Austen heroine. She must have felt distinctly uncomfortable on her pedestal.

The run to Tenerife in the Canary Isles was a good one, although the captain of the *Charlotte* had had some earlier trouble handling his vessel. Now, as promised, the convicts were regularly allowed up on deck and Mary was able to stretch her cramped limbs and breathe fresh air once again. For the first time the convicts could look at each other properly in the light. Friendships were formed and men and women sized each other up and thought of future possibilities. Mary and Will Bryant were able to talk to each other without shouting through bars, exchange memories of Cornwall or possibly of people they both knew. Watkin Tench continued his acquaintance with Mary and was surprised, given the nature of her crime, to find her now so sensible and practical. It appears that Mary may have made a conscious decision not to run foul of the authorities again – her ingenuity and intelligence were to be put to better use.

Once in port, the fleet was besieged by traders in small boats offering fruit and other food. Those prisoners who had managed to keep some funds of their own were allowed to buy, if they could find someone who would do so for them. The convicts did not, however, have a chance to see the islands. They were kept below, looked after by a skeleton crew whilst both officers and men, in watches, were allowed ashore. The store ships already appeared overloaded with long-term rations – salt pork and beef, dried peas, oatmeal, ship's biscuits, butter, cheese and vinegar as well as livestock – but at Tenerife they took on fresh water (the ration was 3.4 litres per day per person), pumpkins and fresh meat. In spite of being battened down in the prison decks, one convict, the enterprising John Powers, managed to shin down the hawser, steal a dinghy, and row over to a Dutch ship. The captain, however, refused to hide him, so he then went ashore, planning to sail to an uninhabited island the next day. Sadly, before he was able to do so, he was recaptured. The convicts discussed the pros and cons of attempting to escape; Mary kept her counsel.

Life was distinctly unfair to Ralph Clark, as he was to record. Why should he, who had so wonderful a wife, who truly respected the sanctity of womanhood, have to spend his waking life surrounded by whores? *All* the convict women were whores to Ralph Clark. The *Friendship* had hardly anchored off Tenerife before four marines broke through the bulkhead into the women's quarters and persuaded four of them to return with them to their quarters. Although the men had initiated the activity, it was, to Clark, entirely the fault of the women concerned – the rebellious Elizabeth Dudgeon, two other Elizabeths, Pugh and Thackerey (the latter, a young married woman, being transported for stealing a silk handkerchief despite the desperate pleas of her husband) and Sarah McCormack from Manchester, aged twenty, who had stolen two gold pieces. When the escapade was discovered, true to the warnings they had been given, the four seamen were flogged and the women put back in irons. The ordering of the punishments had been left to Clark and it was his decision only to 'iron' the women, a judgement he soon regretted. 'I should have flogged the four whores, too,' he noted in his diary. It was at this point that the convict women became, for him, an obsession.

There were nineteen officers in all, some of whom play a particular part in this story. They included Major Robert Ross, an unimaginative martinet commanding the marines, and the

Judge-Advocate, the untrained and legally ignorant Captain David Collins, a handsome, cultivated man, driven by his own relentless ambition, and that of his wife, to ensure he made a 'success' of his new position. Responsibility for the souls of the new colony was in the hands of the Reverend Richard Johnson, a somewhat narrow-minded Evangelical supporter of the Society for the Propagation of the Gospel who was looking forward to bringing the poor natives to God. The cure of the body was in the overall charge of Surgeon John White. Few good doctors wanted to volunteer for such service, leaving the task to the inadequate or downright dangerous. The calibre of the other 'surgeons' aboard the fleet was mediocre, but White was a credit to his profession, highly regarded by his own colleagues, outspoken, fair and very much his own man.

The fleet left the Canaries on 10 June 1787, Phillip despatching a note to the authorities back home that seventy-four prisoners were sick (twenty with fever) and that, so far, seven men and one woman had died during the crossing, and a further man and woman while in port. The condition of the rest, however, was steadily improving, in part because of the fresh air and exercise and better rations. Phillip had loaded antiscorbutics, such as limes, in Tenerife and these were now regularly given to everyone on board.

Once out of port, to their great relief, the convicts were allowed on deck once more, which was as well because before long the weather became intolerably hot and humid. Armies of rats, cockroaches, bugs, lice and fleas crawled out of the woodwork, attacking officers, marines, their families, the sailors and the prisoners indiscriminately. William Fadden, a junior marine on the *Friendship* noted he killed one hundred bugs in a single morning.

Discipline during the voyage was a matter for individual captains under the overall command of Phillip. Some were far stricter than others, resorting to flogging and 'ironing' prisoners for the least offence, when others would merely reprimand. On the *Charlotte* every effort was made to keep the crew from associating with the women convicts, yet on other vessels the captains often turned a blind eye to these liaisons. Sailors openly bragged they could have a woman for a pannikin of rum.

Every night, in spite of the heat, the convicts were battened down in a sickening miasma, a bilge stink made up of urine, vomit, faeces, rotting food, dead rats, perspiration, unwashed bodies and decaying ship's timbers. Convicts on the *Alexander* fell sick from the fumes from the bilges which, noted Surgeon John White, 'had risen by some means or other to so great a height, that the panels of our cabin, and the buttons on the back of the officers [coats] were turned nearly black by the noxious effluvia. When the hatches were taken off, the stench was so powerful that it was scarcely possible to stand over them.'

While there seem to have been fewer sexual liaisons between the crew of the *Charlotte* and the convict women (the male convicts, of course, being unlikely to get the opportunity), John White marvelled that even during tropical rainstorms, when everything was battened down and conditions in the 'stinking holds' were extremely unpleasant, such was human depravity that night after night 'promiscuous intercourse' took place, and that the women were so depraved that neither shame nor fear of punishment 'could deter them from making their way . . . to the apartments assigned to the seamen'.

There was no night-time relief from the horrors of the hold for Mary, now six months' pregnant, the child moving strongly within her. 'The weather was now so immoderately hot,' wrote White, 'that the female convicts, perfectly overcome with it, frequently fainted away, and these faintings frequently terminated in fits.' Some of the clothing promised for the women had been taken on board in Tenerife, but it was of such poor quality that it soon fell apart. However, for the time being they were, at least, moderately clothed.

But for Clark the women appeared always to be flaunting themselves, leaving him wrestling at night with disturbing dreams. On 22 June he wrote: 'Tomorrow, oh my God, three years is it to the day, Betsey Alicia, you made me the most happy of men on the face of the earth for which I shall never forget your goodness, for never did man possess such a Treasure before, as is centred on her, dear Blessed Woman, the most tender, the most best of and beautifullest of her sex, she is all that is sacred, etc . . .'

According to some sources, Mary, from time to time, negotiated on behalf of the other women for improvements in their ration of food and water, the latter now being stale and reduced to three pints a day. Elizabeth Barber went further and wrote a letter of complaint to Phillip on the *Sirius*, for which she was to pay dearly. During the long, hot, airless weeks she and Elizabeth Dudgeon had increasingly been marked out as trouble-makers by the *Friendship*'s captain, Andrew Meredith, one of the strictest in the fleet. Dudgeon had a sharp tongue which she used, to effect, in an interchange with Meredith. He promptly had her lashed to a grating and flogged, a sight watched by Ralph Clark who put in his diary with great relish, 'The Corporal did not play with her, but laid it home, which I was very glad to see . . . she has long been fishing for it, which she has at last got to her heart's content.' That night he dreamed of Betsey: 'I put my hand in her breast, dear sweet dream, it was honey to my soul, so beautiful, so good, so virtuous a woman . . .'

Soon after she had been flogged, Elizabeth Barber, who had somehow acquired rum, got drunk and abused the ship's doctor, shouting out for all to hear, according to Clark, that she knew very well what he was after, 'that he wanted to **** her'. He could not bring himself to use the word even in his diary. She was put in irons, where she turned her attention to the rest of the crew, beginning with the captain, shouting that 'she was no more a whore than his wife' before moving on to the attributes of a Lieutenant Fadden. 'I wonder how she came to forget me among the number,' wrote Clark, 'in all the course of my days I have never heard such expressions come from the mouth of a human being.' Elizabeth Barber was bound and gagged, remaining all night 'in that position until 6 o'clock next morning'. She was then released for a very short while, before her punishment was repeated, the sequence lasting for three days. At one stage Meredith shackled all three difficult Elizabeths – Barber, Dudgeon and Pulley – together but finally let them loose 'to fight it out, which I think is very wrong,' commented Clark.

During July a woman on the *Friendship* gave birth to a child with a crippled right leg and webbed fingers (which the *Friendship* surgeon had to cut), while Sarah McCormack, one of the women found with the sailors, became so ill that all hope for her recovery was abandoned. Clark noted that she was not expected to survive and decided it was her punishment for immorality. The treatment for her disorder was to be bled, sometimes three or four times a day, but despite this she had recovered by the time the fleet arrived off Rio de Janeiro on 5 August. Both she and Elizabeth Pulley, noted Clark in disgust, were now pregnant by sailors. 'I hope Phillip will make the seamen marry them,' he writes, 'and stay with them in Botany Bay.' Clark decided to restrict himself to looking at his wife's portrait only once a week as it was too unsettling, surrounded as he was by 'damned whores' day and night. The poor clothing of many of the women had now virtually disintegrated, leaving them nearly naked again. Clark dreamed of Betsey Alicia 'wearing nothing but a thin white gown and a black kerchief.'

The fleet stayed in Rio for nearly a month, to the delight of the officers and marines and the families accompanying them. Arthur Phillip had known the Viceroy of the Brazils, Don Luiz de Varconcellos, while serving in the Portuguese Navy (possibly when he had shipped the Portuguese transportees to Brazil) and was lavishly entertained at the Vice-regal palace, his men allowed to go wherever they wished. For four weeks they enjoyed themselves ashore, admiring both the exotic birds and flowers (Ralph Clark collected butterflies to take home to Betsey) and the very beautiful and 'lusty' girls of Rio, women with hair so long and thick that it trailed on the floor when they let it down. Whether Watkin Tench found one of the sultry beauties, whose looks so impressed him, accommodating he does not confide to his journal. The men made for the dockside whores, thus adding to the amount of venereal disease carried to New South Wales.

The convicts on the other hand were refused permission even to take their normal exercise on deck and by now Mary must have found the confinement insufferable, as she tried to haul her cumbersome and unwieldy body around the cramped quarters below deck. However, one of the convicts, Thomas Barrett, spent the time forging coins, having persuaded convicts who had brought anything metallic aboard – spoons, shoebuckles, etc. – to let him have them so that he could make quarter-dollar pieces. It was discovered he had been doing this since leaving England and John White was amazed at the high standard of the counterfeit coins. He was also unable to imagine how Barrett had managed to do it as he had had no access to fire and his activities had been regularly checked by the officers both down below and when up on deck.

While in Rio the ships took on further provisions. Realizing that the clothing sent out for the women by Duncan Campbell had been almost useless, Phillip ensured that his purchases of tapioca were delivered in strong sacks made of burlap, which could then be used to make clothes for the convict women, 'many of whom are nearly naked'. It seems that some women, especially those who had been in Newgate and had friends to bring it to them, had brought clothing with them, in some instances handing it to the ship's master for safe-keeping. Others managed to obtain cloth, or clothing such as shirts which could be adapted, from marine officers or even seamen for whom they had made or repaired garments. Even Clark had forced himself into contact with a convict woman in order for her to make him a pair of trousers. (He mused he could happily 'kill' her if she did not do it properly.) Phillip also took on board 10,000 musket balls and barrels of the local rum, a noxious brew which, according to Watkin Tench, would be long-remembered for the hangovers it produced.

On 3 September the fleet set sail again, this time bound for Cape Town, a long fast run before the prevailing westerly winds. Four days out of port, Mary went into labour. Like all of her class she had never been used to real privacy, for even when families had their own homes, parents shared bedrooms with their growing children, young adults with each other. Neither birth nor death was hidden away, but had Mary had her baby back home she would, unless she was very poor, have had a bed of her own in a room from which most people had been cleared, except for her mother and possibly some other female members of the family, there to give her comfort, support and exchange comments on their own childbed experiences. There was no such luxury on board the *Charlotte*. Even though Mary had had to spend almost all of the last eighteen months packed in with others, it must have been dreadful giving birth in such conditions. No special arrangements seem to have been made for the handful of women who were confined on the voyage and Mary seems to have been the only one to have given birth on the *Charlotte*. Presumably she had the shelf-bed to herself for the actual delivery, although if her labour lasted a number of hours even that is by no means certain. There was no room to walk about to hasten the labour on, no old wives' pain relief such as raspberry-leaf tea, no sheets and little water. If she got beyond gritting her teeth then she had to groan or scream out for all to hear. It would have been almost unknown, back in Fowey, for a doctor to be present at a birth; a local woman gifted in these matters was the usual person called in or, at worst, a 'doctor's man'. We do not know who delivered Mary's baby. It may well have been John White himself, for he noted in his medical records of 8 September 1787, 'Mary Broad, a convict, was delivered of a fine girl.' The delivery was normal, mother and child both well.

The weather turned stormy, scattering the ships, some of which entirely lost sight of each other. Once again the convicts were battened down as water broke over the decks, drenching everything. Clark noted that it even washed some of the sailors and their damned whores out of their bunks. The bad weather quietened down the convicts, not least because of the endemic seasickness. A couple of women were put in irons for fighting, another given six lashes for theft. John Powers, the Tenerife escapee, persuaded some of the seamen on the *Alexander* to join him in a mutiny, but they were betrayed by an informer (who had to be transferred to the *Scarborough* for his own safety) and the sparky Powers was put on board Phillip's own *Sirius* and stapled to the deck. Several marines and seamen received anything from one hundred to three hundred lashes for disobeying the rules.

On 15 October the fleet finally reached Cape Town, and on the 28th Mary's baby was christened by the Reverend Richard Johnson in what is described as 'St Phillip's Church'. She called her Charlotte (after the ship) and 'Spence' after . . . who knows? It must have been a poignant moment for her. In Fowey there would have been congratulations and festivities, the baptism in the old familiar church, friendly godparents and the giving away of christening cake, as William and Grace showed off their first grandchild. If it was a first grandchild. Was Dolly now married with a child of her own? There would have been clothes, lovingly sewn, for the new child, gifts from friends, clean linen, very possibly a cradle made by her uncle. Thousands of miles from home, and utterly alone, she handed her baby to the Reverend Johnson wrapped in a piece of burlap sacking.

Phillip knew that the worst part of the voyage was to come and while in port he ensured that all his prisoners had the best diet they were likely to enjoy for several years – fresh fruit, good bread and as many vegetables as they could eat. Mary could not have had her child at a better time. Phillip also took on board oranges, lemons and limes for scurvy, and stocked up on plants, seeds and livestock as this would be their last landfall.

Shortly before they sailed on 11 November, the unruly women from the *Friendship* were removed and distributed among the other five transports. It was a great relief to Clark: 'I am very glad of it for they were a great deal of trouble, much more so than the men.' When sheep were loaded aboard in their place he announced, 'We will find them much more agreeable shipmates than the women,' but in spite of the removal of temptation, he still could not sleep for thinking of Betsey Alicia, 'who I fear I love too much for my own health'.

So the fleet set out on its final leg, wallowing through heavy seas but blessed, if that is the word, by favourable gales. When allowed on deck to peer through the murky weather, the convicts could see little but towering green seas, boiling with foam, while above wheeled gannets, stormy petrels, gulls and albatrosses. Schools of whales and grampuses followed astern. Soon they were battened down below again to experience every movement as the ships pitched and tossed in the mountainous waves. Clark wrote, 'Never was I in a ship which rolled as much as this one does'. The little *Supply*, unable to keep up, lagged behind. Then, on 3 December, the wind suddenly dropped, a thick, cold white fog came down and the vessels found themselves almost stationary in an eerie silence. On 22 December there was 'seasonable' weather, snow and hail. Clark wore a flannel waistcoat, two pairs of stockings and a greatcoat all day in a fruitless attempt to keep warm – the plight of the convicts, especially the women, with little clothing and only a thin blanket each, must have been pitiful.

As the end of the voyage grew near, the main topic of discussion on board became what would await them all on arrival. Among the officers and marines there was much ribaldry about sharing out the women, such small matters as female preference being entirely discounted. The male convicts also made plans, spelling out to the women what was in store for them once they were given the opportunity. It was an unpleasant prospect.

As well as their time on the *Dunkirk*, Will and Mary had had months during the voyage to get to know each other. A few weeks before landing, the convicts were informed that the Governor expected that any of them who had formed what were described as 'irregular liaisons' would put matters right and marry as soon as they had disembarked. It was emphasized, however, that this applied only to convicts, not to any relationships that might have occurred between convict women and seamen. Phillip hoped in this way to minimize any possible fighting over the women, while at the same time keeping the men quiet. In this he was aided and abetted by the zealous Reverend Johnson, eager to put an end to what he saw as gross immorality, who told the convicts that he would be taking the names of willing couples in order to put up the banns.

Intense discussion followed among the convicts. The men weighed up the benefits of having a woman of their own from the start, with the prospect of being tied to that woman for life thousands of miles from home. On the other hand, marriage might well mean better quarters and more food. For the women it was an opportunity to avoid becoming common property.

Whether it was Mary or Will who spelled out to the other the advantages of marriage is not known. It was unlikely they had managed to make love during the voyage in the *Charlotte*, given the efforts made to keep the convicts apart and Mary having recently given birth, so they did not come within the Governor's definition of having an irregular liaison. However, wedlock would offer both of them advantages.

For Mary there would be Will's protection for herself and Charlotte. He was strong, good with his fists, well able to look after himself and a family. By marrying him, she would not find herself bedded against her will to anyone she was unable to fight off, before being handed around to all and sundry. Better still, she would have a man from her own Cornish background who, like herself, was extremely independent and, in his own way, physically attractive. Yes, he would make a good husband, and a good father for little Charlotte. So it was she made the third crucial decision in her life.

For Will, with his eye for the girls, there was the obvious drawback that, as he told his friends, Mary was not conventionally pretty. She also had a child that was not his. On the other hand, the ratio of men to women – four to one and with officers getting the first pick – might well mean that he would have to share a girl with half a dozen other convicts. By marrying Mary, he would secure himself a woman of his own who would look after him, cook and mend for him and who would ensure his sexual satisfaction. Whether love or affection entered into the arrangement for either of them we will never know.

Did Watkin Tench consider the possibilities of Mary during that long voyage? We know he spent time talking to her and he obviously felt attracted to her. He could have arranged for her to be his 'housekeeper' and 'lag wife' during his three-year term in New South Wales. But if he had such thoughts, then he missed his opportunity for, just before the end of the voyage, Will and Mary gave their names to the Reverend Johnson for the banns to be called for their marriage.

By mid-December, as the weather worsened, they might well have thought the decision academic. Gale followed gale, and when the fleet finally arrived off Van Dieman's Land (Tasmania), it ran into such a violent storm that the *Golden Grove* lost its topsails, and the main yard was carried away from the *Prince of Wales*. On 10 January conditions became terrifying enough to drive the women convicts on board the *Lady Penrhyn* to their knees in prayer. Yet, only an hour later, wrote Surgeon Arthur Bowes, 'they were uttering the most horrid oaths and imprecations that could come out of the mouths of such abandoned prostitutes.'

But all voyages come to an end eventually and on the afternoon of 19 January 1788, the lookouts of the First Fleet finally sighted the coast of mainland Australia. It was over. They had reached the Fatal Shore.

CHAPTER NINE

Marriage and Early Days

IT HAD TAKEN them eight months, they had sailed 15,000 miles and only forty-eight people had died – forty convicts, five of their children, a marine, a wife of a marine and a marine's child. Surgeon Arthur Bowes expressed satisfaction at the low death rate: 'It is pretty extraordinary how very healthy the convicts on board this ship [*Lady Penrhyn*] in particular and the Fleet in general have been during so long a passage and where there was a necessity of stowing them so thick together.'

While Governor Phillip had seen to it that the convicts were properly fed and given fruit against scurvy while in port, most of the provisions he had taken on board at Cape Town had been kept back for the fleet's arrival in New South Wales, for he had to face the possibility that it might well be two years before any further help arrived from England. Watkin Tench, however, felt Phillip should have been far more flexible. He, too, thought it quite remarkable that so few people had died on the voyage out but wrote that he wished he could put it down 'to the liberal manner in which the Governor had supplied the expedition'. However many of the 'necessary articles' which would have been given to those sailing only to the Americas were withheld, such as 'portable soup, wheat and pickled vegetables and there was an inadequate quantity of essence of malt which was the only anti-scorbutic supplied'. Knowing this, continued Tench critically, the surprise of the reader of his journal would redouble at the success of the voyage.

'For it must be remembered,' he wrote, 'that the people thus sent out were not a ship's company with every advantage of health and good living, which a state of freedom produces; but the major part a miserable set of convicts, emaciated from confinement, and in want of clothes, and almost every convenience to render so long a passage tolerable.'

Gradually, one at a time, the ships arrived in Botany Bay. The sight that greeted them was not one likely to cheer the spirit. It was the middle of the Australian summer, incredibly hot, and Botany Bay did not in any way fit Captain Cook's enthusiastic description of its suitability for such an enterprise. Phillip had been expecting a sheltered bay and safe anchorage, grassland, good soil, plenty of water and the availability of building materials, such as stone and wood and vegetation for thatch. Instead, the bay itself was shallow and open with no protection whatsoever from the rough seas. There was no grassland, the air was heavy with the scent of eucalpytus trees which stretched away as far as the eye could see. There appeared to be nothing else except a few cabbage palms and some stunted bushes. It was immediately apparent that this was a quite unsuitable site for the building of a new colony. The priority now was to find one that was.

Soon after the fleet had anchored, the voyagers became aware of those who had had no say whatsoever in the founding of a penal colony on their land – the real Australians, the aborigines. Silently, in small groups, the small black men and women lined the shore, following every move made by the newcomers. On the way over Phillip had told his men very firmly that the natives were to be treated in a friendly fashion and left alone. Gratuitous violence would be punished with the utmost severity. Now, as the first party of marines went ashore, they were greeted by the aboriginal men with shouts of 'Warra, Warra!', which meant go away, and by the women 'with a great howl'.

As the historian C. M. H. Clarke writes:

All of them [the English] bore the taint of supercilious intolerance towards all other forms of civilisation – its destructive effect on all primitive cultures with which it came into contact. Not one of the faiths sustaining these men, neither the Christian religion, the 'Enlightenment', nor romantic notions about noble savages, could restrain the rapacity and greed of the white man, nor afford him a workable explanation for the backwardness and material weakness of the aborigine. So when those aboriginal women uttered their 'horrid howl' on first seeing the white men in Botany Bay, that howl contained in it a prophecy of doom, that terrible sense of doom and disaster which pervaded the air whenever the European occupied the land of a primitive people.

Correctly dressed in their suffocating red coats, the marines began searching for water under the eyes of the fast-growing crowd. A native threw a spear, a marine fired over his head with a blank shot. Phillip then put ashore himself to ensure there was no further trouble, carrying with him the usual white man's toys – beads, ribbon, looking-glasses – and then made signs that water was needed. The natives looked at him, according to Tench, 'in fear and trembling,' but pointed to a very fine stream of fresh water. There was a good deal of banter among the marines who were amazed to discover that the aborigines wore no clothes, but, wrote Tench, 'I think it is very easy to conceive the ridiculous figures we must appear to these poor creatures who are perfectly naked.'

For the next few days, while the fleet lay at anchor, regular parties of marines and their officers were sent ashore to reconnoitre and they confirmed what had immediately seemed apparent, that there was no obviously edible fruit or vegetation locally. Gradually the natives became friendlier and, word having obviously got around, more and more arrived on the shore of the bay. Although some initially appeared warlike, they were, again, pacified by the offer of trivial gifts. 'They wanted to know what sex we were,' wrote young Lieutenant Philip King, 'which they explained by pointing out where it was distinguishable. It seems they took us for women, not having our beards grown. I ordered one of our people to undeceive them.' The embarrassed young marine was therefore ordered to drop his breeches and display his white penis, a sight greeted, it seems, 'with a great shout of admiration'. Native women were produced and signs made to the men that they could avail themselves of them if they so wished, however, continued King, 'we decided to decline this mark of hospitality'.

The search for a suitable site for the colony continued with increasing urgency as Phillip became more and more worried about his hundreds of convicts still battened down below in the awful heat. Finally, it was decided to explore the possibilities of a place known as Port Jackson, Phillip himself leading the expedition. Later he wrote to Lord Sydney about what he saw: 'We got into Port Jackson early in the afternoon and had the satisfaction of finding the finest harbour in the world, in which a thousand sail of the line may ride in the most perfect security, and of which a rough survey, made by Captain Hunter and the officers of the *Sirius*, after the ships came round, may give your Lordship some idea.' Phillip's party explored the several coves in the area, finally deciding on the one which seemed to have everything: ample supplies of fresh water, deep water close to the shore where the ships could anchor and firm ground where, 'with very little expense,' quays might be built. He had 'honoured the cove,' he wrote, 'with the name of Sydney.' So, in fact, there never was a penal colony at Botany Bay but, ever afterwards, the name passed into common usage to describe the destination of transportees.

Phillip returned and gave orders for the fleet to weigh anchor the following day, not a moment too soon for when dawn broke the English found they were no longer alone: two large French ships had anchored nearby during the night. England was not at war with France (although it would be eighteen months before the colony received any news of the outside world) but relations between the two countries had not been friendly since the end of the War of Independence. It was better, therefore, to err on the side of caution.

Just what the convicts were making of the delay as they continued to suffer in the stinking holds is not recorded. Unless some thoughtful person like Tench was prepared to give them information, they had no idea what was going on or why they had not already been allowed ashore.

So the fleet set sail on the short journey to Port Jackson and dropped anchor once again. For Tench it was a pleasant sight, a land of gentle hills and little winding valleys, 'covered for the most part in spreading trees'. Flowering shrubs abounded of varieties 'entirely new' and 'surpassing in beauty, fragrance and number all I ever saw in an uncultivated state'. He noted particularly an elegant white flower 'which smells like the English May'.

Phillip knew from what Captain Cook had written that Norfolk Island, midway between Australia and New Zealand, was extremely fertile with plenty of wood, fruit trees, ample supplies of water and, most usefully, a good deal of wild flax, which could be cultivated, harvested, spun and woven into linen of an excellent quality for clothing; Cook had brought samples of it back with him. Concerned about the presence of the French in the area, Phillip decided that Norfolk Island should be colonized without further delay and be officially claimed for the Crown, so while the major task of disembarkation began, he despatched the small *Supply* under the command of Philip King. King was given twenty-two people, six months' rations and some seeds and told to start sewing crops and harvesting the flax immediately.

FINALLY THE hatch covers came off and the male convicts were released. Stumbling and blinking, they were given their orders: ground must be cleared and tents erected for everyone. (Phillip's request, long before the fleet sailed, that an advance party be sent ahead to do just this so that accommodation would be waiting when they arrived had been discounted as too costly.) As this needed to be done as quickly as possible, the convicts would not be 'ironed'. The first boatloads of convicts were put ashore and, almost immediately, one small group escaped into the bush. By chance they stumbled into Botany Bay. The French ships were still anchored there and a party had been put ashore. The convicts pleaded with the French to take them but the Commander, not wanting to risk a diplomatic incident, returned them to Sydney Cove where they were publicly flogged as a punishment and deterrent to others contemplating such an attempt.

A few days later wrote Tench, the scene, 'to an indifferent spectator at leisure . . . would have seemed highly picturesque and amusing. In one place, a party cutting down the woods; a second, setting up a blacksmith's forge; a third dragging along a load of stones or provisions; here an officer pitching his marquee, with a detachment of troops parading on one side of him, a cook's fire blazing up on the other.' Ralph Clark, however, found no humour in the scene, as he was racked with dysentery. His diary entries are sparse, 'shot a duck,' he noted morosely, some days later.

Almost as soon as they landed Phillip had sent for Bryant. By this time Will had established himself as a force to be reckoned with, someone who could act as a bridge between the convicts and their gaolers. On the long voyage from Cape Town the extremely difficult task of sharing out the provisions to all of the *Charlotte*'s convicts had been handed over to him, a labour he had carried out with great success. He had also made sure that Phillip knew that he alone of the entire party could help ensure an immediate food supply for the colony.

'From his having been bred from his youth to the business of a fisherman in the western part of England,' wrote Judge-Advocate David Collins, 'William Bryant was given the management and direction of such boats as were employed in fishing; every encouragement was held out to this man to keep him above temptation.' Once he had helped erect the tents, he would be free to begin setting up the colony's fishing industry. There were small boats (and more could be built), fish hooks and a large seine net. He was at liberty to pick out and train those he needed to assist him. Will agreed to this and then, almost unbelievably, named his own conditions. He was about to marry, a woman who already had a child. Once huts were built, then he wanted one for his family as he did not see why he should have to share the common quarters of the other convicts.

This was agreed. Nor was that all for, as Collins noted, 'he was always presented with a certain part of the fish which he caught, and wanted for nothing that was necessary or that was suitable to a person of his description or situation.'

Mary was no fool, the choice she had made was obviously an excellent one. Cooped up with the other women and still aboard the *Charlotte* she had no misgivings about the coming marriage; but it seems Will did. He started pondering on whether or not it really was a wise move, discussing the problem after work with his friends James Martin and James Cox, both of whom had been on the *Charlotte*. He had, he told them, every intention of getting away once his term of transportation had expired, having already served four years of his sentence. To do so he would sign on as a hand and take the first berth he could on any ship going anywhere, so why take on a wife and family? He might well tire of Mary after three more years, want a plumper, prettier, younger wife, and there was a bastard child as well.

Discussions continued far into the night, including whether a marriage celebrated in New South Wales would count back home, a notion he returned to so often that Judge-Advocate Collins actually once noted: 'Bryant has been frequently heard to express, what was indeed the general sentiment on the subject among the people of his description, that he did not consider his marriage in this country as binding.' In part Will based this view on the belief that the banns had not been called correctly.

Mary was unaware of Will's doubts. While the men were clearing ground and putting up tents, the women had finally been allowed up on deck. The weather was still fine, the shore looked inviting. They were told that they would be landed on 6 February. For the first time for months, even years, they had a chance to wash themselves properly, launder what clothes they had, wander about the deck without irons and with only the minimum surveillance. They hauled up buckets of water to pour over themselves, washed their hair, chatted and gossiped. At least they had arrived safely. As had been the case at Botany

Bay, the arrival of the strangers soon brought large numbers of watching natives on to the scene, a sight which, due to their lack of clothing, provoked the women to much mirth.

Mary was feeling well, little Charlotte was flourishing and on the following Sunday she and Will would be among the first five couples to be married. The past two years had changed her out of all recognition. She was no longer the fresh-faced country girl who had left home to take to the road in such a reckless fashion. She was thin, sallow as a result of her imprisonment and noted for keeping her own counsel – except in the early days when she talked of escape. Even her speech was no longer the same – she now used the common argot of the felons, the thieves' cant, of the London convicts. If you were clever, as she was, you were 'dabby', the 'nubbing cheat' was the gallows, teeth were 'curls', a coachman a 'rattling cove', while there was a vast array of titles for criminals from 'tobyman' (a highwayman on horseback) through those that 'drew the King's picture' (coiners) to the little girl who 'canted the dobbin', stole ribbon or haberdashery. Magistrates were 'beaks' and parsons preached from 'cackle tubs'. If Mary had still spoken as she used to back home then only the handful of Cornish convicts would have understood, for instance, that the 'planchon' meant the floor of the upstairs room, that to do something 'fitty' was to do it properly, that all young Cornish women were automatically addressed as 'maid', and that 'my bird' was a term of endearment. If she had spoken of her longing for Heavy Cake or a Saffron Bun, few would have known what she meant.

The morning of 6 February dawned with high expectations of the coming day. While Phillip had repeatedly complained that there was insufficient clothing for the women, it seems that some clothes had been kept back to give to them before going ashore. Now 'slops' (prison dresses) were handed out to them all, garments so rough that Anne Smith, another trouble-maker during the long voyage, 'upon being given her slops and, at the same time being told of the very indifferent character that she bore and how little she merited the slops, throwed 'em down on deck and would not have anything,' said Ralph Clark. But the rest, the younger women, freed at last from all constraint, behaved as they might have done in the days long before they were first brought to court. Those who had brought extra clothing with them or who had handed it in for safe-keeping thankfully changed out of their filthy dresses, leaving the slops for another time. Possibly Mary had kept back a gown from the days with her lover on the *Dunkirk* and so did not have to go ashore in clothes in which she had lived, eaten and slept for months and in which she had also given birth. The women tied up each other's hair, lent each other ribbons, decked themselves in any tiny piece of finery they had managed to hide away. Chattering and laughing, teasing each other and confiding their hopes and fears, they waited for the boats which would ferry them ashore, excited at the prospect of relative freedom on dry land.

The one person who was not feeling happy, as he considered the unequal sexual balance of his new colony, was Phillip. He alone seems to have had misgivings as to what might happen once the women were put ashore and he ordered that five of them, who had behaved particularly well on the voyage, should be put in a tent near to his own. All of them, noted Surgeon Arthur Bowes, landed looking 'very clean and tidy, some few among them might even be said to be well dressed'. By six in the evening they were all ashore but, ominously, dark clouds had been piling up throughout the day and, continued Bowes, 'they had not been landed more than an hour, and before they all got their tents pitched or anything in order to receive them, there came on the most violent storm of thunder, lightning and rain that ever I saw.'

As if it were some kind of signal, the male convicts then rushed at the women in what can only be described as a mass rape. Screaming women ran this way and that on ground now rapidly turning to mud, only to be caught and thrown down in it, their clothing, so happily put on that morning, ripped from them as they were taken by force. Adding to the mêlée were the seamen from the *Lady Penrhyn* whose master, Captain William Sever, had sent them ashore with his blessing, and a considerable amount of rum, to 'make merry upon the women quitting the ships'.

'The men got to them very soon after they landed,' wrote Bowes, 'and it is above my abilities to give a just description of the scene of debauchery and riot that ensued during the night.' Wrote another commentator: 'The scene which presented itself at this time and during the greater part of the night beggars every description, some swearing, some quarrelling, others singing, not in the least regarding the tempest, though so violent that the thunder shook the ship. It exceeded everything before that I have ever experienced, sailors, marines, all drunk, the heat almost suffocating.'

Those women who had already found themselves their own men were the lucky ones. Whatever doubts Will might have had about marriage, he expected to bed Mary now they were both ashore. She may well have looked forward to it, for she was a normal woman with her own sexual needs, and was about to marry. It can only be hoped that he found somewhere reasonably private for himself, Mary and baby Charlotte. As she regarded the mayhem on the beach Mary must have been deeply thankful that she was not part of it and that Will would not allow anyone else near his woman.

For the rest it was a night of almost unimaginable horror. Young virgin girls in their mid-teens, old women long past childbearing age, all were fair game. Men queued up to gang rape victims held down for them by their roaring, laughing friends. With every realization of the strength of sexual appetites which had been denied any real relief, it is still chilling to read the justification for what happened (that is, if it was thought worthy of mention at all) in the books of the predominantly male historians. What happened was 'only natural', 'only to be expected', even some of the more liberal-minded concluded it was probably all for the best. Thwarted, the men might well have taken their frustration out on their guards. It is an attitude best summed up by Geoffrey Rawson in *The Strange Case of Mary Bryant*: 'Perhaps Phillip and his officers were wise to turn a blind eye to this first mass gratification of lusty appetite. Had he attempted, on this first night, to stem the flood the consequences might have been more serious than they were. Nature was imperious and would not be denied!' Only Robert Hughes in *The Fatal Shore* shows sympathy for the women.

Morning dawned on a desolate scene. The ground of Sydney Cove was nothing but a morass of red mud. Bruised, battered women, covered in mud and blood, sat shivering in the cold, some moaning, some weeping, some hardly able to walk.

In the middle of the morning the marine band summoned all prisoners before the Governor where he sat with Major Robert Ross, the Vice-Governor, Judge-Advocate David Collins, the Reverend Richard Johnson and Chief Surgeon John White. First he read out the Royal Instructions given to him as Governor, then all were told to sit down as he spelt out what the future held. They would be subject to military-type discipline and there would never again be a repetition of the previous night's debauchery. Privately Arthur Phillip hoped that he would not have to fall back on endless hangings as a deterrent in this new world, but he told the prisoners that there was one crime which would carry a mandatory death penalty and that was stealing food; in addition, any men who forced themselves on the women in their quarters would be shot on sight. The regular punishment of the day, flogging, would also obtain here, carried out in military style with the dreaded cat-o'-nine-tails, whenever it was considered necessary. Above all, they were expected to work and work *hard*, all of them. He had already noticed some who were shirking their share of the work. His message was simple: if you do not work then you do not eat. God Save the King! 'God Save the King!' they responded. Three volleys of shots were fired and they were then marched away, to be further harangued by the Reverend Johnson on the question of morals. He was making more lists, he said, of couples intending to put an end to 'irregular situations'.

His was not an easy task, not least because he did not always know who he was marrying, as the convicts often gave aliases when they were arrested. 'The convicts who are married here, I never alter their names,' he confided. 'There would be no end to it. The names they were convicted by in England are the names they go by here.'

On Sunday 10 February, after morning service, the Reverend Johnson christened three babies, two born to unmarried convict couples and the third to a marine and his wife, then turned to the five couples who had agreed to marry: William Parr and Mary MacCormack, Simon Burn and Frances Anderson, Henry Kable and Susannah Holmes, William Hayes and Hannah Green, William Bryant and Mary Broad. Just as Charlotte's christening must have emphasized Mary's plight, this bleak, open-air wedding must have brought back memories of all those weddings back home, the eating, drinking, dancing and singing that would have accompanied such a celebration. Not for her the best dress and new muslin bonnet, the posy of flowers, the love-knots on the church gate. There would be no snug cottage to creep away to, no comfortable bed to search for a furze bush, no laughing friends, merry with drink, to shout jokes outside the bedroom window. For better or worse she was taking Will Bryant as her lawful wedded husband in her old prison dress, holding a baby in her arms, standing on a seashore at the end of the world.

The couples then signed the register, or rather in most cases marked it, for out of the ten only seven could write. William and Mary were the last, Will signing his name firmly, Mary only able to put a cross. The weddings were witnessed by E. B. Perrott, M. S. Freeman and D. Baird.

'Some of the convicts were married yesterday,' wrote Ralph Clark the following morning, 'among them men, some of whom had left wives and families at home. Good God, what a scene of whoredom is going on there in the women's camp! No sooner has one man gone in with a woman but another goes in with her.'

Then, for the first time there is some uncertainty. 'I *hope* the Almighty will keep me free from them as he has hitherto done, but I need not be afraid as I promised you, my tender Betsey, I will never have anything to do with any woman except yourself my dear wife, my true wife, I will be true to you Betsey Alicia . . .'

Before he went to sleep that night Will was, no doubt, still assuring himself that this marriage was not for life but only until he could get away – and he was determined to get away somehow. Lying beside him, still keeping her thoughts to herself, was his new wife. She was, unknown to him, planning on doing exactly the same thing.

CHAPTER TEN

Hunger

A YEAR LATER, by the beginning of February 1789 Mary's overriding concern was no longer escape – although it was still her eventual goal – but simply staying alive. She woke up hungry, went through the day obsessed with the need for food, and slept uneasily at night after soothing Charlotte who constantly demanded more to eat.

It had been assumed that the provisions carried by the ships of the First Fleet would be sufficient to keep the colony fed for up to two years, even supposing no relief ships were able to get through. It had also been taken for granted that within no time at all virgin ground would be broken, crops planted, and after a few months there would be sufficient vegetables available to feed everyone. Then there were the cattle, sheep, pigs and goats which would breed and provide milk, cheese and meat, as well as the poultry for eggs and meat. Those officers who had bought their own stock in Cape Town congratulated themselves on their forethought.

Yet such was the unreal world inhabited by those who had theoretically been in charge of fitting out the First Fleet, that there were no draft animals, no ploughs, no way of easily breaking the ground for cultivation; and hardly any convicts with necessary skills. There were only a couple who had any experience of animal care, only a few who had ever worked the land. The two men who finally proved most successful at working the land were the Reverend Johnson and a Cornish convict called James Rose, convicted at Bodmin Assizes in 1782 who had spent five years on the *Dunkirk* and who by 1789 had served his sentence. He had been a farm labourer in Cornwall and was the first free man to support himself off the land of Australia. He alone, in those early days, successfully grew cereals and vegetables, making compost from vegetable matter and seaweed (the first recorded use). He married a female convict, lived to the ripe old age of seventy-seven and died in 1837, one of Australia's founding fathers.

It seems no lessons were learned from him, however. Cereal crops rotted as they grew, vegetables failed to thrive, and disease, the weather and lack of sustenance decimated the animals. Neither then, nor in the following months when the situation became even worse, did it occur to Phillip and the officers to try to find out how the aborigines managed to sustain themselves from the land.

During the first months most of the male convicts were set to work building housing, first for the Governor, then the officers and marines and finally for themselves, but this took so long, due once again to lack of skills, that all the original plans had to be modified. At first walls were made of wattle and daub, as in medieval times, but these proved unsuitable for the weather – the strong winds and rain blowing right through the huts, causing them to collapse. Finally suitable clay was found for making bricks – at least there were a couple of brickmakers among the felons. There was, however, a lack of carpenters.

'As there are only twelve convicts who are carpenters,' wrote Phillip to Lord Sydney in May 1788, 'as many as can be procured from the ships have been hired to work on the hospital and storehouses. The people were healthy when landed, but scurvy has, for some time, appeared among them and now rages in a most extraordinary manner . . . several of the convict carpenters are now sick. The rains fall heavily.'

The rations of old salted meat, weevily flour and dried peas continually had to be cut and by the New Year of 1789 the only difference between the food ration for officers and the male convicts was that the officers were allowed half a pint a day of 'Rio Spirits'. The female convicts received two-thirds the allowance for the men, the children considerably less. Some of the officers were attempting to grow their own vegetables, a few using islands just offshore, but even when they were successful it was almost impossible to stop the resultant small crops from being stolen, both by convicts taken over there to work or even by fellow-officers.

However much Phillip might have wanted to avoid the use of capital punishment in his new colony, it was not to be. At first those caught stealing food were punished by flogging, but even as the severity of the punishment increased from a hundred to five hundred, even a thousand, lashes, so the number of thefts from the scant vegetable patches and the stores increased. Finally, in February 1789, seventeen-year-old Thomas Barrett, originally sentenced at Exeter Assizes in 1782, when he was only eleven, for stealing a watch, a steel chain (value 3 shillings), a watch key (value 1 penny), a hook (also valued at 1 penny) and two shirts (valued at 8 shillings) and who had had his death sentence commuted to transportation, paid with his life for stealing some butter, dried peas and salt pork from the general store at Sydney Cove. Shocked and white, he had been led trembling to the gallows where he apologized for having lived 'a very wicked life'.

There was only one natural, nourishing source of fresh protein and that was fish. Mary Bryant could reflect, a year after landing that, in spite of the privation and hunger, the bargain she had made with Will had been more than justified. Her life, compared with that of most of her First Fleet sisters, was a comparatively good one, apart from the hunger, and occasionally there were even ways around that. She was very fortunate. True to his promise, Phillip had allowed Will to build his own hut, which he did as soon as was practicable, choosing Farm Cove, a site well away from the main convict camp. He had then been given the nets and lines brought from England for setting up a fishing industry, a task he set about with a will. Vitally, in view of what was to come, he was allowed almost unlimited use of the Governor's own boat, the only good-sized, sturdy sailing craft in the colony.

Most of the early fishing was carried out with seine nets. Like huge string bags, these nets can either be slung between several boats, then pulled in when there is a sufficient catch, or held between fishermen standing in the water. Not surprisingly, there were insufficient small boats available for the fishing, once the ships of the First Fleet sailed away taking their own boats with them. And strange as it may seem, there were problems too finding enough convicts who could be forced into helping Bryant, for the simple reason that many were deeply suspicious of eating fish. They had rarely eaten it back home and were only prepared to eat it now through sheer necessity. Yet there was a wide range of fish available from the familiar, such as rock cod, skate, grey mullet, bream, horse mackerel, with here and there the odd sole or John Dory, to the exotic, 'innumerable others,' wrote Tench, 'unknown in Europe, many of which are extremely delicious and many highly beautiful; top of these we call light horsemen . . .'

Never one to let time lie heavy on his hands, Tench would often go down to the shore with Will and Mary and help bring in the seine nets. Twenty to thirty men and women (but mostly men) would wade out up to their thighs or waists in the clear dark water, each holding a piece of the seine, Will calling to them to pull and haul at the right moment. Tench wrote that he 'did many nights of public service from 4 p.m. to 8 a.m., hauling the seine in every part of the harbour of Port Jackson and, after a circuit of many miles and twenty or thirty hauls, seldom more than a hundred pounds of fish were taken, only seldom was there a glut.' Had there been sufficient small boats for the task there would obviously have been enough fish for all, as they would have been able to fish further out. Building more boats was a priority but there were no boatbuilders and all the carpenters were fully occupied on housing.

Mary's practical skills from her Fowey days stood her in good stead. She could work a seine net as well as any man and she almost certainly knew how to repair nets for everyone fished back home. If she did not, then Will would soon have taught her. She would also have known how to gut then salt down fish.

There was a rough affection between the pair even though privately Will continued to tell his friends that he did not consider himself legally married. Just as their impending marriage had saved Mary from the excesses of the first terrible night ashore, the marriage itself kept her from a great deal else. She did not have to share the women's quarters, first in tents, then in cramped, leaky huts; she was not put out as a servant to one or more officers, with all that entailed; she did not have to fight off physically either admirers or other women. Increasingly the women were turning to violence against each other, fighting over food, drink (especially hard spirits) and their pathetic few possessions. Not surprisingly, Mary made enemies among the women who did not have her advantages. She was considered a 'deep one', unfairly privileged, the object of envy. Contemporary commentators writing of her independence, her steadfastness, accorded her a grudging respect. Treated from the first as whores, and used as such on arrival, the other women's own estimation of themselves was very low. It is not surprising that many resorted to drink when it was available, seeking oblivion from lives that were almost unendurable. Mary, thanks to Will, had been spared any such indignities and remained, as a result, very much her own woman.

While there was more than enough for the male convicts to do, insufficient thought had been given to the tasks to be allotted to women. Some provided servant labour, but that still left many with little or no employment. Communal cooking was minimal, small groups of convicts cooked their own food, or that of those sharing the same hut or tent, on shovels over open fires. Some women were detailed to do the laundry for the officers and male convicts, which meant taking it down to a stream, pounding it on stones, then laying it over bushes to dry. As most convict clothing was badly made from cheap cloth it very soon fell apart under such treatment. The clothing of the officers fared little better.

Once building was under way, however, the women were soon set to work cutting and fetching rushes for thatch, making the wooden 'ties' (pegs) for tiles and collecting seashells which could be burned to provide the only source of lime with which to make mortar; tasks which Mary would have also had to undertake unless she was otherwise occupied with activities related to the fishing. By the standards of what was to come later in the female convict factories of Parramatta and Tasmania where they used the treadmill, they were fortunate. The treadmill, which was also used in some English prisons, was like a huge waterwheel, with wooden treads about nine inches wide. In Australia, convicts were made to work it to grind corn, though in both countries it was also used simply as a punishment. A number of prisoners would be put on it at once and as the wheel was set in motion so they had to keep walking up the treads. If they missed a step they risked injury. It was very heavy going, particularly as most still wore their irons. It was particularly hard on women. Many who were pregnant miscarried, and menstruating women often haemorrhaged. Sadistic overseers would not even allow them cloths to staunch the flow.

There was a steady, but small, trickle of convict marriages (some men gave up the idea once it became apparent there were few, apart from sexual, advantages, and an even steadier stream of births, for it proved impossible to keep the men out of the women's quarters. At first ridicule was used to try to curb this. 'This day,' wrote Ralph Clark, 'our carpenter, one sailor and a boy were caught in the women's tents and were drummed out of camp to the tune of the Rogue's March, playing before them, and the boy had petticoats put upon him. All had their hands tied behind them. The anarchy and confusion which reigns and the audacity of the convicts, both men and women, is arrived to such a pitch as is not to be equalled by any other set of villains on the Globe. Men seize upon any sailors near the women's quarters and beat them unmercifully. I hope this will be a warning to them for coming into the whores' camp. I would call it by the name of Sodom, for there is more sin committed in it than in any other part of the world.'

Mary no longer spoke openly of escape. In the early days four women had run off into the woods and had been shot at by sailors (Clark was sorry they had not been hurt). Three were recaptured, one was never seen again. Mary would chat to the other women as they washed clothes or took their turn at collecting rushes or seashells, but she was never fully accepted once she had left the *Charlotte*.

Talk often hinged on who was sleeping with whom, which men were good to their women, which treated them with violence. There was a certain amount of admiration for those, such as Elizabeth Barber, who cheeked officers and refused to be subdued. Such rebels were regularly brought up before either Clark or, if the offence were more serious, before Judge-Advocate Collins. Most often it was for being drunk and disorderly, petty pilfering, quarrelling or being found among the men late at night. Certainly there were women who, well aware of their scarcity value, played men off against each other, causing frequent fights. Preferences changed, liaisons broke up leading to a welter of accusations, not least ones of theft. Men accused the women of stealing their shirts so that they could make shifts or petticoats, the women would respond that they had been given them either as a free gift or in exchange for domestic tasks. Two men were sentenced to several hundred lashes for lying in wait for the women when they went to bathe after work, one actually being found grappling with a half-naked woman on the ground while her companions tried to pull him off. There was growing gossip, too, that even the most moral and serious-minded of the officers were beginning to look with new eyes on the convict women.

At first women were merely reprimanded for their misdeeds, but as the months went by they too fell victim to floggings, usually twenty-five or fifty lashes, at the cart's tail, a punishment that had been used for women since Elizabethan times. The women would be tied behind the back of the cart which was then driven slowly along with her walking behind. When it reached the place where the punishment was to take place she would be tied to the back of the cart and whipped. Women were not flogged at the triangle, a dreaded device which stood in the middle of the camp, to which male offenders were lashed for their more drastic punishment. It consisted of three stout posts, set up tepee-fashion, the victims' wrists being bound to the top of it, each foot then tied to two of the uprights.

'The very small proportion of females makes the sending out of an additional number absolutely necessary,' wrote Phillip in one of the many despatches which would take months to reach England, 'for I am certain your Lordships will think that to send for women from the Islands, in our present situation, would answer no other purpose but that they would pine away in the misery.'

Nearly all those in authority were now feeling the strain of being so very far from home and everyone, from Governor Phillip down to the lowliest marine, appears to have loathed Major Ross who was officially Vice-Governor. Within months he and Phillip were barely on speaking terms and Ross was described by one of his own officers as being 'without exception the most disagreeable commanding officer I ever knew,' a view echoed by Watkin Tench who narrowly escaped a court martial at his hands. Ross hated the country, the natives, the marines, the convicts and, most of all, his staff, writing home:

> that in the whole world there is not a worse country. All that is contiguous to us is so very barren and forbidding that it máy with truth be said that here nature is reversed; and if not so, she is nearly worn out, for almost all the seeds which have been put in the ground have rotted, and I have no doubt but will, like the wood of this vile country, when burned or rotted, turn to sand . . . If the minister has a true and just description given him of it, he will surely not think of sending any more people here. If he does, then I shall not scruple to say that he will entail misery on all that are sent, and an expense on the mother country that, in the days of her prosperity, she was not equal to, for there is not one article for the use of man that can ever be necessary, but which must be imported into this country . . . it is full of timber but the only use that can be made of it is to fire the cooking pots. All but two of those coming out with me now want to get away.

The Reverend Richard Johnson wrote personally to Evan Nepean, telling him of the convict couple (the woman already pregnant when sentenced) who had been taken from Norwich to Plymouth and whom he had married on their arrival. Their friends in Norwich had been so horrified at their plight that they had collected twenty pounds and spent it on necessities for them in their new life, the goods being given to the ship's captain to look after until they reached New South Wales. However, on arrival, all the goods had disappeared and Johnson points out that as so much interest had been shown in the couple's welfare, there might well be trouble if it ever became known in Norwich. 'Their child is still living, but of a weakly disposition, but a fine boy . . .'

He continued with a saga of bad luck: 'Thunder and lightning killed all the sheep belonging to the Lieut. Governor and others. The "fresh water" seems to bring on dysentery and worms.' There was much strange wildlife, kangaroos, opossums, 'a spotted animal of the cat kind but larger,' flying squirrels and three sorts of rats.

Surgeon John White begged for supplies for his 'hospital', a large ramshackle hut, through which the wind blew and where the walls collapsed as water dissolved the poor mortar. 'We have no sheets or blankets for the hospital,' he wrote. 'We need sugar, sago, barley, rice, oatmeal, currants, spices, vinegar, soap, tamarinds, raisins and more saucepans.' Phillip sent another urgent despatch: 'The cloaths for the convicts are in general bad and there is no possibility of mending them, for want of thread; it is the same with the shoes, which do not last a month; as regards the ration, the women have $\frac{2}{3}$rds what is allowed to the men, and the children one third. The children's allowance is, I think, too little and I have been obliged in several instances to order them half the men's allowance, or two thirds as the women are allowed.' No extra allowance seems to have been given to nursing mothers.

The convicts who had landed so relatively healthy began, very steadily, to die; first the very old and the very young, then those already vulnerable to sickness. Finally death made inroads into every age group. Nearly all the colony, marines and their wives, the officers, as well as the convicts, were weakened by scurvy. Cholera, dysentery and influenza abounded. At first the convicts stopped work to attend the funerals of their fellow felons, but soon the funeral processions to the graveyard became so commonplace that they hardly commanded notice.

Disease did not stop with the settlers. It soon spread to the unfortunate aborigines whose bodies were found on the beaches, under the trees, along the paths where they had dropped. Phillip did everything during his period as governor to see the aborigines were properly treated, but he never succeeded in overcoming the prejudices of the marines and convicts, many of whom looked for excuses to treat them as they thought they 'deserved', for the hostility of some tribes, and their lack of basic 'decency'. Unused to theft, the aborigines would leave their artefacts lying around and the sailors and marines often stole tools and weapons as souvenirs. In May 1788 a convict working on water tanks at a place called the Tank Stream was speared dead, and two weeks later two convicts collecting thatch were found stabbed to death, in retaliation, it was said, for marines stealing the aborigines' canoes.

Watkin Tench was almost alone in never deviating from his interest in, and sympathy for, the real Australians, and among the facts he noted early on was 'the ease with which the tribes understood each other,' though possibly what sounded like different languages was in fact dialects as 'each in speaking preferred their own tongue'. In December, Phillip decided that the only way to communicate effectively with the natives was by capturing an aboriginal, making a 'friend' of him and setting him up as an interpreter. To that end, at the end of December 1788, a young male was caught and brought into the colony. At first he was called 'Manly' (as Phillip considered that to be one of his qualities) but eventually this was changed to the nearest phonetic approximation to his own, Arabanoo. His story is brief and sad for, after a period of liveliness owing to the novelty of his situation, he began making attempts to escape, on one occasion nearly drowning after jumping off the *Supply*, which had been kept by the colony to use as a ferry to Norfolk Island.

'When brought back aboard,' writes Tench, 'he appeared neither afraid nor ashamed of what he had done, but sat apart, melancholy and dispirited, and continued so until he saw the governor . . . the dread of being carried away, on an element of whose boundary he could form no conception, joined to the uncertainty of our intention towards him, unquestionably caused him to act as he did.' It is not known whether Will and Mary made friends with Arabanoo, but what we do know is that they had unusually close relationships with other aborigines brought in by the marines and with their families who remained outside. This would prove essential to them in the future.

Phillip had remained true to his promise that Will could always keep a small portion of the fish he caught and this was noted in the colony records; but by February 1789 there was too little food available for this to continue. Will deeply resented the loss of such a privilege, a resentment shared by Mary. While they may have kept many of their personal thoughts and feelings from each other, Will and Mary were always united in their attitude to camp authority: they would not bring unnecessary punishment on themselves by pointless rebellion, they would live their own lives in their own way to the best of their ability, they would use the system for all it was worth and they would do anything necessary to survive. Neither were against breaking rules, but if they were broken then it had to be for good reason. Starvation certainly provided one.

At the beginning of February, sick with hunger, Will decided to take a risk. From a comparatively good catch of fish, he kept a few back. Some the family ate themselves, the others he swapped with another convict who was tending what was left of the vegetables. For once, the Bryants dined well.

For a long time solidarity had prevailed among the convicts. Phillip, Collins and Clark had found it very difficult to get any of them to inform on the others. For example, in the early days, a sheep had been roasted whole to celebrate the birthday of the Prince of Wales; it had vanished before the officers could get near it and although Phillip had offered a reward, no one had ever 'peached'. A year later, however, things had changed: hunger and want produced a small but persistent core of informers. Add to this that the Bryants were already the subject of envy owing to their free lifestyle, almost as free as any of the marines, their superior living accommodation and the ability to turn their skills to good advantage, and there was the making of a disaster.

Someone (later identified as Joseph Paget) learned of the 'stolen' fish and the swap and told the Judge-Advocate. There was only one possible outcome. It seems that initially there was even talk of hanging Will Bryant as an example, but even if it was not Mary who pointed out to the Governor the folly of this course of action (and it has been suggested that she did), it must have finally dawned on the officers that the inevitable consequence of his death would be the accelerated starvation of everyone else.

On 4 February 1789 Will was brought before Judge-Advocate David Collins and the informer stepped forward to testify. His name was Joseph Paget and he had been sentenced at the very same Exeter Assize as Mary. The details of his crime are not known, but possibly there was some element of jealousy involved as he and Mary had not only been together on the *Dunkirk* in Devonport but he had sailed with the Bryants on the *Charlotte*, but now had to receive his rations from the hand of Will. Not only did Paget tell of the theft and subsequent swap, he embroidered his account by relating to the court that he had 'often' sold stolen fish for Bryant, who then pocketed the proceeds. At this point Surgeon John White spoke up for Will, saying that he found this hard to believe as to him Will had always seemed 'strictly honest'. Not surprisingly, however, Will was found guilty and sentenced 'to receive 100 Lashes; to be deprived of the Direction of the Fish and the Boat; and to be turned out of the Hut he is now in along with his family.'

Yet again the convicts were lined up in the centre of the camp to witness a punishment. However hardened, few could remain unmoved at watching a man's flesh ripped from his back. The marines stood each side of the wooden triangle, beating their drums as Will was brought out and the sentence read. His shirt was then removed and he was tied to the triangle. A hundred lashes was mild by the standards of the day. Men, even in Australia, were subsequently sentenced to up to two thousand, some dying before that number was reached, others being taken away halfway through to allow their backs to heal so that they could later endure the rest of their punishment. It was the custom for children to be made to watch too, and it is likely that little Charlotte witnessed the man she thought of as her father being punished in this way.

The marine detailed to administer the beating raised the cat-o'-nine-tails with its tarred and knotted strings and, on a count from an officer, began the beating. There is no description of Will's ordeal but there are plenty of others. Almost immediately the skin would be lacerated, even twenty-five lashes could flay a man's back. An account of a hundred-lash flogging comes from Alexander Harris's *Settlers and Convicts* published in 1847.

> I had to go past the triangle where they had been flogging incessantly for hours. I saw a man walk across the yard with the blood that ran down from his lacerated flesh squashing out of his shoes at every step he took. A dog was licking the blood off the triangle, and the ants were carrying away great pieces of human flesh the lash had scattered upon the ground.
>
> The scourger's foot had worn a deep hole in the ground by the violence with which he whirled himself around on it to strike the quivering, wealed back, out of which stuck the sinews, white, ragged and swollen. The infliction was a hundred lashes, at about half-minute time, so as to extend the punishment through nearly an hour. The day was hot enough to overcome a man merely standing that length of time in the sun . . . I know of several poor creatures who have been entirely crippled for life by these merciless floggings.

At first the men would do their best not to cry out, then they would scream, finally, almost insensible, they hung from their slack wrists, swaying with each lash. For Mary, standing for an hour in the February sunshine, it must have seemed interminable. Eventually Will, now almost unconscious, was cut down and dragged to one side and left to his wife. Mary would have had nowhere to go, as she could not even take him back to their hut to see to his wounds.

Some of the women at least must have been sufficiently sympathetic to bring cloths, water and salt, the latter being the only antiseptic available. Mary would then have had to clean Will's lacerated back, trying to wash it with the salt water while he was still semi-conscious. There is no record of just when she began her long and sustained campaign to persuade him that the only course now open to them was a properly planned escape, but it seems very likely that the turning point came as she sat in the sun with her moaning husband, her hands covered in his blood. What is certain is that later she was to tell people that it was only the possibility of getting away – even if she died in the attempt – that enabled her to survive the desperate months that followed.

CHAPTER ELEVEN
'For Our Country's Good'

L ITTLE ALLOWANCE was made for convicts who had suffered
punishment and as soon as he could get about Will was
put to work digging, and then dragging in the clay to make
bricks, while Mary was given supervised work with the gangs
of convict women making lime or the ties for the roof tiles. She
and Charlotte now had to share the huts of the other convict
women while Will joined the men.

The conditions in which she had to live were well described
in a letter from 'a female convict'. Several convict letters from
those early days were published, either in full or in part, in
newspapers of the time, but always anonymously and the names
of the writers now seem to be lost. The unknown woman begins
with a brief recital of the rigours of the voyage over, then
continues:

> We now have two streets, if four rows of the most miserable
> huts you can possibly conceive of deserve that name. Windows
> they have none, as from the Governor's house, etc. now nearly
> finished, no glass could be spared so that lattices of twigs are
> made by our people to supply their places. At the extremity of
> the line, where since our arrival the dead are buried, there is a
> place called the churchyard; but we hear, as soon as a sufficient
> quantity of bricks can be made, a church is to be built, and
> named St. Phillip after the Governor.

After expressing her fear of the natives she writes:

> As for the distresses of the women, they are past description,
> as they are deprived of tea and other things they were indulged
> in during the voyage by the seamen, and as they are all totally

unprovided with clothes, those who have young children are quite wretched. Besides this, though a number of marriages have taken place, several women, who have become pregnant and are since left by their partners, who have returned to England, are not likely even here to form fresh connections . . . Something like ground ivy is used for tea; but a scarcity of salt and sugar makes even our best meals insipid. The separation of several of us to an uninhabited island was like a second transportation. In short, every one is so taken up with their miseries that they have no pity to bestow on others. All our letters are examined by an officer, but a friend takes this for me privately.

Whoever she was, she could write of her life as well as any of those in authority over her.

Women were now experiencing harsher punishment. Five days after Will received his flogging, a number of women were similarly sentenced, mostly for insolence – Elizabeth Hayward (thirty lashes), Charlotte Ware (thirty lashes for fighting), Ann Thornton (twenty lashes), Mary Marshall (twenty lashes) and Judith Jones (who received twenty-five for creating a disturbance). Judith Jones, also known as Anne Davis, regularly appeared on the list of punished offenders.

With no end in sight to the food crisis, Phillip had sent the only sizeable ship left to him, the *Sirius*, to Cape Town for flour and cereals. He decided to send more convicts to Lieutenant Philip King on Norfolk Island and in a note explained that the rigours facing the colony in New South Wales left him with no alternative. On 17 February the *Supply* sailed with twenty-one male convicts, six female convicts and three children who, wrote Phillip, 'are of an age that, if left with the convicts, they will be lost. The mother of the girl is the most abandoned in the settlement [Judith Jones/Anne Davis, according to one source]. The boy's mother died on the passage.' Venereal disease was now added to the other woes, he noted, 'It is a more severe scourge, and has gained such a footing in this Settlement, that I now doubt if it will ever be done away.' It was most probably this voyage which the female convict referred to in her letter as the 'second transportation'. 'The Cove is now left for the first time without a ship,' reported Watkin Tench.

In early March sixteen convicts left their work at the brick kilns without permission, marched to Botany Bay and attacked a band of natives with the intention of stealing their fishing tackle and spears. Will Bryant was not among them. They had armed themselves with their working tools and had made large clubs. They walked straight into an ambush, however, for they had been watched all along the route. The aboriginals killed one man and severely wounded seven others before the marines could be called to rescue the remainder. Phillip was furious. At first the convicts told him they had merely gone in search of leaves of the 'sweet tea' (the vine used for brewing up, referred to earlier) and they had then been assaulted without provocation, but finally they confessed. Each was given 150 lashes and ordered to wear leg irons for a year. Arabanoo, who was summoned to watch, does not appear to have appreciated the benefits of white civilization and justice. Tench writes: 'Arabanoo was present at the infliction of the punishment and was made to comprehend the cause and the necessity of it; but he displayed on the occasion symptoms of disgust and terror only.'

Later in the month there was a far more serious trial. For a long time there had been constant pilfering from the stores and extra watches had been kept over the convicts, without the culprits being discovered. The reason for this finally became apparent when, on 18 March, seven marines were found taking food after procuring a duplicate key. One, Joseph Hunt, promptly turned King's Evidence and informed on the rest. On 26 March they were brought to trial and summarily sentenced to death, for this was the penalty Phillip had promised for such a serious offence, whoever had perpetrated it, though he had hoped he would never have to carry it out. A gallows had already been built in anticipation of the sentence and at ten o'clock the next morning the six marines, less Hunt who had been pardoned for his part in their conviction, mounted the scaffold. The marines did not take their deaths penitently, all blamed Hunt, saying he 'was the occasion for their deaths, as he was the first that began the said robbery, but he had received a free pardon. There was hardly a marine present but what shed tears, officers and men,' wrote an observer.

By the beginning of April Phillip had no option but to take Will off the brick kilns and put him back in charge of the fishing, for it had proved impossible to manage without his skills. But he would, Collins noted, be kept under surveillance at all times to ensure there was no repetition of his offence. The immediate effect of this was that he and Mary were allowed to move back into their original hut, which made life considerably more tolerable for them, even if their escape plans had, for the time being, to be shelved.

Not all the women left behind by Mary in the women's camp were hard-drinking, hard-swearing viragos. There was, for instance, Susannah Holmes, who had been sentenced to death, at the age of nineteen, for the theft of household linen and silver, her sentence then commuted to seven years' transportation. While in Norwich gaol she had met a young man from Suffolk, Henry Kable, who had kept watch while his father and a friend had robbed a country house. He had been sentenced to transportation but had been forced to witness the public hanging of his father outside the gaol. Susannah and Henry became lovers and in 1786 she had a son, but they were refused permission to marry.

As the First Fleet was being made ready to sail Susannah was sent from Norwich to Plymouth by coach, travelling outside, clutching her child, 'a very fine babe which the mother had suckled from birth'. Kable's desperate entreaties to travel with her were refused. After waiting for three hours on Sutton Harbour to be put aboard the *Friendship*, she was finally put into a small boat, at which point the gaoler, who had come with her from Norwich, told her she would have to give up her baby as it had not been listed for the voyage. Susannah had to be taken on board by force but the gaoler, an unusually decent man, left the child with a reliable woman and then, on his own initiative, went to the home of Lord Sydney himself to put the case, begging His Lordship's secretary to make out an order to restore the child to Susannah. Amazed at his persistence, Lord Sydney saw him himself and was 'much moved' by the story, so much so that he signed the order for the return of the child and another for Kable to accompany Susannah on the *Friendship*. Only years later was it discovered that this was the couple who had had money collected for them in Norwich, referred to by the Reverend Johnson. When Henry Kable was finally made a free man he took the matter of the stolen goods to the colony's first civil court and received fifteen pounds in compensation. Susannah went on to have another ten children and died at the age of eighty-four.

The more astute women used whatever means they could to better themselves. Anne Innett, convicted in Worcester for stealing a dimity petticoat, three handkerchiefs, a silk gown and some haberdashery, had already become the mistress of Lieutenant King on Norfolk Island. She bore him two children in two years, then married a fellow convict in 1792 who was granted a free pardon and land by King, who, having become Governor of the Colony and having married a Devon girl while home on leave, was anxious to hush the matter up.

Esther Abrahams, a seventeen-year old Jewish milliner, abandoned, pregnant and destitute, had stolen several yards of black lace and was sent to Newgate where she gave birth to a daughter. Both sailed on the *Lady Penrhyn* on which she met an officer, Lieutenant George Johnston. He and Esther lived together almost from arrival at the colony and had several children. Johnston had to return to England owing to a court case and was away for some years, during which time Esther built up a fine property with orchards, gardens, pastures, bakery, its own forge and stores. He eventually married her, built a mansion for the family, and she became one of the wealthiest women in early Australia.

Mary just missed the arrival of a woman really after her own heart, for Mary Haydock sailed from England with the Third Fleet. She was brought up by her grandfather in Cheshire and was, like Mary, considered a tomboy by her neighbours, not least because she liked to dress as one. When her grandfather died, none of her relatives wanted the responsibility of her so, at the age of fourteen, she took to horse thieving and was finally caught, arrested and sentenced as James Burrows, the name of the dead son of a neighbour. She kept up the pretence throughout her imprisonment, almost until it was time to sail, but then confessed. Her relatives were given the chance of standing surety for her good conduct if she were released but none of them wished to do so. She therefore sailed for New South Wales where, uniquely for a convict woman, she married an employee of the Dutch East India Company who later made a fortune. She ended her days as Mrs Reiby, a tremendously wealthy widow, the owner of farms and land and a successful coastal trading business. She was also famed for the dashing way she drove her carriage and pair around Sydney.

On 18 May there was, finally, a glimmer of relief for the starving colony when the *Sirius* returned from Cape Town with supplies of seed, wheat, barley and four months' flour (some 127,000 pounds). She had made the passage to Cape Town round Cape Horn in ninety days. However she brought no news of further supply ships, there was no word of them in any port of call. In fact, there was news of disaster – sickness had affected the crews of all the First Fleet ships on their return journey, to the point where it had been necessary to combine the crews of the *Alexander* and *Friendship* and then sink the latter off Batavia, in the East Indies. The extra food would at least 'procrastinate' famine, wrote Tench. Smallpox was now raging through the colony and it carried off poor, unfortunate Arabanoo who was 'much regretted by everyone, as it was supposed he would have been of infinite service in reconciling the natives to us,' wrote Tench. 'He was,' wrote Bradley, 'a great loss and quite familiarised, and very happy: quite one of the Governor's family and had got some of our language as well as communicating much of theirs. He was remarkably good tempered and had he lived would no doubt have been of infinite use to us.' Arabanoo was buried in the Governor's own garden outside his new house at Rose Hill, later known by its native name of Parramatta.

Although other aborigines were taken and captured for the same purpose, none proved as docile and helpful as Arabanoo.

Most of 1789 passed without incident for those in the new colony, day succeeding identical day, always against a background of hunger and punishment. But to celebrate the King's birthday that June there was a novel and startling event, for a group of convicts were allowed to present a play. The only script in the colony, which belonged to one of the officers, was Farquhar's comedy *The Recruiting Officer*, and its production was later the inspiration for a novel, Thomas Keneally's *The Playmaker* (1987), and also a splendid play, *Our Country's Good* (1988) by Timberlake Wertenbaker. Both assign leading roles to named convicts, including Mary Bryant, but, sadly, there are no details of who played what. Neither Keneally nor Wertenbaker were able to discover if Mary truly was involved, though both thought she ought to have been. Nor do we know whose idea it was, who selected the convicts and who rehearsed them. Keneally gives the honour to Ralph Clark but this seems unlikely in view of his personality and known views, and he would surely have noted such an unusual enterprise in his journal. The most suitable would have been Watkin Tench but we know he was only in the audience, his being one of the two brief accounts, the other by Collins, of what the production was like. Collins writes: 'The Governor received the compliments due to the day in his new house, of which he had lately taken possession as the Government House of the colony, where his excellency afterwards entertained the officers at dinner, and in the evening some of the convicts were permitted to perform Farquhar's comedy of *The Recruiting Officer*, in a hut fitted up for the occasion. They professed no higher aim than "humbly to excite a smile", and their efforts to please were not unattended with applause.' Tench wrote:

> In the evening the play of *The Recruiting Officer* was performed by a party of convicts, honoured by the presence of his excellency and officers. Every opportunity of escape from the dreariness and dejection of our situation is not to be wondered

at. The exhilarating effect of theatre is well known and I am not ashamed to confess that the distribution of three or four yards of stained paper, and a dozen farthing candles stuck in bottles around the mud walls of a convict hut failed not to diffuse general complacency on the countenances of some sixty persons of various descriptions who were to applaud the representation. Some of the actors acquitted themselves with great spirit and received the praises of the audience. A prologue and epilogue, written by one of the performers, was also spoken on that occasion which, though not worth inserting here, contained some tolerable allusions to the situations of the parties and the novelty of stage representation in New South Wales.

The lines of the original prologue written for the production of *The Recruiting Officer* are no longer extant. The lack was supplied by Wertenbaker in her own play and, in doing so, she gives them the cynicism which the original writer must have felt:

> From distant climes o'er widespread seas we come,
> Though not with much eclat or beat of drum,
> True patriots all; for be it understood,
> We left our country for our country's good,
> No private views disgraced our generous zeal,
> What urged our travels was our country's weal,
> And none will doubt but that our emigration
> Has proved most useful to the British nation . . .

The play was a triumph of the human spirit over the most appalling conditions. Almost certainly one of those involved was a Robert Sideaway, who had escaped in Tor Bay from the convict ship bound for Nova Scotia, been recaptured along with the other mutineers and sent to Botany Bay, for, when he had served his sentence, he remained in New South Wales where he established the colony's first playhouse. It proved successful enough for him to buy a farm and land, on which he lived with his wife, also a former convict.

By that June there was another reason why, apart from the close watch being kept on them, the Bryants had to abandon any immediate escape attempts, for Mary was pregnant again, this time by Will; her condition, coupled with the continuing lack of food which meant they could not possibly hoard any for future use, ensured they would have to await a change of circumstance.

Two reports from the court records sour the last months of that year, both connected with women. On 10 September Private Henry Wright was

> indicted for that he not having the Fear of God before his Eyes, but being moved and seduced by the Instigation of the Devil, on the 23 Day of August, with Force and Arms at a certain Place near Long Cove, in the County of Cumberland aforesaid, in and upon, one Elizabeth Chapman, spinster, in the Peace of God and our said Lord the King, then and there being, violently and feloniously did make an Assault, on her, the said Elizabeth Chapman, and then and there feloniously did ravish and carnally know, against the Form of the Statute in that Case made and provided, and against the Peace of our said Lord the King, his Crown and his Dignity.

Behind the pompous language lies an appalling incident, for Elizabeth Chapman was barely eight years old. She was playing in the bush when Wright leapt on her, tore off her clothes and raped her with extreme brutality. Despite her tender years, Elizabeth was required to give evidence at Wright's trial. She was questioned by Collins:

> How old are you?
> A little more than eight.
> Do you know that it is wrong to speak an untruth?
> Yes.
> What will happen to you if you do?
> Go to the Devil.
> Where do you expect to go if you speak the Truth?

To heaven.
Can you say your catechism?
Yes.
The Lord's Prayer?
Yes.

She repeated it and was then taken, sobbing, through a graphic description of the rape. A number of Wright's fellow soldiers, as well as convict women, also gave evidence against him. Elizabeth's mother said that Wright 'had the Character for doing such things with Children'. He was found guilty and sentenced to death, but the papers were marked 'recommended for mercy'. Sexual assault and ravishment of a child was considered less serious than robbing the stores. Collins wrote that this recommendation was accepted and he was sentenced to serve the rest of his time in the colony on Norfolk Island. Concluding the case Collins says: 'This was an offence which did not seem to require an immediate example; the chastity of the female part of the settlement had never been so rigid as to drive men to so desperate an act; and it was believed that beside the wretch in question there was not in the colony a man of any description who would have attempted it.' The reprieve was duly noted on 11 September.

No such mercy, however, was extended to Anne Davis/ Judith Jones. Two years of imprisonment, flogging and ironing had had no effect on her drunken and disorderly behaviour, her torrents of abuse or her compulsion to steal everything she came across. Today she would, most likely, be considered mentally ill: in the penal colony she was thought to be downright evil. In the November of 1789 she went on a wild, and foolish, burgling spree. While the male convicts were at work, she entered their huts and took away just about anything she could lay her hands on, whether it was useful to her or not. It was obvious she would be found out. She removed virtually all Robert Sideaway's clothes, along with those belonging to Mary Marshall with whom she was living, and some money, along with goods from the huts of at least ten others, all of whom gave evidence against her. When the various objects were found in her possession she claimed it was the fault of another notorious troublemaker, Elizabeth Fowles, who had asked her to carry them away on her behalf.

She was not believed. She was tried, found guilty and sentenced to death. Says Collins: 'On receiving sentence, the Prisoner declared she was with Child.' It was usual, back home in Newgate, for women to make 'the belly plea', for the authorities were loath to hang a woman with child as it would mean the killing of an innocent soul along with the guilty. It was a common ploy and women then industriously set about getting pregnant to bear out their claim. They could be hanged after birth, but there was always the chance of something turning up, even that they would be pardoned, in the meantime. On this occasion, the ploy did not work. 'A Jury of Twelve Matrons were then impanelled and sworn to try if the Prisoner is Quick with Child. On their Return into Court, the Foreman delivered in their Verdict that the Prisoner at the bar is not with Child.' In fact the woman who brought back the result of the examination to the Court said Anne Davis was no more pregnant than she was herself.

On 23 November Anne Davis, alias Judith Jones, was executed 'acknowledging', noted Collins, 'at that fatal moment which generally gives birth and utterance to truth, that she was about to suffer justly, and that an attempt which she made, when put on her defence, to incriminate another person (a woman whose character was so notorious that she hoped to establish her own credit and innocence upon her infamy), as well as her plea of pregnancy, were advanced merely for the purpose of saving her life. She died generally reviled and unpitied by the people of her own description.' She was the first woman to be hanged in Australia.

By the end of the year the food situation was as bad as ever. Mary was by now six months' pregnant. However the Bryants were no longer being watched as they fished; quite simply, there were not enough fit officers to do so.

CHAPTER TWELVE

The Second Fleet

A<small>T THE END</small> of 1789 Phillip had sent the little *Supply* to Norfolk Island to find out how Lieutenant Philip King and his colony were faring. King wrote back asking desperately for help, especially for livestock, and on 8 January the *Supply* returned again carrying the only animals that could be spared as so many of the original stock had died – two pigs belonging to Phillip himself. The Governor also informed King that he was shortly to be relieved of his post and brought back to Port Jackson to enable him to return to England carrying despatches at the first opportunity.

The only industry now flourishing was fishing and Collins noted that Phillip, after a particularly good haul of fish at the end of January, had agreed that his own boat be used for that task three nights a week 'for the public good' and that as a result fish was served as part of the ration a number of times. Happily released from surveillance, Will set about his task with enthusiasm, gradually going further and further out from shore in search of larger catches.

Phillip wrote a series of reports to go to England which emphasized that without more aid there would soon be little left of the new colony. 'In addition to the loss of provisions which we had sustained by rats [on the voyage] a very considerable quantity of flour, rice etc. has been lost and damaged . . .' He described his own corn harvest at Rose Hill and how the corn was 'exceeding good', about two hundred bushels of wheat, sixty of barley and a small quantity of flax, Indian corn and oats, all of which were being preserved for seed, otherwise there was insufficient food grown to feed the colony. Smallpox, he reported, had proved a scourge and he could not understand how this had come about as nobody had suffered from it on the voyage from England.

In spite of all the problems, regular inland exploration continued. Ralph Clark found whole settlements of aborigines suffering from smallpox. He was asked to bring in a native to replace the much missed Arabanoo, but admitted to his journal that he could not do so as removing the able-bodied male provider of a family might well result in his children starving to death. On another trip he found a skeleton which could not have been that of a native and he deduced it to be that of 'Mr Hill, a Midshipman, belonging to the *Sirius* who was either killed by the Natives or lost in the woods. I brought its head home with me and sent it to the Hospital, to see if they could inform me if it was a natives [*sic*] or one of the people that has been missing . . . perhaps a convict that was lost from Rose Hill near a twelve month since.' The surgeons decided it was probably the convict's head 'and wanted for me to give them the skull, but I would not. I told them that I would carry it back and collect the rest of the bons [*sic*] and Bury them and the Head.'

By now, the tone of Ralph Clark's remarks had changed from his earlier journal entries. He seems to have been genuinely concerned for the starving aboriginal children and was conscientiously determined to give the bones, whoever they belonged to, a decent burial. He had almost stopped writing of 'damned whores', and also of the perfections of Betsey Alicia; in fact he was soon to give up keeping his journal altogether for over a year, the reason being that the moral Ralph had finally succumbed to the lure of the flesh and had taken himself a convict mistress, a lag wife. Mary Branham had been sentenced at the Old Bailey in 1784, at the age of thirteen, for stealing two petticoats, a pair of stays, four yards of cloth, a pair of stockings and some breeches from her employer, John Kennedy. She had been ordered to be transported 'to Africa' but instead had sailed with the First Fleet on the *Lady Penrhyn*. During the voyage, she had become pregnant by a sailor, whose son she bore on arrival. He was always known as 'Small Willy'. She was only nineteen at the time she became involved with Clark.

On 17 February, Clark was invited to dinner by the Governor. His delight at being asked, however, soon turned to dismay. How would Clark like to go to Norfolk Island in place of Lieutenant King? 'I made him no answer at all,' says Clark, who was appalled at the prospect of leaving his colleagues to live in a community made up largely of convicts. Major Ross then intervened. 'He said that I *am* going. I said it was impossible.' Ross was not interested in the impossibility or not of Clark's preferences, he and Phillip both thought Clark was the man for the job and that was that. He, Ross, was also planning to spend some time on the island in order to write a report on behalf of the marines, a decision which was given every encouragement by Phillip who saw relief, at least for a few months, from the deputy he now loathed.

So Clark went away and made his arrangements. He visited his little island garden on one of the islands of Port Jackson for the last time, noting that his corn was now coming on, and returned to where he had found the skeleton, carrying its head, 'where I buried it on a point of land in Lane Cove. I have named it Skeleton Point.' He then went inland and picked a bag of the 'sweet tea' leaves to take with him to Norfolk Island.

The *Sirius*, which had been cleaned and repaired, was to go on from Norfolk to China leaving despatches there to be sent back to England, before loading up with supplies and returning to Port Jackson as quickly as possible, while the *Supply* would return at once with Lieutenant King. Clark, in his last mention of Betsey Alicia, noted that he wrote 'a letter to my Beloved' to go with the *Sirius* to China, in which he expressed the hope that the reason he and his party were being sent to the island was that Norfolk 'has more resources in it than this place, in Fish and Birds, for I find that there is no more from the first of next month than thirteen weeks of provisions left in store. God help us. If some ships do not arrive, I don't know what will.'

When the *Sirius* finally sailed on 5 March she carried ninety-six male convicts, sixty-five female and twenty-five of their children. The little *Supply* took a further twenty men, two women and three children. The women had been particularly chosen for their good behaviour. Among them, of course, was Mary Branham who, the following year, bore Clark a daughter whom they called Alicia after his wife. Anne Yeates, sentenced for stealing 36 yards of cotton voile at York Assizes had been listed to go but had asked if she might remain behind. Her wish was granted, not surprisingly, as she was now the mistress of the Judge–Advocate David Collins; in England, meanwhile, his wife wrote him letters demanding he bring their separation to an end. The ships sailed on 5 March, and on the same day, according to the Colony's records, 'George Johnston, the son of Lieutenant George Johnston and Esther Abrahams, a convict, was christened after church.'

On or about 31 March Mary gave birth to a son and on 4 April he was baptized with the hopeful name Emmanuel. In spite of all the privation she had undergone, and the lack of nutrition, the baby was strong and thrived. Whatever modest celebrations there might have been that day, however, were soon overshadowed by the events of the morrow.

For week after weary week the colony had watched the horizon for the appearance of the desperately needed supply ships from England. At last, at 8 o'clock on the morning of 5 April, news was brought that the flag on South Head had been hoisted. Watkin Tench had a premonition that it was not good news from England

for I could see nobody near the flag-staff except one solitary being, who kept strolling around unmoved by what he saw. I well know how different an effect the sight of strange ships would produce.

The governor determined to go down to the harbour and I begged permission to accompany him. Having turned a point about half way down, we were surprised to see a boat, which was known to belong to the *Supply*, rowing towards us. On nearer approach, I saw Captain Ball make an extraordinary motion with his hands, which too plainly indicated something disastrous had happened; and I could not help turning to the Governor, near whom I sat, and saying 'Sir, prepare yourself

for bad news!' A few minutes changed doubt into certainty; and
to our unspeakable consternation we learned that the *Sirius*
had been wrecked on Norfolk Island on the 19 March.

The ships had arrived off the island on 13 March and all the
people had landed straightaway, but the weather had changed
the next day and there was a severe gale. The *Sirius* had had to
stand off, for fear of being embayed and wrecked, and it was
five days before her captain felt it safe to bring her back in again
and start offloading the provisions and other goods. Then,
suddenly, a sharp wind had sprung up with the incoming tide
and the ship had begun to drift towards the shore. Alarmed,
Captain Hunter tried to sail his ship out into open waters again
but she would not go about, and although every effort was made
to save her, she struck a reef and was immediately wrecked.
Wrecked with her was all hope of getting news of the plight of
the colony to England and also of bringing back the stores to
Port Jackson. A proportion of the provisions were saved, a
number of casks and barrels being washed up on the beach, but
most of the officers lost their few possessions. Major Ross sent
back a message that he had put the island under martial law in
view of the privations that were to come.

That afternoon Phillip called the whole colony together and
told them what had happened. It would now be necessary, he
said, to reduce the rations still further, to $2\frac{1}{2}$ pounds of flour, 2
pounds of pork and 2 pounds of rice per day between seven
people. This would be everyone's ration, without distinction, but
even so there was now only flour enough to last until November,
pork until the end of July and rice until September. In future,
when it looked as if the fishing might be good, everything else
would be dropped and all those capable of work would be put to
it. Meanwhile the *Supply* would be sent to Batavia, a long journey
for such a small vessel, to fetch flour, and also so that her captain
could try to charter a ship to bring back some more food.

It was not only the lack of food that was soul-destroying, it
was the monotony of a diet without green vegetables or fruit
and with very few other fresh vegetables. The colony was still

deeply suspicious of trying anything strange found in the forests around them, but the surgeons had taken the risk of giving scurvy victims 'acid berries' from nearby bushes, with promising results. Soon they were also being offered as a prophylactic. Punishments for theft of food were now draconian, ranging from floggings of eight hundred to a thousand lashes, to hanging. Once again Phillip sat down and wrote a series of despatches to be sent with the *Supply* to Batavia in the hope the Dutch would forward them from there. The ship also took a number of desperate personal letters as well.

Captain Campbell of the marines wrote:

I early and late look with anxious eyes towards the sea, and at times, when the day was fast setting and the shadows of the evening stretched out, have been deceived with some fantastic little cloud, which, as it has condensed or expanded by such a light, for a little time, has deceived impatient imagination into a momentary idea that it was a vessel altering her sail or position while steering in for the haven . . . surely our country-men cannot have altogether forgotten us or been vainly led from any silly, sanguine representations hence to trust we could make it out tolerably well without their assistance . . .

An unidentified officer wrote a letter which was finally published in *The Oracle* on 25 April 1791:

By the time this reaches you, the fate of this settlement and all it contains, will be decided. It is now more than two years since we landed here, and within less than a month of three since we left England. So cut off from all intercourse with the rest of mankind are we, that, subsequent to the month of August 1788, we know not of any transaction that has happened in Europe and are no more assured of the welfare or existence of any of our friends than of what passes on the moon. It is by those only who have felt the anguish and distress of such a state that its miseries can be conceived.

He followed this with an account of the wreck of the *Sirius* and the resultant lack of almost all food apart from fish. 'We use every means to get fish, and sometimes with good success, which is an incredible relief. Our fishing service, the officers, civil and military, take it in turns every night to go out all night with the fishing boats; and the military, besides, keep a guard at Botany Bay, and carry on a fishery there, taking it three days and three days, turn and turn about.' It seems that, once again, Will was allowed a small proportion of the catch, a Godsend to Mary now suckling Emmanuel. 'Were the ground good,' continued the unknown writer, 'our gardens would be found of infinite use to us in these days of scarcity, but with all our efforts we cannot draw much from them.'

'I find I am spending the prime of my life,' wrote David Collins to his father, 'at the farthest point of the world, without credit and without profit, secluded from my family . . . my connections, from the World, under constant apprehensions of being starved. All these considerations induce me to embrace the first opportunity that offers of escaping from a country that is nothing better than a Place of Banishment for the Outcasts of Society.' Even he felt uneasy about sentencing a man to death for some scraps of dried-up pork and a handful of peas. Convicts, trying to do their work, fell where they stood and 'an elderly man, dropped down in the store, whither he had repaired with others to receive his day's subsistence. Fainting with hunger, and unable to hold up any longer, he was carried to the hospital.' The man died and, 'on being opened, his stomach was found quite empty.'

Watkin Tench waited with increasing impatience for news from Europe, noting in his diary that 'from intelligence, from our friends and connections we had been entirely cut off, no communication with our native country since the 13 May 1787. Famine was approaching with giant strides, and gloom and dejection overspread every countenance . . . we were on the tiptoe of expectation. If thunder broke in the distance, or a fowling-piece of louder than ordinary report resounded in the woods, "a gun from a ship" was echoed on every side and nothing but hurry and agitation prevailed.'

The Reverend Richard Johnson noted that 'Mrs J. has had our second child. Our first was a boy, but Still Born, the latter a girl, a sweet Babe about five weeks old.' Another unknown correspondent, voiced his feeling of total isolation.

> The dread of perishing by famine stares us in the face; on the day I write we have but eight weeks provisions in the public stores, and all chance of a reinforcement under seven months is cut off, unless ships from England, notwithstanding the lateness of the season, should come to us. The hope of this is, however, very feeble, for, without the most shameful and cruel inattention . . . ships must have left England by the 1 August last, to come here; and if so, they have undoubtedly perished on their route. Even this alternative, dreadful as it is, is less afflicting than to believe that our country would send us out here as a sacrifice to famine.

The convicts were no longer fit to work full days on their puny rations and Phillip ordered that they be employed only during the morning and left to tend their gardens in the afternoons. He was also worried about the health of the growing children and, in spite of the rapidly diminishing food supply, ordered that their ration should be increased. Corporal punishment was also reduced, for now any flogging could kill a man. It might well have been because of the weakness of those involved that, after several days of successful fishing, the seine net, nearly full of fish, was dropped by those holding it with the loss of most of its contents, yet 'upwards of 2000 fish pounds of fish was taken in the course of this month (May),' wrote Collins, 'which produced a saving of 500 lbs of pork at the store, the allowance of thirty-one men for four weeks.'

Then, on 3 June, the cry of 'the flag's up' rang through the colony. 'I was sitting in my hut, musing on my fate,' wrote Tench, 'when a confused clamour in the street drew my attention. I opened my door and saw several women, with children in their arms, running to and fro with distracted looks, congratulating each other, and kissing their infants with the utmost passion and extravagant marks of fondness. I needed no more; but instantly started out, and ran to a hill, where, by the assistance of a pocket-glass my hopes were realised. My next door neighbour, a brother-officer, was with me; but we could not speak; we wrung each other by the hand, with eyes and hearts overflowing.'

Tench raced down to the beach as a large English ship, colours flying, began to beat into port. He persuaded Phillip to take him with him and together they set out in the Governor's boat to board the vessel. She was the *Juliana*, out of England, the first to arrive from the Second Fleet, which had sailed out of Plymouth eleven months previously in July 1789. 'Letters! letters!' was the cry, said Tench, as he tore open his mail with trembling fingers. The *Juliana* brought news indeed, news of the French Revolution which had begun on 14 July 1789, 'with all the attendant circumstances of that wonderful and unexpected event,' noted Tench, who had never lost the beliefs he had first acquired during his early years in Paris, beliefs strengthened by his sojourn in America. Later, he would retire to his hut and drink to its success. Among other items was the news that the King's madness was said to be caused by the disease porphyria.

The apparent failure of the government to send supplies was soon explained, for the special supply ship, the *Guardian*, carrying much food and stores, along with twenty-five male convicts who were all either farmers or artificers, two experienced gardeners and seven superintendents for the convicts, had struck an iceberg on her passage and had managed to limp back to the Cape of Good Hope only with the utmost difficulty and with the loss of many lives, all the cattle and most of the stores and food. This had happened in December 1789.

The *Juliana* carried 225 female convicts and two years' provisions for them. There was no extra food, for it had been assumed that by the time the Second Fleet arrived, it would have been preceded by the fast-sailing *Guardian* and that crops and animals in the new colony would now be flourishing; but at least the extra supplied could be stretched to cover the immediate needs of all the colony. Most of the women on the *Juliana* were reasonably well and, although Phillip's heart sank at the prospect of the rest of the fleet arriving with only sufficient food to cover the newcomers, he was soon cheered by the totally unexpected arrival of the next ship, the *Justinian*, from Falmouth, which carried a full load of stores and also a portable hospital.

Then, on 29 June, the *Neptune* and the *Scarborough* warped into Sydney Cove, followed by the *Surprise*. Nothing could have prepared the officers for the sights they witnessed, sights which resulted in a flurry of letters being sent back to the authorities in England. Once again the transportation and victualling of the ships had been put out to private contract, this time to Messrs Calvert, Camden and King of London. They were paid £17 7s 6d for the transportation and feeding of each convict but how they spent this money was entirely unsupervised by the British government. The contractors, noted slavers, had opted for the cheapest solutions.

'The irons used upon these unhappy wretches were barbarous,' wrote Captain William Hill, who sailed on the *Juliana*, in a letter to the great abolitionist, William Wilberforce. 'The contractors had been in the Guinea Trade and had put on board the same shackles used by them in that trade, which are made with a short bolt, instead of chains that drop between the legs and fasten with a bandage around the waist like those in different gaols; these bolts were not more than three-quarters of a foot in length (nine inches), so that they (the convicts) could not extend either leg from the other for more than an inch or two at most; thus fettered it was impossible for them to move but at the risk of both legs being broken.'

The *Neptune*, he continued, was in no fit state to have been put out to sea and took in water constantly. For much of the time the 'unhappy wretches' in the holds, unable even to stand, were up to their waists in water, there was no fumigation of the quarters, men lay in their own filth for months. Of 900 male convicts embarked at Plymouth, 370 had already died and 450 were desperately ill 'and so very emaciated and helpless that very few, if any of them, can be saved by care or medicine, so that the sooner it pleases God to remove them, the better it will be for this colony, which is not in a situation to bear any burden, as I imagine the medicine chests to be nearly exhausted and provisions scarce . . . The slave trade is merciful compared to what I have seen in this fleet.' At least the overseers were paid for every healthy slave they delivered to their destination; with transportees they made money out of deaths for they could dispose of the corpse's goods and keep the allowance for themselves.

David Collins wrote: 'It was shocking to behold the deplorable condition to which the poor wretches were reduced by dysentery and scurvy . . . the miserable state to which the poor wretches were reduced by perpetual confinement below throughout the passage put it beyond the power of art to restore many of them. The sole direction of them on board was left to the masters of the transports who, either from inclination or want of knowledge, denied them any of those indulgences which might have been a means of preserving their health, or at least preventing so great a mortality.'

Those newcomers who could think at all were also dismayed to find they had arrived in a colony on the brink of starvation. However the first priority was to get the convicts off the transports and this was soon put in hand, beginning with the women on the *Juliana*. All the women in the colony, and many of the male convicts, were summoned to help care for the sick and dying. Wrote Collins:

> By noon . . . two hundred sick had been landed from the different transports. The west side afforded a scene truly distressing and miserable; upwards of thirty tents were pitched in front of the hospital, the portable one not being yet put up; all of which, as well as the hospital, were filled with people, many of whom were labouring under the complicated diseases of scurvy and dysentery, and others in the last stage of either of these terrible disorders, or yielding to the attacks of an infectious fever.

The appearance of those who did not require medical assistance was lean and emaciated. Several of these miserable people
died in the boats as they were rowed on shore, or on the wharf
as they were lifted out of the boats; both the living and the
dead exhibited more horrid spectacles than had ever been
witnessed in this country. All this was to be attributed to
confinement, and that of the worst species of confinement in a
small space and in irons, not put on singly, but many of them
chained together . . . It was said that on board the *Neptune*
several had died in irons; and what added to the horror of such
a circumstance was that their deaths were concealed, for the
purpose of sharing their allowance of provisions, until chance,
and the offensiveness of the corpse, directed the surgeon, or
some one who had authority in the ship, to the spot where they
lay.

Fortunate indeed were the women who had sailed on the
Juliana for only five women and two children had died on the
way over. Forty-two men died on the *Surprise*, sixty-eight on
the *Scarborough* (which had had such a good record in the First
Fleet) and 151 men, sixteen women and four children on the
terrible *Neptune*, where even women in labour had had trouble
persuading the overseers to unlock the irons which shackled
their ankles only nine inches apart.

The stores were also landed from the ships and food prepared
for all, the colony and newcomers alike, and search parties were
sent into the bush for more supplies of the acid berries for the
scurvy victims. Tench gave the number landed sick at Port
Jackson as 486 (none from the *Juliana*) of whom 124 died almost
at once. By 30 June there were 349 sick or dying people in the
hospital, and every morning saw a procession to the graveyard
carrying those who had died in the night.

Governor Phillip had the captains and overseers of the three
transports brought to him. He raged at them, telling them that
full details of what had happened would be sent back to England.
He accused them of being little less than murderers and that he
would see them punished. In future he would do everything that

lay within his power to ensure that each transport had a government representative aboard 'to ensure such a thing never happened again'. Fortunately, the efforts of Phillip, and the avalanche of letters and reports which reached home, did ensure that never again would a fleet sail under such conditions.

Gradually the survivors were nursed back to health and strength. There was cloth aboard the *Juliana* and the new female convicts, along with the other women, were put to making badly needed clothes for themselves and others and, for a few weeks, rations were increased all round. But Phillip stared into an abyss, for the other news brought by the captain of the *Juliana* was that the Third Fleet, bearing a thousand convicts, was even now on its way, with only minimal new supplies.

During the autumn Will and Mary finally began to think seriously of plans of escape. Over the years a number of convicts had run off into the bush, but had either never been heard of again or had been brought back dead. Building a boat would not only take time but be impossible to conceal. It seems it was Mary who came up with the idea that the best boat in which to make a substantial journey – for Will realized that the nearest landfall would be the Dutch East Indies – would be the Governor's own boat.

Such a plan would have required outside help and it seems likely that, in part, they were aided by the aborigines. Unlike their fellow convicts, Mary and Will had continually made contact with the natives, and most especially with a man called Bennelong. Soon after the death of Arabanoo, two natives had been captured from a tribal party on a beach and brought back to be used as interpreters. One had escaped almost at once, the other, Bennelong, had been caught trying to do so. For some time he had pretended to accept his fate but finally, when sleeping in a room in the Governor's house, he had crept out and run away. Some months later, he and Phillip made contact again, and after various misunderstandings (including the Governor being wounded by a native who panicked, thinking he was going to be taken away) some kind of *modus vivendi* was agreed between them so that now Bennelong and his family came and went much as they pleased. They were frequent visitors to Phillip at Rose Hill – and also to the creekside hut of the Bryants. Bennelong's wife and sister would take their children to play with Charlotte Bryant and the two native women would sit and do their best to communicate with Mary.

Possibly they were able to make themselves sufficiently understood to explain their own methods of navigation by the night sky of the southern hemisphere. We now know that aborigines could cross their continent using what they called 'song lines'. Certainly they could show, in a practical way, the currents and reefs along the coast. Soon, to everyone's amazement, Will Bryant was seen taking Bennelong's family out on fishing trips with him.

The final piece of the jigsaw fell into place in December 1790 when the little *Supply* finally returned from Batavia with a cargo of food. The captain had searched around for a ship to charter which would bring in more stores and the only one available was a Dutch vessel known as a 'snow' – not, as usually reported, a translation of its name, the *Waaksamheyd* (which actually means 'The Good Lookout'), but a type of sailing ship. Her captain, Detmer Smith, had driven a hard bargain, which had taken time and she did not finally arrive in Port Jackson until the 17th of the month, where she was to stay for several weeks while various wrangles took place between Smith and Phillip as to whether or not she was to be chartered again. Smith knew he had a strong card to play for by this time the transports of the Second Fleet had left Port Jackson.

Neither the Governor nor the officers took to Captain Smith, who was therefore cold-shouldered and left very much to his own devices. So he was glad of the company offered by the only convict who could freely come and go as he pleased – William Bryant – and he was even more charmed by his new friend's dark-eyed wife who kindly offered to do his laundry, fetch and carry for him between the colony and his ship and who, helped out by the captain's food and spirits, was only too happy to entertain him in their hut over supper.

CHAPTER THIRTEEN

Escape

THE PROSPECT facing the Bryants was truly daunting. The Governor's cutter was a serviceable craft with three sets of oars and a sail, but any escape which was to have a chance of success would mean sailing hundreds, possibly thousands, of miles in largely unchartered waters, not knowing what they would find at the other end. It would have been frightening enough if Will and Mary had been on their own, but there was no question of Mary agreeing to go without the children; Charlotte was now three and a half, Emmanuel not yet a year and still at the breast. (For obvious reasons convict women suckled their children for as long as possible.)

Here there is something of a mystery. Will's sentence would have expired by the end of March 1791 and, with his skills, he stood a very good chance of being taken on as a hand by the next ship of any nationality which put into Port Jackson. His past record would certainly not have stood in his way, especially if such a vessel were exceptionally short-handed through sickness. So, theoretically, he could have cut and run and had, indeed, publicly discussed the possibility. But Will had a classic failing. He was what we would call colloquially a 'loudmouth'. It took very little to make him air his views, however tactless or dangerous this might be, and alcohol, especially spirits, made it worse. His views on his Australian marriage, freely expressed at the time it took place, had now resurfaced and had even reached Governor Phillip.

'It having been reported to the Governor,' wrote David Collins, 'that Bryant had been frequently heard to say that he did not consider his marriage in this country as binding, His Excellency caused the convicts to be informed that none would be permitted to quit the country who had wives and children

incapable of maintaining themselves and likely to become bur-
densome to the Settlement.'

Mary, on the other hand, still had a further two years of her
sentence to run and two very small children totally dependent
on her. Since the government had made no provision for
allowing convict families to return home she was faced, as she
always had been, with what amounted to a life sentence in New
South Wales. The stores from the Second Feet and the *Waaksamheyd* had meant the colony had been marginally raised above
starvation level but there was no guarantee that within months
the situation would not be as bad again. Even when she ceased
to be a convict, all life would hold was the prospect of scratching
a living from the land. Many men and women eventually
thrived, as has already been detailed, but Mary was not prepared
to take that risk, especially as she must also have been aware
both of what Will was saying again about his marriage and that,
whatever the Governor might proclaim, a ship's master desperate for a seaman might well have given Will a passage in the
knowledge that there was very little that could be done once it
was a *fait accompli*.

Why then, the cynic might ask, did Will jeopardize the
chance of a successful escape by bringing along a young woman
and two small children? One theory has been that Mary told
Will that if he did not agree to take them she would inform the
Governor of what he was planning. This is possible, but goes
against all that we know about Mary and can glean of her
personality. A more likely explanation is that in spite of the
obvious handicaps, Will actually needed Mary to help ensure the
success of the plan. Mary could handle a boat as competently as
most men and that would be a great advantage; more to the
point, in the immediate planning stage she could be used to liaise
with Detmer Smith – who both saw as the linchpin to the
success of the enterprise – organize the collecting of all the
necessary stores, and carry information back and forth between
those who were to make the voyage with them, without
arousing the amount of interest Will would have done in similar
circumstances.

They had always recognized that they could not make the escape alone, but who else should they involve? Three men were obvious choices: James Martin, the Irish thiever of lead from the Powderham Estate who had been sentenced at the same assize as Mary, and James Cox and Sam Bird, who had sailed with the Bryants on the *Charlotte* and remained close friends ever since. The other four are more surprising, for William Allen, Nathaniel Lilly, William Moreton and Samuel Broom were relative newcomers from the Second Fleet. It is possible that they secured their passage through blackmail, for, once again, Will's tongue had run away with him and in February 1791 David Collins wrote in his report that Bryant had been 'overheard discussing an escape attempt with other convicts'. It is likely, however, that Collins added this after the event since it seems incredible that if such a rumour had reached him he did not take immediate steps to ensure Will was given no such opportunity.

The prolonged wrangle between Phillip and Detmer Smith over charter costs was a boon to the conspirators. While the unproductive meetings continued, Mary was continually seen in Smith's company, something which occasioned surprise among her fellow convicts. Mary had never shown any signs of being unfaithful to Will and he was known to be possessive of her, whatever he might have to say about the legality of his marriage. Yet here she was, apparently making up to the Dutchman – a man generally disliked in the colony – while Will not only sat complacently by, but went out of his way to befriend the man. There is no doubt Smith found Mary attractive and he may well have harboured hopes that the relationship could be put on a more intimate footing. There are suggestions that Mary 'sold herself' in exchange for Smith's assistance, but there is no proof of this. She might well have decided it was worth it, if it was the only way of assuring his help, but it is more likely that she was just a clever actress.

By the beginning of February, the Bryants felt they could trust Smith sufficiently to reveal their plans to him. He proved sympathetic, not least because he felt he had been slighted by Phillip. Also, like other Dutchmen, he had little sympathy with the British desire to establish a prison colony on the other side of the world. He was also hard-headed and prepared to do deals. Will had always kept a small amount of money by him for there had been nothing on which to spend it in Port Jackson. Mary negotiated with Smith for navigational instruments and he told her he would sell them a compass and a quadrant. Whether Will had enough money in hand to buy these, whether he acquired it from the other conspirators or, as some sources suggest, 'sold' fish from his catch, he raised sufficient cash to buy them along with a hundredweight of rice, 14 pounds of salt pork and a hundredweight of flour. Smith also threw in two old muskets and a quantity of ammunition – telling Will he might well need it if they had to put in at a hostile shore – a 10 gallon barrel for fresh water and, most crucially of all, a chart. The most hopeful landfall, Smith told him, was the Dutch East Indies – three thousand miles away.

The seven other would-be escapees were told to save everything they possibly could from their rations, however meagre, and Will, no doubt with skills acquired during his smuggling days, built the kind of cache in his hut that could have been found in a large number of Cornish cottages of the day – a sizeable square hole, lined with wood, which was then hidden by a false floor. In this the Bryants secreted the stores bought from Detmer Smith, along with all the other goods, to which were added the rice, flour and dried meat given to Mary by James Martin and the others. In spite of what had previously happened when he had been found bartering fish for vegetables, Will stepped up this practice, exchanging fish from his catch for a wide range of other foodstuffs. To some extent this was now easier for, with the influx of new prisoners from the Second Fleet, it had become far more difficult to stop illicit sale and barter. Indeed, on 11 February 1791, a general order was issued proclaiming:

> Although repeated Orders have been given, to prevent the Convicts from Selling or Exchanging their Provisions issued from the Public Stores, for money, spirits or tobacco, that

practise is still continued, and those who sell their own Provisions must then support themselves by stealing from others . . . it is the duty of every Individual to Endeavour to Stop this Practise . . . No Provisions are ever to be purchased or received from a Convict, on any Consideration whatever, and the Commissary is directed to give thirty Pounds of flour as a reward for discovering any Person who may in future be guilty of this Order.

Will had already realized that any escape attempt would have to take place soon, before the weather began to deteriorate significantly, a view borne out by Detmer Smith and, possibly, the aboriginal Bennelong, with whom Will was still spending a considerable amount of time. The last possible opportunity would be the end of March, after which the regular autumn gales would set in. So, initially, the attempt was scheduled for the end of February or the first week of March.

Then, on 28 February, there was a near disaster. Will had gone out fishing in the Governor's cutter, taking with him Bennelong's sister, her two children and 'a little girl' (possibly Charlotte). On their way back, a sudden strong wind had blown up and, because the boat was heavily laden (for Will had a crew aboard as well), he had been unable to take evasive action quickly enough and had either failed in his attempt to go about or had unexpectedly gybed. The hooks supporting the sail broke and the boat wallowed in the sea before filling with water, heeling over and finally capsizing. Bennelong's sister immediately hoisted her infants on to her shoulders and struck out for the shore, while a member of the crew swam with the little girl. Will stayed behind in the water, desperately trying to right the boat on which all his hopes rested. The incident was witnessed by Captain John Hunt, late of the wrecked *Sirius*.

'Several of the natives,' he wrote, 'seeing this accident as the boat drove towards the rocks, gave them every possible assistance, without which, in all probability, one of the crew [presumably Will] would have been drowned. After clearing the boat, they collected the oars and such articles as had been driven on shore in different places; and in these friendly offices Bennelong was very assiduous: his behaviour gave Governor Phillip an opportunity of receiving him in a more kindly manner than he had done since his previous bad behaviour. The natives then towed the boat up to the cove.'

There was now no question of being able to leave until substantial repairs had made the boat seaworthy again. On the other hand, this did ensure that it was in the best possible condition and, because it was the Governor's own boat, the repairs were given priority. The damaged planking was stripped from the cutter and replaced and she was given a new mast, sail and tackle. What the accident had shown was that while it might be the largest and strongest boat in the colony, it could easily be upset when carrying a full load of adults and equipment, even close in to the shore.

After mentioning the incident with the boat, Hunter noted that matters had marginally improved in the colony although everyone was suffering from the heat, which had risen to 106 degrees Fahrenheit, so hot that birds dropped out of the air as they flew. 'The wind was from the northwest, and did much injury to the gardens, burning up everything before it. Those persons whose business compelled them to go into the heated air declared that it was impossible to turn the face for five minutes to the quarter from whence the wind blew.'

Governor Phillip, in his journal, noticed a great increase in the number of bats, owing to the hot weather. He saw one with a wingspan of upwards of 'four feet' and kept a female bat as a pet, 'that would hang by one leg a whole day without changing its position; and in that pendant situation, with its breast neatly covered with one of its wings, it ate whatever was offered it, lapping out of the hand like a cat.' A second store-house had been completed, he reported, built of stout brick with a tiled roof, although it was only half full as the crops were suffering from the dry weather. The marine barracks at Rose Hill was also nearly finished and the officers' wing ready for tiling.

Finally, at the beginning of March, Phillip grudgingly

accepted the charter deal offered by Detmer Smith for there seemed to be no other alternative. The *Waaksamheyd* would, therefore, be officially chartered on behalf of the colony and fitted up accordingly. She would take to England with Captain Hunter and the crew of the wrecked *Sirius* (but not apparently Lieutenant Philip King), and others whose time was now up, such as Surgeon John Altree and a Lieutenant Bradley, along with a vast number of despatches, reports and letters from the colony. A Lieutenant Thomas Edgar, who had come out on the *Juliana*, was put in charge of seeing that everything was done to Phillip's satisfaction.

The fitting out continued during March, taking up a great deal of time and energy, which was very useful to the Bryants as it deflected attention away from them, although the continuing delay also brought them ever nearer to the monsoon deadline, after which it would be suicidal to attempt the escape. Then, with every week that passed, the risk grew that one of the men might be tempted to confide in their woman who in turn might inform on them in the hope of keeping her man with her. In Will's opinion, it was the women who were most likely to betray them, though there was no foundation for his thinking this.

On 27 March the *Waaksamheyd* finally sailed out of Port Jackson with her homeward-bound passengers, waved off by the hundreds left behind on the shore. She carried with her the full story of the terrible first three years of the penal colony, along with desperate requests for more help. One of these was from Surgeon John White, begging for urgently needed medicines and other medical equipment, for which he had been asking in vain for many months. The hearts of those who saw her go were, as their journals show, consumed with envy, but all echoed Private John Easty who wrote 'and may God send them a good voige [*sic*] I Pray.'

It was decided that the sailing of the *Waaksamheyd* would provide the distraction for the escape, for there was now no more time to delay. How they managed to conceal the last-minute preparations, the removal of goods from the cache and the organizing of how and where they would all meet up, without a talkative three-year-old becoming aware of it and chattering about it, or casual visitors to the Bryants' hut sensing something strange was going on, is quite amazing. It is possible, though, that there were people who had a good idea of what was in the wind but kept their thoughts to themselves.

As soon as darkness fell on the evening of 28 March 1791, a handful of the conspirators arrived at the Bryants' hut and the goods and equipment concealed under the floor were distributed among them. The rest of the crew were to wait at agreed points on the way down to the beach. For the last time Mary looked around the little hut Will had built for them and which had been their home, apart from the brief spell after Will's punishment, for nearly three years. Then, carrying the sleeping Emmanuel and clutching a large bag of the leaves of the 'sweet tea' vine, which she had picked during the previous week, she fell in behind the others as they slipped noiselessly, like shadows, down to the shore.

It is said that Bennelong played a vital role at this point, and willingly helped his white friend get away. The Governor's cutter was anchored well out in the cove in deeper water and had to be brought much nearer in if they were all to embark quickly. In any event either Bennelong or one of his tribe swam out to the cutter, cut the hawser which anchored her, and then towed her in as near to the shore as was possible, holding her fast while the escapees went aboard. Silently, just before midnight, the first of the party waded out to the boat, then the children were handed in, followed by the stores, navigational equipment and the muskets. Will took the chart in his pocket.

Still there was no sign of life on the shore. Will signalled to his helper on the rope to let go. They could not risk the sound of oars which would carry across the water for miles and therefore had to rely on the tide to take them out towards the sea. Just after midnight they slipped quietly and unseen past south Head, where, fortunately, they were not sighted by the sentry. Once round the point, Will felt it safe to hoist the sail. Gradually the wind filled it, it bellied out and the cutter swept out triumphantly on a fair reaching wind to the open sea and freedom. Laughing and weeping, the occupants of the boat hugged each other, drunk with their success. They had done the impossible, they had stolen the Governor's own boat and got away with it, and they were now safe from any possible pursuit. It had been a masterpiece of organization and co-operative effort.

IT WAS not until six o'clock the next morning that the escape was discovered. Then all hell broke loose, as marines ran about trying to find what had happened to the convicts. Next the cry went up that the Governor's boat was missing. The first that Sergeant James Scott, the unfortunate marine on duty at the lookout on South Point, knew of the affair was when a sergeant and a party of marines arrived in a long boat 'in persute of Bryant a convict and the principal Fisherman for Government'. The unhappy man had to admit he had seen and heard nothing. 'It seems they have got off, God knows where.'

Young Private John Easty wrote:

Today 8 men with 1 woman and 2 Children Convicts toke a kings boat of 6 oars with a large quantity of provisions which they had got from time to time by work and a new Seene [seine] for fishing with a large quantity of carpinters tools of all Sorts for enlargeing the boat with beds and Mathäckmattick instruments and Cumpus, New sails and Masts and oars and 6 stand of Arms and Everything that was nesariey for Making thare Escape which was Executed between the hours of 9 and 12 it was Supposed that thay intinded for Bativee but having no vessell in the habour thare was no Pursueing them so thay got Clear of, but it is a very Desperate attempt to go in an open Boat for a run of about 16 or 17 hundred leags and pertuclar for a woman and two Small children the oldest not above three years of age but the thoughts of Liberty from Such a place as this is Enough to induce any Convicts to try all Skeemes to obtain it as they are the same as slaves all the time thay are in this country.

Many others shared Easty's view, if not his idiosyncratic spelling. He was right about the pursuit. There was no boat left in the colony remotely capable of catching up with a large cutter with six hours' start, apart from the *Supply*, which was, once again, at Norfolk Island.

'They were traced from Bryant's hut to the Point,' wrote Collins in his official account of the escape, 'and in the path were found a handsaw, a scale, and four or five pounds of rice, scattered about in different places, which, it was evident, they had dropped in their haste. Near the point where some of the party must have been taken in, a seine, belonging to the government was found which, being too large for Bryant's purpose, he had exchanged for a smaller that he had made for an officer, and which he had . . . excused himself from completing and sending home.' Thus Will had ensured they would be able to fish for food on the voyage.

After listing the names, offences and sentences of those involved, Collins continued: 'So soon as it was known in the settlement that Bryant had got out of reach, we learned that Detmer Smith, the master of the *Waaksamheyd*, had sold him a compass and a quadrant, and had furnished him with a chart, together with such information as would assist him in his passage northward.' So *someone* had obviously been in the know, since Collins was able to glean this much.

On searching Bryant's hut, cavities were found under the floor where he had secured the compass and such other articles as required concealment: and he had contrived his escape with such address, that although he was well known to be about making an attempt, yet how far he was prepared, as well as the time when he meant to go, remained a secret.

Most of his companions were connected with women; but if these knew anything, they were too faithful to those they lived with to reveal it. Had the women been bound to them by any ties of affection, fear for their safety, or the dislike to part, it might have induced some of them to have defeated the enterprise; but not having any interest either in their flight, or in their remaining here, they were silent on the subject. For one woman, Sarah Young, a letter was found the next morning, written by James Cox, and left at a place where he was accustomed to work in his leisure hours as a cabinet maker, conjuring her to give over the pursuit of the vices which, he told her, prevailed in the settlement, leaving to her what little property he did not take with him, and assigning as a reason for his flight, the severity of his situation, being transported for life without the prospect of any mitigation, or hope of ever quitting the country, but by the means he was about to adopt.

Three of the escapees, in fact, were serving life sentences and so had little to lose. 'It was conjectured they would steer for Timor, or Batavia, as their assistance and information were drived from the Dutch snow.'

The previous September a convict called Tarwood and four others had stolen the boat belonging to the lookout from the beach and, without planning or supplies, had sailed off into the unknown and had never been seen again. Unlike Tarwood and his associates, continued Collins:

Bryant had long availed himself of opportunities given him by selling fish to collect provisions together, and his boat was a very good one, and in excellent order; so that there was little reason to doubt their reaching Timor, if no dissension prevailed among them, and they had but prudence to guard against the natives wherever they might land. William Morton was said to know something of navigation; James Cox had endeavoured to acquire such information on the subject as might serve him whenever a fit occasion should present itself; and Bryant and Bird knew perfectly well how to handle a boat.

He either did not think to add, or perhaps did not realize, that Mary was equally at home and handy in a boat. 'What story they can invent on their arrival at any port, sufficiently plausible to prevent suspicion of their real characters, is not easy to imagine,' Collins concluded.

The air now rang to the sound of the bolting of stable doors after the horse had gone. In future, wrote Collins, *any* rumour of an escape attempt, however unlikely, was to be reported at once. From now on sentinels would be placed on each wharf every night, and an officer of the guard had to be 'spoken to' before any boat of whatever size could leave the cove. In addition to this new regulation, it was directed that the names of everyone employed in the handling and use of boats, and most particularly those concerned with night-fishing, should be given, in writing, to the officer of the guard 'to prevent any convicts not belonging to officers or to the public boats from taking them from the wharfs under the pretence of fishing or other services . . .'

Tench, unofficially, wished the escapees well for

> I every day see wretches pale with disease and wasted with famine, struggle against the horrors of their situation. How striking is the effect of subordination; how dreadful is the fear of punishment! The allotted task is still performed even on the present reduced subsistence: – the blacksmith sweats at the sultry forge; the sawyer labours pent-up in his pit; and the husbandman turns up the sterile glebe . . .
>
> But toil cannot be long supported without adequate refreshment. The first step in every community which wishes to preserve honesty, should be to set the people above want. The throes of hunger will ever prove too powerful for integrity to withstand. Hence arose a repetition of petty delinquencies, which no vigilance could detect, no justice reach.

THE CONDITIONS which drove William and Mary Bryant and their companions to escape were appalling. Yet they, and those who survived the First and Second Fleets, were fortunate compared with the sufferings of those who would come after, even though the years 1788–91 are known as the Starvation Years. Norfolk Island, after Ralph Clark left, became synonymous with sadism, cruelty and torture. It even pioneered sensory deprivation with its special bunker cells, built without windows to keep prisoners in the dark, and walls over three feet or more thick, specifically designed to prevent any sounds from reaching those inside.

NOW WELL out at sea and no longer in sight of the land, Mary Bryant, her baby on her knee, settled herself in the stern of the cutter and took her turn on the tiller.

CHAPTER FOURTEEN

'This Wonderful and Hazardous Voyage'

T HERE WERE, at one time, two personal journals of the Bryants' remarkable voyage in existence, one a day-by-day account written by Will during the time they were at sea, the other by James Martin, mostly written in retrospect after his return to England. Right up until 1937 when Professor Frederick Pottle, the great editor of the works of James Boswell, published his small monograph *Boswell and the Girl from Botany Bay*, it was assumed that both were lost. Some years later the 'Martin Memorandum' surfaced among the Jeremy Bentham collection of papers and is now safely held by London University. Bryant's has never been found and we only know of its existence due to a series of remarkable coincidences, one of which had a great effect on the voyagers.

On 27 April 1789 an event took place which has captured the public imagination ever since and given rise to a host of books, plays and films – the mutiny on the *Bounty*. As is well known, Captain William Bligh also made a remarkable journey in an open boat and, like Bryant and his band, headed for East Timor, arriving there in the June of that year. There is nothing in the papers of the day to prove whether or not the Second Fleet brought news of the mutiny to the penal colony, but certainly Detmer Smith did so. Two years later Bligh returned to East Timor and was there shown Bryant's journal, some tantalizing details of which appear in Bligh's unpublished papers held by the Mitchell Library. The journal was shown to Bligh on 2 October 1792 after he had finally 'teased the Governor' into showing it to him. It was, he writes 'a hand-written and very ingenious account' entitled *Reminescences [sic] on a Voyage from Sydney Cove, N.S.W., to Timor* by William Bryant. Bligh attempted to make a précis of it, using some quotes from Will, but 'I was too ill and the time was too short for me to copy the Journal. I however employed a person about it, but he did not get the fourth part through it.' The account that follows, therefore, is based on the written accounts of Martin and Bryant and the oral information given later by the survivors.

From all these it is clear that, once they left sight of land, there was a change in the attitude of the others to Will and Mary, for it is apparent that it was Mary's inspiration that carried them through. From her arrest in Plymouth, through her imprisonment on the *Dunkirk*, the voyage to New South Wales and the time in the penal colony, Mary's priority had been survival and, to that end, she had played the game by the only rules available to her: rules which meant deferring to, and accommodating, men. She had taken an equal part in the organization of the escape, not least in acting as the essential go-between with Detmer Smith, and she had also seen to the procuring and concealing of essential supplies. Once the cutter was out of sight of land, however, it was she and not Will, as one might have assumed, who proved to have the strength and fortitude necessary for such a voyage. While they were all to be deeply indebted to Will for his undoubted navigational skills and seamanship, he seems to have lost heart very quickly each time the going became tough, and again and again it was left to Mary to rally and encourage the men.

Only the desperate would have risked such an undertaking. To reach East Timor, Bryant had to navigate his craft north along almost the entire eastern seaboard of the Australian continent, run for miles between the Great Barrier Reef and the shore, then sail safely through the Torres Strait, before turning west into the uncharted Arafura Sea. With so many people in such a relatively small boat it was vital that they should be able to put ashore at frequent intervals during the first part of the voyage, not least to take on fresh water, but again and again they were to be frustrated by the sight of splendid sandy beaches on which, due to continual and heavy surf, landing was impossible.

After several hours at sea on that first day and as soon as they felt safe from pursuit, an inventory was made of the goods they had smuggled on board. Martin says there was a hundredweight each of flour and rice, some dried pork and about eight gallons of fresh water in the cask given to them by Detmer Smith. Bryant, according to Bligh, adds that as well as the seine net, compass, quadrant and chart, he also had the forethought to include nails, a grapnel, and rosin and beeswax for caulking the seams of the boat since he anticipated that there might well be problems with it after the recent accident.

For two days they sailed steadily northwards within sight of land, propelled, according to Bryant, by steady north-northeast winds, but two days later the wind became contrary, so they put into a little cove about two degrees north of Port Jackson, where they stayed for two days. Mary at once organized a hunt for fresh food, saw to the replenishment of the water cask and found a kind of cabbage, the leaves of which they could cook with some grey mullet they had pulled in with their seine net. They also found something else, for Bryant wrote: 'Here we caught grey mullet and repaired our boat, then, walking along the shore towards the entrance of the creek, we found several large pieces of coal. Seeing so many pieces we thought it not unlikely to find a Mine and searching about a little we found a place where we picked up with an axe as good coals as any in England took them to the fire and they burned exceedingly well.' Martin says that a handful of interested natives arrived while they were there and that he offered them some of his own clothing so that 'they went away much satisfied'. They named their first landfall Fortunate Cove.

This first landfall was to set a pattern to be repeated whenever possible: several days of sailing, followed by a two-day respite to collect food and water and see to the boat. It rapidly became apparent that while the cutter might have been suitable enough for rowing the Governor around Sydney Cove and fishing in good weather, it was far from ideal for a long voyage. Bryant was right to have been unhappy about the repairs: it leaked continually from its seams and, being so low in the water due to the weight of those on board, took in water every time the wind picked up.

At about 6 a.m. on 31 March they set off again, still hugging the coast, Bryant noting that on 1 April they were in the latitude of 33°20 south. On the afternoon of the 2nd, they discovered a fine harbour, and went ashore to explore. Bryant described the harbour as being 'superior to Sydney' and, says Martin, it seemed to run up the country for many miles and was a quite commodious anchorage for shipping. As they were working their way along an unmapped coastline, it is not possible to be definite about their ports of call – Port Stephen, Port Macquarie and Moreton Bay are three that have been suggested.

Bryant's concern regarding the state of the boat had now turned into serious alarm about its seaworthiness. He decided that it must be hauled ashore so that its seams could be caulked with the rosin and beeswax. There were abundant supplies of fresh drinking water and the delay allowed Mary to cure and dry their surplus fish and to add to their stocks of the leaves of 'sweet tea'. She also washed and dried their clothes. As they went about their business they were, once again, watched by natives who made no effort to drive them away – the last time this would happen. From now on they were to be the object of deep suspicion and outright hostility.

It seems they kept track of the dates and days with care, for Martin noted that the following Sunday they tried to put ashore again, as Will was still unhappy about the state of the boat, but that their first attempt was thwarted by an offshore wind and heavy surf. Eventually they found a suitable spot and had just begun to unload their goods from the cutter, preparatory to working on it, when a large number of natives appeared throwing spears. While Mary took the children back to the boat, some of the men tried to explain to the aborigines that they intended no harm towards them, but the natives continued their attack. Finally, in desperation, Bryant took one of the muskets

Detmer Smith had sold him, and fired over their heads, thus driving them away. They then took to the sea again without making any further attempts to repair the boat.

They continued much in this way for the first two weeks or so, going ashore whenever they could and sailing as far as possible in between. The navigation was shared between Bryant and Will Moreton, both of whom took their turn on the tiller, along with Mary and James Cox. Whenever possible they used the cutter's two sails to move them along, but it was also necessary for everyone to take their turn at the oars, either to supplement the sails when the winds were light or to keep the boat going when they dropped off all together.

After the reception they had received from the aborigines at their last port of call, they decided that in future, as well as searching for a safe beach on which to land, they should also look at its potential from the point of view of a hostile attack. This having been decided, the next landfall was 'a little white sandy island' in the middle of a fine natural harbour. There the boat was hauled up and further repairs made to her hull. As there did not seem to be any sign of natives, two days later they rowed over to the mainland to fill their water cask and pick more 'cabbage' leaves. As they were leaving, a handful of natives appeared, who, according to Martin, were quite different to any they had seen before, having skin and hair of 'a marked copper colour'. These natives had canoes with them made of bark but they did not attempt to follow Bryant's party.

So far the weather had been kind to them and Bryant had begun to think that he had, after all, managed to escape in time to avoid the impending monsoon. Now he saw he was wrong, for the weather was deteriorating and showing every sign of the seasonal pattern which was the monsoon's forerunner. For several days they were driven by strong offshore winds which made it impossible for them to land. They made one attempt, but the surf was so 'hard and strong' that it proved impossible. The state of the small children can well be imagined, crying and shivering with cold and fear; indeed all the party were in a parlous state.

This was the first occasion when Will seems to have become pessimistic about the likely outcome of the enterprise. Mary would have none of it, spurring them on to greater effort, encouraging them all to hang on. They needed all the inspiration they could get, even when the wind lessened, the surf still made the wrecking of the boat a real possibility if there was any attempt to put in to the land. So Will anchored just outside the surf, while two of the men very bravely attempted to swim ashore with the water cask to find fresh water. To their despair, they were seen and chased off by natives and returned empty-handed.

It was now only with the greatest difficulty that they could keep the boat afloat as it was taking in water both above and below the waterline. Finally they found their way into a little river, after surmounting the problem of getting the boat over the shoals in the river mouth where the water was only five or six feet deep. Bryant wrote that 'it was with difficulty I got the boat into the creek, there being shoal water across it,' but, noted Bligh, 'he tacked the Boat in skilfully, without it receiving damage.' There was no beeswax or rosin left for running repairs but the resourceful Martin had brought along some soap which was used instead to good effect. They found water on the shore of the creek but no shellfish or other fish and so set out again, this time making a fast twenty miles, still keeping an eye out for a suitable place to land and hunt for food.

Then the monsoon hit them with its full force, bringing with it strong winds and torrential rain. Mountainous green seas, with wave piled on wave, towered above the boat. So much water was taken into it that they were forced to throw overboard all their personal possessions and clothing 'to lighten the craft'. The winds remained strong and contrary, keeping them out of sight of land for eight days, fearful that they would not reach it again before their food and water ran out. 'All of us,' wrote Martin, 'were much distressed for lack of water and food.' Yet Mary, he says, again rallied them all through it. One can only marvel at how Mary also managed to keep Charlotte and Emmanuel relatively content. Both children must have found much of the voyage very frightening.

Their first attempt to go ashore once the wind died down was abortive again due to the strong surf. However, as night was falling, Bryant decided to anchor off shore, using both the anchor and the grapnel to hold them fast, while they waited to see if it subsided during the night; but, in the small hours of the morning, both anchor and grapnel gave way and 'we stared death in the face,' Martin wrote, 'as we thought the only outcome was for the boat to be staved in and for us to drown.' However, the next day, they did make a safe haven where they found fresh water and an abundance of shellfish, which they cooked and ate. They were also able to dry out their clothes.

But, in spite of all these setbacks, they were making steady progress northwards. At the place they christened 'White Bay', where they stopped next, they found two native women sitting by a fire with their children and on this occasion Mary was able to reassure them that no harm was meant and to persuade them to part with a 'firebrand' so that she could light her own fire.

White Bay proved a very safe and pleasant spot, but the voyagers knew they dare not rest there for long. They still had hundreds of miles to go and the weather could only get worse. So, reluctantly, they pushed their boat out and again set off northwards. The weather then turned against them with a vengeance, and they ran into a storm compared with which the earlier one paled into insignificance. The seas ran 'mountains high'; one minute they were down in a trough with the waves towering above them, the next precariously clinging to the crest of a mighty breaker. They reefed in their mainsail and tried to use it to keep some way on the boat but with only minimum success, so that 'all night we stayed with her head to the sea thinking every moment to be our last, the seas coming on us so heavy,' Martin remembered later.

It was then that the men seemed to give up all hope of a successful outcome to the voyage, resigning themselves to their deaths. Mary simply refused to give in. Snatching up a hat belonging to one of the men, she began to bail, calling on the rest to follow suit. What was the matter with them? What kind of men were they to sit bewailing their fate while the boat sank under them, not even making an attempt to fight for their lives? They must bail with anything that came to hand, as fast as they could and as long as they could. Once she had organized the bailing, she took the tiller, straining against the huge seas. She told them, as they laboured, that she had no intention of drowning and nor should they. So, with a mixture of bullying and encouragement, shouting the while above the howling wind, she finally got them bailing out the water, allowing them no let-up until the storm subsided. She was their shining light and, as Martin writes, in spite of the very real distress she must have been suffering as the condition of 'her two babies' deteriorated rapidly through the continual cold and wet, she never once gave way to her own fears. According to Bligh, Bryant wrote that Mary and the children bore the danger and the fatigue 'wonderfully well'.

At a point when even Mary must have thought the tempest would never end, they ran into the calmer waters between the shore and the Great Barrier Reef, an area with a different kind of hazard, dotted as it is with hundreds of what were then uncharted islands and coral atolls. This time they were forced to put their fear of natives aside, as without more food or water they would die anyway. With some difficulty they managed to find a safe landing place on a small island, only about a mile in circumference. Here, they eventually managed to light a small fire, on which they cooked some of their rice in the remaining water before going out to look for more. The islet, however was without a spring of any kind; nor were there any edible shellfish. But when the tide dropped, they saw they could walk out to a reef of rocks about half a mile away and a party set off to see what they could find – it turned out to be a large group of turtles that had come ashore to lay their eggs. They turned five unfortunate creatures on to their backs and lugged them across the sand to their camp as the tide began to come in again. One was killed immediately and, that night, they dined off its flesh, the first large hot meal they had achieved since leaving the colony; to add to their delight, it rained during the night, enabling them to collect several pints of drinking water in the sails from the boat which they had spread out for that purpose.

They rested up on their islet for six days, recovering from their ordeal, but all the time shadowed by the knowledge that they would soon have to press on, leaving the relative safety of their present waters for the Arafura Sea. They killed more turtles, twelve in all, smoking the flesh to take with them. They found fruit growing on thick bushes 'like unto a Bellpepper,' which tasted good, and there were also various kinds of fowls which stayed at night 'in holes in the ground'. Once again they caulked the seams of the leaky cutter with soap, finally putting to sea again at eight o'clock in the morning, in the latitude of 26°27, according to Martin.

Protected from the worst of the ocean by the Great Barrier Reef, they continued to pick their way through islands, sometimes landing briefly in search of more turtles, without success, although they did find shellfish and were able to fish with the seine. Had it not been for the turtles and shellfish, says Martin, they would certainly have starved nor would they have survived had they not continued to find fresh water.

At last they reached the extent of the east coast and passed through the Torres Strait into the Gulf of Carpentaria where, again, there were numerous small islands, most of which seem to have been the home of natives who were distinctly unfriendly. On the first occasion they tried to go ashore, the natives, who had been watching from the beach, immediately took to their canoes. In each sat a man who paddled, while a second stood, spear poised, ready to attack. Frightened of being overwhelmed, the escapees once again fired muskets into the air to scare away their pursuers but this time the aborigines refused to be put off. Downing his spear, each warrior then produced a bow and arrow and began firing at the cutter. 'As God would have it,' wrote Martin, none of the arrows actually landed in the boat, but many dropped alongside. They were about eighteen inches long, with sharp, barbed points and could obviously have caused a considerable amount of damage. These aborigines were taller, broader and blacker than any seen previously. More canoes appeared, apparently from nowhere, one containing a person whom they thought must be a chief, as he wore an elaborate necklace of shells around his shoulders.

Burdened as the cutter was with so many people, it took them some time to get away but eventually they managed to haul up the sails and outstrip their pursuers. However this still left them with a very real dilemma: they had to find water and take on board as much as they could as the time was now rapidly approaching when they would have to make the final run to Timor. This being the case, they went ashore at the next possible opportunity, in spite of the obvious proximity of a native village made up of twenty huts, thatched with grass, each big enough to hold at least six people. They took on some water and left, as they thought, unobserved, sailing a little way down the coast to spend the night. But the next day, when they returned for more water and supplies of fruit and cabbage leaves, they ran into an ambush.

At first, as they approached the beach and village, the scene seemed exactly as they had left it the previous day. Then, to their horror, as they came closer, they saw two enormous war canoes, huge fighting proas, putting out to sea. These were very different craft to any they had seen before, each holding from thirty to forty warriors, powered by banks of paddles and sails made of some form of matting. On the decks of each were substantial fighting platforms. Soon the first pair were joined by others. 'We tacked about with what water we had,' says Martin, 'determined to cross the Gulf which is about five hundred miles across.' The canoes pursued them for several hours until they were finally left behind. Aware now that they had to make Timor if they were to survive, they risked putting in one final time for fresh water and were therefore able to replenish their supply before sailing out into the open sea. It was with trepidation that they embarked on the last leg of the voyage.

We have no written account of the final three weeks, although, according to Bligh, Bryant did leave one. Tantalizingly, it was in the three-quarters of the journal which Bligh had asked his clerk to copy but which he had been unable to complete in the time available. 'The latitudes and distances run throughout,' wrote Bligh, 'are not regularly kept up so as to ascertain the different places they stopped at, but the Journal in other respects is clear and distinct and shows the writer must have been a determined and enterprising man.' It was remarkable that in spite of the rigours of the voyage 'not one person died'.

The account was also read by a Lieutenant Tobin, who was accompanying Captain Bligh and who remarked: 'This enterprising man [Bryant] had with him in the boat his female partner and her two children, who, he observed, 'bore their suffering with more fortitude than any among them.'

All we know of the home run was that the winds were favourable at last, that rationing of both food and water was severe and that, patently, the boat held together in spite of all its defects. So, on 5 June 1791, sixty-nine days after leaving Port Jackson, they finally sighted land again. In ten weeks, less a day, they had sailed 3254 miles, the last 1200 across uncharted ocean. It remains one of the most remarkable journeys ever made in an open boat, easily rivalling that of Bligh himself, especially when one bears in mind that Bligh was a first-class, highly experienced ocean navigator and that among those with him was the *Bounty*'s own sailing master. While both Bryant and Will Moreton were competent seamen, as navigators they were not in the same league as Bligh and his sailing master. In the words of one sailing authority, 'On the side of pure navigation, this passage stands in a class by itself.'

Towards the evening of 5 June, Bryant finally tied the cutter up to the wharf at Kupang. Like Bligh, two years and nine days before him, he had made an exact landfall. It is the true stuff of legend.

The fears and horrors of the voyage were behind them. As the *London Chronicle* was to report later, 'It was impossible for them to form any idea of the distance they would have to run or what dangers, independent of those of the sea, they might have to encounter; added to this the monsoon had just set in and the wind was contrary. Yet, under these circumstances, they rather chose to risk their lives on the sea, than drag out a miserable existence on the farther shore.'

CHAPTER FIFTEEN
When the Luck Ran Out

URING THEIR weeks in the boat, the convicts had had
plenty of time to work out a believable explanation as to
who they were and why they had arrived in such a manner.
Obviously the simpler the story the better. As the coral seas had
claimed countless victims it seemed sensible to tell the authorities
that they were the survivors of a wreck. Will would take Mary's
maiden name and call himself Will Broad, mate of a large whaler
(which would explain why he had been able to have his wife and
children aboard), which had sunk somewhere off the Great
Barrier Reef.

Their arrival in an open boat, with an account so similar to
that of Captain Bligh, was totally accepted by everyone, including the Dutch Governor, Timotheus Wanjon. Will went into
some detail as to the supposed wreck, colouring his story still
further by saying that he thought all hands had escaped drowning and that they might expect more survivors shortly, since the
captain and other crew members had got safely into the other
ship's boat, but that the two had then become separated. He
could not know that this extra piece of unnecessary 'information'
would help towards their undoing. Will's party were obviously
desperately in need of food, clothing and accommodation.
Wanjon said that he could certainly provide all they needed and
presumed that Will, as a merchant seamen, had the authority to
sign the necessary bills which would later be sent to the British
government. Will agreed and carefully signed them all in the
name of 'William Broad'.

Wanjon, says James Martin in his Memorandum, 'behaved
extremely well to us and filled our bellies and clothed us.' The
men were soon able to find work, presumably on the docks and
quays, and they were all, according to Martin, 'very happy' for

the next two months. Mary's fame soon spread throughout Kupang, her courage, inspiration and sheer dogged determination were praised to the skies by all – even Will, at first, although he soon began to grumble about her to the others. Even without any knowledge of the real situation, the Dutch took to their hearts the young mother who, from the accounts of the rest of the party, was largely responsible for their survival, not only by taking her turn at the tiller and the oars, but by refusing to allow them to give in to despair.

Now, as the men worked, she was able to recover and, most importantly, build up the strength of the two small children, both of whom had been considerably weakened by the long voyage. East Timor was a beautiful spot in which to recuperate, with a climate considered to be very pleasant, especially compared with that of the white man's grave of Batavia. A naval surgeon described the island as the 'Montpelier of the east, to the Dutch and Portuguese settlements in India; and from the salubrity of its air, it is the favourite resort of valetudinarians and invalids from Batavia and other places.' It was fertile, he continued, its countryside variegated by beautiful hills and dales and was as large as Great Britain. Its principal trade was in wax, honey and sandalwood but its strategic importance was as the major trading centre of the Dutch East India Company. Kupang teemed with people of many races and religions – it even had its own Chinatown.

It was then, just as the convicts were recovering from their ordeal, able to relax at last in congenial surroundings, exhilarated by the success of their escape, that, by the cruellest of ironies, their luck finally ran out.

As has already been mentioned, it was to Kupang that Captain Bligh sailed his boatload of survivors from the mutiny on the *Bounty*. He and they had arrived back in London in March 1790, with the full story of the mutiny, a tale which shocked both government and Admiralty to the core. It was obvious that the mutineers must be made examples of, so a punitive mission was put in hand immediately, under the command of one of the most unpleasant captains in the British Navy. Whatever differing views might now be held as to the rigorous regime imposed by Bligh on his men, no such doubts surround the ensuing conduct of Captain Edward Edwards, whose name was to become a byword for inhumanity.

Edwards was given the warship HMS *Pandora*, which had been fitted out with seventy-four guns. His orders were to proceed first to Tahiti (which was considered by Bligh to be the most likely landfall for the mutineers) and, if there was no sign of them there, then to search further afield, first in the Friendly Isles then in neighbouring groups. As we now know, the original band of mutineers had split into two by this time, some remaining on Tahiti while the rest, under the command of Fletcher Christian, had settled on Pitcairn Island.

In his introduction to *The Voyage of HMS Pandora*, the edited logs of Captain Edwards and George Hamilton (the surgeon quoted above) naval historian Basil Thomson writes: 'With a roving commission in an ocean studded with undiscovered islands, the possibilities of scientific discovery were immense, but he faced them like a blinkered horse that has his eyes fixed on the narrow track before him, and all the pleasant byways of the road shut out. A cold, hard man, devoid of sympathy and imagination, of every interest beyond the straitened limits of his profession, Edwards, in the eye of posterity, was almost the worst man that could have been chosen.' We owe much of our knowledge of Edwards's subsequent behaviour to young Lieutenant Corner, who wisely kept his own counsel while still under his command, though gave evidence against him later.

Pandora also carried a Lieutenant Hayward, who had been one of Bligh's men and who had his own vindictive reasons for volunteering for the *Pandora*. Surgeon George Hamilton is described in one account as 'a coarse, vulgar and illiterate man, more disposed to relate licentious scenes and adventures, in which he and his companions engaged, than to give information of proceedings and occurrences connected with the main object of the voyage,' but on reading his account this seems unfair. Certainly he enjoyed his food and drink, and any pretty woman he might find accommodating, but his descriptions of the voyage itself and the places subsequently visited are clear and straightforward.

The voyage of *Pandora* was dogged by ill luck from the start. The crew Edwards had taken on board turned out to be already infected with a fever which had reached epidemic proportions in the English ports and, as the ship was crammed with stores for a long voyage, there was nowhere to put the sick men except on deck. That most of them recovered and that none later suffered with scurvy, Hamilton believed was due to his dosing the men regularly with the essence of malt and hops and brown sugar put aboard for brewing, and by giving them as much sauerkraut as they could eat.

Edwards decided to make the voyage via Cape Horn which he succeeded in rounding safely. He then sailed westwards, propelled by strong, favourable winds. Had he been able to stay on this course, then Pitcairn Island would have been his first landfall but, fortunately for the mutineers, when he was within twenty miles of it the wind backed round to the north so that he was forced to pass it by. Instead he continued, as planned, for Tahiti. There were still fourteen mutineers left on the island, most of whom had taken native wives. They had built themselves a small schooner on which they planned to move to a less accessible island once they had fully provisioned it, but there had seemed to be no hurry.

Suddenly, to their horror, they woke up one morning to find a British ship-of-the-line anchored offshore. It was obvious why she was there. The fourteen mutineers immediately took to their schooner, hotly pursued by the *Pandora*'s boats, but the mutineers soon outsailed them only to realize that they had put to sea without any food or water. Foolishly, they decided to risk returning to Tahiti at dead of night to stock up with both. It proved their undoing. The *Pandora*'s crew were waiting for them and, after a chase up into the mountains and a fight, they were all recaptured.

It was now that Edwards showed his contempt for even basic human decency. He had a 'round house', some eleven feet long, built on the quarter deck of the *Pandora*, the only access to which was through the nicknamed 'Pandora's Box'. Later Edwards was to say he had had the prison specially built to save the prisoners from being battened down below in the tropics, but for those incarcerated this was a mere nicety. Heywood, a midshipman mutineer from the *Bounty*, describes how they were kept 'with both hands and both legs in irons, and were obliged to eat, drink, sleep and obey the calls of nature, without ever being allowed to get out of this den.' In no time they were crawling with vermin as they lay in their own ordure. Most of them had taken native wives and the women had had to be torn away from them on their arrest. Heywood's girl, who had recently had his baby, pined away and died, leaving behind the first child of mixed race to be brought up on the island. The native Tahitians could only look on in helpless astonishment at the way the white men treated their own kind.

Next, Edwards fitted out the mutineers' schooner and sent men off to the nearby islands to see if they could find any more of the *Bounty*'s crew – without success for the mutineers had deliberately misled him as to where the remainder of the party were likely to be and much time was wasted in fruitless searching.

So, several weeks later, Edwards again set sail in the *Pandora*, to look further afield. It was now that his own pig-headed obstinacy and refusal to heed advice were to bring disaster. He had decided to make for New Guinea and the Torres Strait, a passage known as a graveyard for sailing ships. He had been warned that should he attempt this route, then the only safe way to do so was by hugging the New Guinea coast; indeed Bligh himself had only made the passage with difficulty and had given Edwards details of how he had accomplished it, along with the necessary navigational information. Edwards ignored it all. Not only that but, in spite of the advice that night sailing should never be attempted in such waters (a point reiterated by the famous French navigator, Bougainville, who only ever sailed in daylight), Edwards pressed blindly on, not only *through* the Torres Strait but through that strait *at night*. The outcome was inevitable.

'How fatuous a proceeding this was,' writes Thomson, 'in unsurveyed and unknown waters may be judged from the fact that in coral seas that have been carefully surveyed, all ships of war are now compelled to keep the lead going whenever they move in coral waters.' Thomson, who was writing in 1915, was referring to the 'lead' with which depth soundings were taken before the days of radar and echo sounders.

On 25 August Edwards arrived off the Murray Islands and tried to force a passage between them but was unable to do so. He followed the Barrier Reef southwards, almost reaching the safe waters used by Bligh, but then, on 28 August, he decided he had found a channel big enough through which to take his ship, in spite of falling darkness. The wind and current drove the ship on to the reef, tearing a huge hole in her planking. She immediately began to fill with water and, for the next eleven hours, all hands were put to the pumps.

How Edwards then treated the mutineers was to haunt him at his subsequent court martial, at which Lieutenant Corner testified that while three of them had been unchained to allow them to work the pumps, the rest, in spite of their pleading and promises not to escape, had been refused permission for their irons to be removed; not only that but Edwards had put two sentries to stand over them, threatening to shoot the first man who attempted to free himself and hang from the yardarm anyone who felt moved to assist him.

The ship stayed afloat throughout the night until finally Edwards gave orders to abandon it. It seems all too likely that had he given the order earlier, there would have been far fewer deaths. At this point, writes a witness, 'the wretched prisoners, seeing the officers going into the boats by the stern ladders, begged that they might not be forgotten.' That only four of them drowned was almost entirely due to the bosun's mate who, contrary to orders, went down into the Box and freed three mutineers, Muspratt, Byrne and Skinner. Skinner was released from his leg-irons, still with his hands chained together. Another seaman, Morrison, then changed places with the bosun's mate and began releasing the rest, at which point Edwards ordered the hatch to be put back, locking him in with the remaining convicts. He managed, however, to knock the irons off two of the others, while one man succeeded in releasing himself. They then begged either Edwards or the Master at Arms to open the hatch, but were refused.

At that point the *Pandora* heeled over and the Master at Arms and his sentries went with it. The captain was seen swimming to his pinnace. The sea poured into the Box and the bosun's mate, who was now in one of *Pandora*'s boats, hearing the agonizing cries coming from it, climbed back on board the sinking vessel and knocked off the hatchway. In spite of this, several mutineers went down still ironed hand and foot, while Skinner, one of the first to be released, also drowned as his handcuffs had prevented him from swimming.

So it was that some eighty-nine surviving crew members, plus ten mutineers, were finally loaded into four boats. Nearby was a coral islet and here the party was evenly distributed, then led by Edwards to the shore of Queensland, where natives showed them a source of water. Finally, on 15 September, Edwards brought his small flotilla into Kupang harbour, the third such party to arrive there in open boats. It was then that he was told he had been expected, and greeted with the news that the rest of his crew, including his mate and the latter's wife and children, had already preceded him, indeed had been there for two months! At the same time Will and the rest of *his* party were told that their captain had now arrived.

FOR MARY memories of her stay in Kupang must have been very mixed. It was a time of ease in a lovely setting, a time when she was happily accepted into society. There must have been an underlying strain, however, that she had to be careful what she said, but no doubt she was able to talk happily about her childhood in Cornwall, her parents and her sister. It would have been more difficult to ensure Charlotte did not say anything untoward, for she must have played and chatted with other children. Fortunately Emmanuel was only just learning to talk.

In the event, it was neither Charlotte, the children, nor the other convicts who were to bring about disaster, but Will himself.

It may well be that as time went on, and no further survivors from the supposed whaler arrived, that there would have been some who were suspicious as to the true origins of the boat party, but if that was the case they seem to have kept quiet about it. Will, however, though having praised Mary's part in the exploit, became weary of the esteem in which she was held by his colleagues. He had always believed that women should know their place, and Mary had got well above hers. He wanted a 'proper' woman, one who would treat a man right. Once again he began to talk about finding a berth in a ship bound either for England or the Cape of Good Hope, leaving Mary and the children to fend for themselves. As he grew more morose so he turned to what had always been his Achilles' heel – drink.

Soon, according to James Martin, there were open quarrels between Will and Mary, as Mary became increasingly alarmed by Will's heavy drinking and the consequent loosening of his tongue. Will had never been able to take criticism from anyone, least of all a woman. It was disastrous that it all came to a head just as Edwards and his party arrived in Kupang.

Edwards soon made it clear to Governor Wanjon that all his crew and mutineers were accounted for, dead or alive. Therefore the party in the small boat had nothing to do with the wreck of the *Pandora*. Accounts conflict wildly as to what happened next.

Martin says that after a particularly vicious quarrel with Mary, Will went off 'and laid information' against the rest, but this seems improbable as he would have had nothing to gain from such action. It is far more likely that after a blazing row he took himself off to a bar, got drunk and, having had his original story questioned as a result of the arrival of Edwards, bragged about the amazing escape he had masterminded, about how they had stolen the Governor's own boat and how his brilliant seamanship had brought them safely into Kupang. From what is known of him, it would have been quite in character.

Whatever the truth of the matter, within days of Edwards's arrival, Wanjon had sent out a party to arrest the convicts.

According to Martin and Surgeon Hamilton, Mary escaped into the jungle with her children, but was eventually captured and sent to join the rest in the 'castle gaol'. Wanjon questioned the convicts closely and they finally admitted who they were; however he seems to have been a humane man since he allowed them out on bail, two at a time, on a daily rota. It was the last trace of humanity they were to experience for a long time.

For Edwards the discovery of the escaped convicts was a bonus, something he could set against his disappointment at not having retrieved all the *Bounty* mutineers. His immediate task was to charter a ship large enough to take the whole party – seamen, mutineers and convicts – as far as Batavia, where he hoped he might find a suitable vessel or vessels for the next leg of the journey, to the Cape. He finally selected the *Rembang*, which was about to leave for Batavia carrying a cargo of spices and despatches from the East India Company's accountant, B. C. Roset, to his Directors in Batavia; thus it was that the details of the Bryants' escapade came also to be recorded in the Dutch *Colonial Archive* in The Hague.

In the despatch dated 30 September 1791 Roset writes:

> With regard to alien shipping in these waters, we notify your Right Honourables, most humbly, that besides the two English warships, which arrived here on the 6 January of this year, there arrived here again in June an English boat with eleven persons on board, among which were a woman and two children. They professed to have lost their ship approximately off New South Wales, not far from New Holland. Also that the captain and the rest of the crew probably would follow in another boat.
>
> However, later on, it has now been discovered that they had run away from New Holland. Unfortunately we have not been able to find out the reason of their running away for lack of an interpreter. So, therefore, they are placed at the disposal of your Right Honourables and will be sent off with this ship 'Rembang'.
>
> If similar visits as the above mentioned would recur in the

future, our humble request is to be informed how to act in such cases.

Roset then went on to add that also sailing in the *Rembang* would be another group of survivors '. . . being the crew of the warship *Pandora*, wrecked in the Pacific, which was sent out to find the ship *Bounty*, under the command of Lieutenant William Bligh, who visited this port two years ago. The *Bounty* was not encountered but 14 mutineers of this ship were found on the island of Othaheite [Tahiti], of which 4 drowned when the *Pandora* sank. The remaining 10 arrived here with the crew of the *Pandora* and all of them will be sent with the deliverer of this letter.' A short summary of the cargo was also enclosed.

Edwards chose the *Rembang* in part because she had an extra deck running along two-thirds of her length. There were no portholes, lighting or ventilation on this deck. He had it divided into three by screens, the small section aft for the mutineers, the middle for the crew of the *Pandora* and the foreward space for the convicts. To all intents and purposes, it was a repeat of 'Pandora's Box'. In bad weather the occupants would be battened down; in fine weather the hatches would be left open to let in some light, at which time the sailors would be allowed on deck. No such mercy was shown to either the mutineers or the convicts.

When the captain of the ship heard the party was to include a woman with two small children, he immediately offered a cabin in the aft part of the vessel, saying he thought it quite wrong for them to be confined on the 'tween deck, even if the woman was a convicted felon. But Edwards refused, just as he also set himself firmly against any discussion of washing facilities for the prisoners or the provision of food and water for them. So far as he was concerned the convicts and mutineers he was taking back to England were merely gallows' fodder, and as such deserved only sufficient food and water to keep them alive. They certainly did not deserve any comfort, even if they included a woman and children.

Mary could only have felt desolation. For years at Port Jackson she had survived on the belief that one day, somehow, she would escape. All of them had accepted that they might be discovered making the attempt and while that would have been a dismal end to the venture, it was nothing like as devastating as recapture after they had been so sure they were finally free. Even death in the open boat on the way to Kupang might well have seemed preferable, than to have gone through so many hardships and achieved so much, only to have freedom snatched away from them. All they could now look forward to was an appalling voyage back to England followed, if they survived, by retrial and probable death on the gallows as escaped transportees.

Just before Edwards left, Wanjon presented him with the bills Will Bryant had signed in the name of Broad, for the cost of their food, clothing and housing while in Kupang. At first Edwards refused to have anything to do with them, but was finally forced to accept them when Wanjon told him that if he did not do so then he would prevent any provisions from being put aboard the *Rembang* for the coming voyage. He was deaf to the claims of Edwards that Bryant's bills were invalid, since they had been signed in his wife's maiden name. Edwards duly presented them to the British government on his return, but there is no record that they were ever honoured. When it finally came to signing for the provisions for his voyage, Edwards only agreed to a minimum amount – he would lose no sleep over his prisoners being half-starved.

On 5 October Wanjon formally handed over the convicts to Edwards who duly signed for them. At that stage they were all in good health. Edwards immediately had them confined below. 'He put us in irons called the "bilboes",' writes Martin. This was a long bar made of iron, with sliding shackles fixed to the prisoners' ankles, the whole locked to the floor at one end. The *Rembang* sailed for Batavia the next day.

It would seem that Will, whether or not he was entirely to blame for their betrayal, was now treated as a pariah by the rest of the party, battened down in that confined space. Whether it was because his spirit was broken is not known, but his health deteriorated rapidly as did that of little Emmanuel, who had not recovered from the deprivations of the voyage as quickly as Charlotte, in spite of the beneficent air of Kupang, nor could his diet be supplemented any longer with breast milk. He had to take his chance with the rest so, whatever Mary made of the situation in which she now found herself, her first concern was for the baby.

As a result of the conditions they were kept in, the prisoners were soon soaked through. Off the island of Flores the ship ran into a cyclone of which there are two contrasting accounts, one Dutch and one English. According to the Dutch archive, the ship was brought safely to Batavia due to the skill of the Dutch seamen, while the *Pandora*'s crew remained below decks playing cards; according to Surgeon Hamilton, it was the other way round:

> In a few moments, every sail of the ship was shivered to pieces, the pumps all choked and useless, the leak gaining fast upon us; and she was driving down, with all the impetuosity imaginable, on a savage shore, about seven miles under our lee. This storm was attended with the most dreadful thunder and lightning we had ever experienced . . .
>
> The Dutch seamen were struck with horror and went below. The ship was preserved from destruction by the manly exertions of our English tars whose souls seemed to catch redoubled ardour from the tempest's rage. Indeed it is only in these trying moments of distress, when the abyss of destruction is yawning to receive them, that the transcendant worth of a British seaman is most conspicuous. The Dutch would fight the devil should he appear to them in any other shape but that of thunder and lightning.

It is a matter of choice which account is to be believed.

Within days, all the benefits of good treatment and sunshine in Kupang went for nothing as the convicts became ill with fever. No doubt their past experiences had left them vulnerable to disease.

'I arrived at Batavia on the 7 November,' writes Edwards, 'and on application to the Governor and Council, my people were put aboard a Dutch East India Company's ship that was lying in the Road, to be kept there until they could be sent to Europe, and the sick were ordered to be received in the Company's hospital at Batavia.'

Shore leave in Batavia, especially in its hospital, was hardly a boon. Captain Cook had warned that Batavia was a place 'Europeans need not covet to go to, but, if necessity obliges them, they will do well to make their stay as short as possible, otherwise they will soon feel the effects of the unwholesome air of Batavia which, I firmly believe, is the death of more Europeans than any other place upon the globe.' He had put in to the port, he says, with as healthy a ship's company as could be found anywhere, leaving it some three months later 'in the condition of a hospital ship besides the loss of seven men.' The Dutch told him he was lucky to get off so lightly. The port's notorious reputation was already known in Port Jackson and the homeward bound Watkin Tench was to write that 'Death, to a man who has resided in Batavia, is too familiar an object to excite either terror or regret.'

Surgeon Hamilton thought it to be the last place God made, noting that 'under the muzle [sic] of the sun, a Dutchman cannot exist without snuffing the exhalations from stagnant water to which they have been accustomed from infancy.' He blamed the fevers which raged continually around the port on the amount of stagnant water to be found in it, due to the fact that the Dutch 'are intersecting it [the town] so fast with canals, that in a year or two this beautiful town will be completely damned . . . the first thing we did was to send to hospital the sickly remains of our unfortunate crew. Some dead bodies floating down a canal struck our boat, which had a very disagreeable effect on the minds of our brave fellows, whose nerves were reduced to a very weak state from sickness.' He did not mention the state of the convicts. 'This,' he continued, 'was a *coup de grâce* to a sick man on his premier entrée into this painted sepulchre, this golgotha of Europe, which buries its whole settlement every five years.'

Hamilton took a dim view of the Dutch, blaming them for just about all the world's ills; nor was he liberal in his view of non-Europeans. 'The Chinese here are the Jews of the East, and as soon as they make their fortune, they go home. Let the amateurs of the Republican system read and learn.' The hospital he summarily dismissed as a stinking hole.

It was to this same hospital that Mary was sent with the mortally ill Emmanuel. We are not told if she was allowed to take Charlotte with her. She was soon to be joined by Will, who was now also seriously ill. Emmanuel died in Mary's arms on 1 December 1791 and was buried at once with scant ceremony. Infant death was too common to be of any interest. He was not yet two years old.

Three weeks later, on 22 December, his father, who had been so strong, joined him in the grave. Will had survived the years on the hulks, the long voyage out, the privations of life in Port Jackson, a savage flogging and the rigours of the open boat, finally to die of 'fever', coupled (though not, of course, mentioned on the register of his death) with a combination of bad conditions, overwhelming disappointment, and the knowledge that just as he had been the prime mover in the original escape, he was also the weak link that had finally betrayed his wife, family and friends. At a time when a relatively small lift in spirits can make the difference between life and death, it seems Will gave up.

Throughout those last three weeks Mary nursed him as he slipped further and further away. She must have felt very torn. To a large extent Will had kept to his side of the bargain, providing for her and protecting her throughout their time in the penal colony. She had also kept hers, and given him a son, a son who was now dead and who might have been alive but for Will's drunken stupidity. They had gone through so much together, not least the planning and carrying through of the successful escape. There is no record as to whether or not they were finally reconciled before Will's death.

CHAPTER SIXTEEN

Desolation

G OVERNOR PHILLIP had written to the Home Office on 5 . November 1791 giving, somewhat belatedly, the details of the escape from Port Jackson, concluding: 'As there is a probability that the boat may go to a Dutch settlement, the names and descriptions of the people are enclosed. The getting back of any of these men is much to be desired.' Before leaving Kupang, Edwards had also sent off a list to the Admiralty Office in London of the escapees he had taken on board:

WILLIAM MORETON
WILLIAM BRYANT – says the term of his transportation is expired
WILLIAM ALLEN
JOHN BUTCHER
JAMES COX – says the term of his transportation is expired
NATH. LILLEY
JOHN SIMMONS [*sic*]
JAMES MARTIN
MARY BRYANT
EMMANUEL BRYANT
CHARLOTTE BRYANT

They might indeed have got away with it, writes David Collins, 'had it not been for the fortunate discovery and delivery of these people to the captain of a British man o'war. Had this not been the case, the evident practicability of reaching Timor in an open boat might have operated with others to make the attempt, and to carry off boats from the settlement. It is now hoped that the certainty of every boat which should reach that or any other Dutch settlement, under similar circumstances, being suspected and apprehended, would have its due effect here.'

Edwards had sent a small advance party to the Cape of Good Hope on 19 November on a Dutch East Indiaman, the *Zwan*. He then set about negotiating with the Dutch for passages for the rest to Holland or, failing that, to the Cape, 'at no expense to the Government further than for the officers and prisoners, which appeared to me to be the most eligible and least expensive way of getting to England.' He succeeded in finding three ships which could take extra passengers. He and those he described as 'the pirates' were to sail on the *Vreedenburg*, while Mary, Charlotte and William Allen, along with some of the *Pandora*'s crew, sailed on the *Horssen*. The rest of the sailors and other convicts – James Martin, Nathaniel Lilley, John Butcher (alias Samuel Broom), John Simms (alias Samuel Bird) and William Moreton – are listed as being taken on the *Hoornwey*, although there are discrepancies in the various accounts as to who, apart from Mary, actually travelled on which vessel.

Mary had little time to mourn. As a convict, Will had received only the most cursory of ceremonies at his burial, after which she was immediately returned to the Dutch guardship anchored off the harbour, preparatory to being transferred to the East Indiaman. James Martin says that all the convicts were kept 'in irons again there [in Batavia] . . . we lost the child and six days after the father of the child was taken bad and died, which was both buried at Batavia. Six weeks after we was put on three different ships bound to the Cape of Good Hope which we was three months on before we reached the Cape.'

Edwards had laid down the regimen for the prisoners with the Dutch captains before leaving Batavia. They were to be kept below and in irons. Every evening, at five o'clock, they could be brought up on deck for an hour's exercise and to allow them to perform their natural functions. At four bells they were to be taken below and chained up again for the night. Accordingly their health, already far from good, deteriorated still further, undermined by privation, semi-starvation and intense mental anguish. All, according to reports, became 'lethargic'. It was very hot but water was rationed to one quart a day each.

The fever which raged in Batavia had followed them aboard

and now stalked the decks of all three vessels during what Surgeon Hamilton described as 'this tedious passage'. It carried off both Dutch and English sailors, along with Samuel Bird and William Moreton, Will Bryant's fellow navigator on the voyage to East Timor. While passing through the Straits of Sunda, Mary lost her last direct link with Will, for James Cox, maddened by fever and the pain of a festering leg where the irons had rubbed a wound, jumped overboard during his brief exercise time. It is unlikely that he reached the shore, as his wrists were still handcuffed, but there is a faint possibility that he might have done as the distance was only about two miles. It was Cox who had left the note to his girlfriend, later found by Collins, giving her his few possessions and warning 'do you give over those vices that I have caught you at more than once, or you will come to a bad end.'

Both Mary and Charlotte became ill and the Dutch captain, in defiance of Edwards's orders, released Mary from her irons so that she could care for the child.

Captain Edwards, with the rest of the vessels close behind, reached Table Bay on 18 March 1792 and found there before him a British ship, the HMS *Gorgon*, under the command of Captain John Parker. She had arrived on 11 March direct from Port Jackson, carrying with her a number of marine officers and men whose time had expired and who were now bound for England and war with France. Included among them were Lieutenant Ralph Clark and Watkin Tench, who was now a captain.

The following day Edwards wrote at once to the Admiralty: 'Sir, Agreeable to my intentions which I did myself the honour to signify to you in a letter addressed from Batavia and sent by a Dutch packet bound to Europe, I embarked the remainder of the Company of His Majesty's ship *Pandora*, the pirates late of the *Bounty* and the convicts, deserters from Port Jackson, on board three Dutch East India ships.' He then gave details of the arrangements he had made and a description of the voyage to the Cape.

'I found His Majesty's Ship *Gorgon* here on her return from

Port Jackson, and on account both of expedition and greater security I intend to avail myself of the opportunity to embark on board of her with the ten pirates for England, and I request that you will be pleased to communicate the circumstances to my Lords Commissioners of the Admiralty.'

Edwards then appended a list of the others he proposed taking aboard as well: 'A list of the convicts, deserters from Port Jackson, delivered to Captain Edward Edwards of His Majesty's ship *Pandora* by Timotheus Wanjon, Governor of the Dutch Settlements at Timor, 5 October 1791.

WILLIAM ALLEN
JOHN BUTCHER
NATHANIEL LILLEY
JAMES MARTIN
MARY BRYANT, transported by the name
   of Mary Broad

On board His Majesty's
Ship *Gorgon*

WILLIAM MORETON Died on board the Dutch East India
   Company's ship *Hornwey* [*sic*]
JOHN SIMMS
WILLIAM BRYANT Died 22 Dec'r. 1791, hosp'l. Batavia.
JAMES COX Died (fell overboard), Streights [*sic*] of Sunda

So, some six months after falling into the hands of Edwards, the survivors were transferred to the *Gorgon* to find, by a coincidence worthy of a historical blockbuster, that she was carrying the very marine officers they had left behind in Port Jackson and, in the case of Mary and James Cox, two of those who had sailed out with them in the First Fleet. There was also a cargo of plants and animals from around the settlement, the deck being crowded, according to Captain Parker's wife, 'with kangaroos, opossums and every curiosity that country produced. The quarter deck was occupied with shrubs and plants, while our cabin was hung around with the skins of animals. We had also procured a variety of birds.'

As well as Mrs Parker there were a number of other women on the ship accompanying their husbands. As the *Gorgon* left for

England on 5 April 1792, Mary experienced the first kindness she had been shown since Kupang.

But Charlotte was now desperately ill and Mary was experienced enough to read the signs. Captain Parker was no Edwards and it was he who was in command of the ship. He insisted that, convict or not, Mary should have proper accommodation and somewhere to nurse her dying child. She must have already known some of the women on board, even if she had never spoken to them and it seems they behaved well to her. She was given adequate food and drink for herself and her child, and Charlotte was attended by the ship's surgeon. But it was too late.

On 22 April Ralph Clark noted in his journal: 'Very hot. At night, below the lower gun deck, there is hardly any living for the heat.' Between then and 2 May he recorded the deaths of five of the children born to marines and their wives. 'The children are going very fast, the hot weather is the reason for it. Another child died on 4th May, another on the fifth.'

The entry for Sunday 6 May reads: 'Squally weather with great deal of rain all this day. Last night the child belonging to Mary Broad, the convict woman who went away in the fishing boat from Port Jackson last year, died at about 4 o'clock. Committed body to the deep.'

So, for the third time, Mary heard the familiar words of the burial service read for one of her family, this time for a burial at sea. Charlotte, the child conceived on board the *Dunkirk* of an unknown father, had followed her brother and stepfather into oblivion.

One account speaks of Mary being stony-faced and showing no emotion as Charlotte's body, sewn in a piece of sackcloth, slid over the side. This may well be true. She must have been emotionally and physically drained; she had nothing left. She had suffered so much, come within a hair's breadth of success in one of history's most amazing escapes, only to lose it all – husband, children and liberty. All that awaited her now at the end of the road was the gallows.

Did she contemplate ending it all then? She would have had

both time and opportunity during the long voyage home, for she was not imprisoned like the rest of her fellow convicts. We will never know what gave her the strength not to kill herself, at the point where she had reached the very nadir of despair. Especially since she would later say that she would prefer death on the gallows to further, long-term imprisonment.

WHILE WE are obliged to Ralph Clark for the information on the death of Charlotte, he was by no means as open or prolific in his journal musings on his homeward voyage as he had been on the way out. Nor did he have much to say about women. When he was first posted to Norfolk Island he continued to write in much the same vein as previously about the convict women, in spite of having taken Mary Branham to his bed: 'Gave orders for a jail to be built and neck collars made for the women. Never came across such a cross set of D*** B****'s in all my life, they make me swear my very soul out. I shall order the women to be locked up in the jail every night.' He'd also proclaimed that any woman who went anywhere without his leave would be sentenced to twenty-five lashes.

But by the time he returned home he had stopped musing on the women in his life, even on Betsey Alicia, and there is no reference whatsoever to the girl who would have been, according to his earlier ramblings, no better than a whore and who, up until the time he left, had been his official mistress. During his later years on Norfolk Island, there is a huge gap in the journals and it is not known whether this is because he felt unable to write much during that period or whether the relevant papers have been lost. Mary Branham gave birth to his child in the summer of 1791 and sailed back with him to Port Jackson at the beginning of December. The baby was christened Alicia (after the perfect wife) on 16 December 1791. Three weeks later, on 6 January 1791, Clark left Australia on the *Gorgon*. Neither Mary Branham nor Alicia Clark are ever referred to in his papers. It is yet another irony of fate that if Alicia survived, she would prove to be his only descendant.

Watkin Tench picked up some of the threads of his friendship with Mary during that long voyage home. Had he really been Charlotte's father, as has been suggested, one cannot imagine so kind and humane a man would not have made some note to that effect or shown some sorrow at her death; unless there was another, secret diary which did not survive, for he made it clear that his journals and notes had been kept for publication at some future date. Almost alone among the marine officers who sailed with the First Fleet and who were not accompanied by their own women, he is not recorded as having taken a mistress while in Port Jackson; yet he seems to have been both attracted by, and attractive to, them.

From Mary he learned a good deal of the convicts' history subsequent to their escape. 'It was my fate to fall in again with this little band,' he writes. 'In March 1792, when I arrived on the *Gorgon* at the Cape of Good Hope, six of these people, including the woman and one child, were put aboard to be carried to England. Four had died, and one had jumped over-board, at Batavia.'

He describes how their boat was sailed along the coast of Australia and the different harbours they put in to and what had happened to them there. His version of the story they told Wanjon differs slightly from the version of the Dutch Governor himself: 'Treated by the Dutch with kindness and hospitality, they pretended they were from a ship, on passage from Port Jackson to India, which had foundered.'

It is not surprising that the sympathetic Tench with his love of liberty and the cause of freedom should continue:

> I confess that I never looked at these people without pity and astonishment. They had miscarried in a heroic struggle for liberty; after having combated every hardship and conquered every difficulty.
>
> The woman had gone out to Port Jackson in the ship which had transported me thither and was distinguished for her good behaviour. I could not but reflect with admiration at the strange

combination of circumstances which had brought us together again, to baffle human foresight and confound human speculation.

If this was a romantic novel it would end here, with these two remarkable and independent people, so close in spirit, winning through and living happily ever after together. Unfortunately, this is not fiction. Whether Watkin Tench was tempted to throw caution (and his career) to the wind and offer Mary a permanent relationship, he does not say. Even if he had considered it, it is unlikely that she would have been in any state to appreciate such an offer.

The rest of the voyage passed without incident and with all on board, even the prisoners, in relatively good health. Captain Parker allowed both the mutineers and the convicts on deck for regular exercise. This humane naval captain, a credit to his service, died not long after the voyage, leaving his wife to write an account of it. It seems remarkable that nowhere in this does she mention Mary Bryant and her unique history. It seems that for Mrs Parker, Mary was a non-person.

Just before the *Gorgon* arrived, Edwards wrote a further letter to the Admiralty in case the one he had sent from the Cape had gone astray.

I beg leave to inform you that I found His Majesty's Ship *Gorgon* at the Cape of Good Hope on my arrival there in the *Vreedenburg*, a Dutch East India Company's ship from Batavia, and I thought it proper to remove the pirates late belonging to His Majesty's armed vessel, the *Bounty*, and the convicts, deserters from Port Jackson (whom I had under my charge on board the Dutch East India Company's ships) into His Majesty's said ship, for their greater security, and I took the same opportunity myself to embark on board her for England and I hope that these steps will be approved of by their Lordships.

I gave you an account of my arrival at the Cape of Good Hope and my intentions to embark on board the *Gorgon* with the pirates, convicts, etc. in a letter which I did myself the honour to address to you from thence and sent by the *Baring*, Thomas Fingey Master, an American ship bound for Ostend.

Inclosed [*sic*] is the state of the company of His Majesty's Ship *Pandora* at the time I left the Cape of Good Hope, and the manner in which they were disposed of on board the Dutch East India Company's ships in order to be brought to Europe and also a list of the pirates late belonging to the *Bounty*, and of the convicts, deserters from Port Jackson, delivered to me by Mr Wanjon, the Governor of the Dutch settlements in the island of Timor, now on board His Majesty's Ship *Gorgon*.

On 18 June 1792 the *Gorgon* anchored off Portsmouth and Edwards was put ashore. He dated his letter the following morning, 'June, 19th, 1792' and added to it: 'I arrived yesterday evening at St. Helen's, and left the *Gorgon*, and landed at Portsmouth last night and I am now in this office awaiting their Lordships' Commands.'

To this missive Edwards attached a copy of the list of convicts, and their fate, which he had sent with the despatches to Ostend, to which he added:

EMANUEL BRYANT. Died 1st December 1791. Batavia

CHARLOTTE BRYANT. Died 6th May 1792 on board H.M.S. *Gorgon*

} Children of the above William and Mary Bryant

The convicts were to remain on board while the *Gorgon* sailed for London. Joy at seeing the shore of England again was now over-shadowed for all of them by fear of what was to come.

It was just five years and six months since Mary had left Devonport for the Fatal Shore.

BOOK THREE

LONDON

CHAPTER SEVENTEEN

Enter James Boswell

IT IS THE 3rd of July 1792, a fine sunny morning. A gentleman sits drinking his coffee and perusing the columns of the *London Chronicle*; a commonplace scene. He is rather overweight and wheezes when he breathes. He has a florid complexion, his face covered with the thin, red, broken veins of the heavy drinker. James Boswell is fifty-two but looks older. He is a not very successful lawyer, a widower with growing children, but he has recently achieved what he has always thought was his due – fame and a certain amount of recognition among his contemporaries.

Boswell's place in literary history has been assured over the years by his *Life of Samuel Johnson*, an account of the life, times and sayings of the great man who was his guide, mentor and friend, to which he had put the final touches a year previously. Little more was known about him until the nineteenth century when the amazing cache of his personal papers was discovered in Malahide Castle in Scotland. Among these were the journals he had kept for many years. However, at the time of writing, only the *London Journal*, which deals with his early years in the capital, is readily available to the interested reader. The rest were only published in an extremely limited edition, copies of which remain locked in the safes of libraries. As a result, his involvement with Mary Bryant, the story of which appears in his last journal, remained unknown for nearly two hundred years.

James Boswell was born in Edinburgh on 29 October 1740, the eldest son of Alexander Boswell, eighth Laird of Auchinleck in Ayrshire. According to Frederick Pottle's introduction to the *London Journals*, the family traced its descent back to a sixteenth-century Boswell, Thomas, a favourite of James IV of Scotland, who gave him a barony, before both were killed, side by side, on Flodden Field in 1513. The family remained devoted to the Stuart·cause thereafter, firmly supporting the claim of Mary, Queen of Scots, to the English throne. However they were very canny. While not becoming ennobled themselves, they did the next best thing, by making a whole serious of advantageous marriages into the Scottish aristocracy.

Boswell remained to the end of his days a terrible snob, claiming acquaintance with every nobleman of great estate with whom·he came into contact on the basis of his family connections. His grandmother was a Bruce, daughter of the Earl of Kincardine, his mother Euphemia Erskine descended, if indirectly, from the great Earl of Lennox who was the grandfather of Lord Darnley, the weak and unfortunate second husband of Mary Stuart. 'Boswell, therefore,' writes Frederick Pottle, 'could (and did) claim that the blood of Robert the Bruce flowed in his veins, and on one occasion felt free to remind George III that he was his cousin . . .'

His father, Alexander, was a very distinguished lawyer, a member of the Faculty of Advocates, elevated to the bench as one of the fifteen judges of the Court of Session, Scotland's supreme civil court. A year later, in 1755, he 'took the double gown', becoming one of the five judges of the High Court of Justiciary, the supreme court for criminal cases and, through these honours, assumed the title Lord Auchinleck, although he was not actually a peer. He had an enormous country estate (he could ride for ten miles without leaving his own land) as well as a fine town house in Edinburgh, where James was born.

Not surprisingly, he wanted his eldest son to follow in his footsteps and go into the law and James's whole education was bent towards that end. Instead of attending Edinburgh High School like other members of his class, the young James was sent to a strict private school, before being entered at university at the age of thirteen. It was still not uncommon for boys to go up to college at such an early age and his father saw no reason why James should not as he could live at home while he studied. It is hardly likely that James considered that an advantage. The three Boswell boys were given a rigorous and puritanical upbringing in a dour household where there was little relaxation and no real affection. A series of domestic tutors, or crammers, lived with the family to ensure the three boys were kept up to the mark in their studies. Inevitably, the end result was not the one their father might have wished.

Although James had been a timid and shy child, as he grew older he began, not unnaturally, to rebel against his father's strict regimen. From being puny and undersized he put on weight – already rather too much weight – and became vain of his appearance, in particular his dark hair and eyes. He fell in love with the theatre, wrote poetry and chased the girls. In fact chasing women was to remain a lifelong activity. While Lord Auchinleck foresaw a rosy future for his son as a distinguished lawyer, that son now had other ideas. He began to dream of a red coat, a commission in a royal regiment, preferably the Guards. He saw himself set up in fine lodgings in London, in his splendid uniform cutting a dashing figure with the women. His father refused even to discuss the possibility and eventually there was so much antagonism between the two that, after he matriculated, James ran away to London, announcing when he arrived that he planned to be received into the Roman Catholic Church. His family were shell-shocked at the suggestion.

It seems that Boswell not only went so far as to be received into the Church but also toyed with the unlikely notion of becoming a monk. However he soon distanced himself from Catholicism for reasons he never explained but which become understandable when it is learnt that as the law then stood Catholics could not become army officers, let alone barristers or advocates. He could not even have inherited his father's estate. Auchinleck, appalled at the activities of his errant son, made hasty arrangements for the disposal of the estate should James not recant, then followed this up by asking an old friend, Lord Eglington, to take young James in hand. He certainly did, but hardly in the way Auchinleck intended. Soon James was experiencing the kind of lifestyle which previously he had only dreamt about. For a brief spell he was a friend and confidant of the young and notorious Duke of York, he regularly attended the races, dined in high society and spent his evenings in theatres, gambling clubs and brothels.

Lord Auchinleck remained adamant that his son would have no career in the army. So, as James's overriding concern was that he should, somehow or other, persuade his father to let him remain in London, he decided to be entered at the Inns of Court. He had recently made friends with Thomas Sheridan, the father of the playwright, who kindly offered to make the necessary arrangements. So sure was James that Auchinleck would agree to this change of plan that he asked Sheridan to go ahead and it was arranged that he should start at the Inner Temple in the November of 1761. But this did not please Auchinleck either. Rumours of his son's wild lifestyle had reached him in Scotland, not least that he was heavily in debt. He ordered James home.

Father and son spent months wrangling about James's future before Auchinleck finally admitted defeat. How hard James worked at his law studies is unclear, but he does tell us what he was doing in his spare time: 'Adventure with P., the most curious young little pretty, though all out . . . no opportunity for a long time,' he noted, cryptically, in his diary for January 1762. On 3 March he wrote, gleefully, 'Finally made it out.' The 'curious young little pretty' was Peggy Doig, probably a servant or a sempstress, and by July James was deep in discussion with Dr Cairnie, Kirk Treasurer of Canongate, as to what provision he would be making for her and the coming child now that he was to return to London.

Boswell seems to have been genuinely delighted at the prospect of becoming a father, leaving money for the care of Peggy and for the upkeep of his child and giving details of where and how the baby should be baptized and who should stand godfather. He was certainly very happy to give his name to the infant. The baby boy, born after Boswell left Scotland, was christened Charles. 'Poor little creature,' he wrote on hearing the news. 'I wish from my heart that I had seen him before I left for England. His resembling me is the most agreeable thing . . . He shall always find me an affectionate father, and I must indulge many fond – perhaps foolish – ideas of his making a figure in life. I am determined that nothing shall be wanting to accomplish him for whatever his genius leads him to.' Touchingly, he planned a life for his little son with a kind nurse who 'would love him,' school in 'some pleasant village in England where his parentage should not be known, as the scoffing of his companions might break his spirit,' secondary education of whatever kind he desired, in fact all those things he had not experienced himself. Sadly none of this was to be, for little Charles died at the age of two without James ever having seen him, to the latter's great distress.

Once in London, his debts settled and with a private income of two hundred pounds a year, Boswell threw himself with enthusiasm into everything except the law. His pursuit both of the aristocracy and women was relentless. The former were ruthlessly sought out, visited and forced to make his acquaintance: James seems to have been impervious either to insults or indifference. The latter he chased obsessively, thinking nothing of having a sixpenny whore in an alleyway on his way to dine or noting frankly in his journals the physical attributes of girls who took his fancy. He was particularly keen on girls with big breasts. He describes, with relish, an encounter with 'a monstrous big whore in the Strand, whom I had a great curiosity to lubricate, as the saying is. I went into a tavern with her, where she displayed to me all the parts of her enormous carcass; but I found her avarice was as large as her ★★★★, for she would by no means take what I offered her.' He had a passionate affair with an actress called Louisa, from whom, he claims, he caught the clap (venereal disease), but as he had already suffered with it on several occasions he was, perhaps, being unkind to her. He ate and drank hugely and continued his studies as and when he felt like it.

But there was another side to him, a side which directly led to his intervention in Mary's life. During those early years in London he paid a visit to Newgate prison and saw his first public execution. Both were to have a lasting effect on him. At a time when hardly anyone cared what went on in prisons and most people were hardened to executions, indeed saw them as entertainment, his views and feelings do him credit. He described Newgate as 'surely the most dismal of places with three rows of cells, four in a row, all above each other. They have double iron windows, and within these, strong iron rails; and in these dark mansions are the unhappy criminals confined.'

He saw and spoke to the felons who were shortly to be hanged, including Paul Lewis, a highwayman whose description fits that of Captain Macheath in *The Beggar's Opera* (young, handsome and beautifully dressed in a white coat embroidered in silver and with a blue silk vest, his hair 'neatly queued and a silver lace hat smartly cocked') and a young woman called Hannah Diego, who was to be hanged for theft. He returned home desperately depressed, 'Newgate being upon my mind like a black cloud. Poor Lewis was always coming across to me . . .' He lay sleepless all night 'in sad concern'. Feeling that he had to carry his interest through to the very end, he took himself off to Tyburn the following morning. 'In my younger years I had read in the *Lives of the Convicts* so much about Tyburn that I had a sort of horrid eagerness to be there.'

A friend found him a place near the scaffold after they had pushed their way through the huge crowd of spectators. What followed 'terribly shocked' James. Lewis went to his death bravely, gallant to the last, but poor Hannah Diego was dragged to the rope screaming and, just before her execution, managed to get her hands free and actually struck her executioner. While the crowd laughed and jeered, James was physically sick and later that night invited himself round to a friend's house for 'gloomy terrors came upon me so much that I durst not stay by myself; so I went and had a bed (or rather half a one) from honest Erskine, which he most kindly gave me.'

Boswell never changed his views on executions, a contrast to Dr Johnson who complained bitterly when some of the spectacle was taken from the procession to Tyburn. It was during these early years in London that he met and became firm friends with Samuel Johnson, a friendship which would later bear such fruit with the *Life*.

James Boswell never did succeed in becoming the famous and distinguished lawyer his father envisaged. Nor did he make the expected advantageous marriage. When he finally decided to settle down, he married his cousin Margaret, who had no money of her own. They had two sons, Alexander and James, and three daughters, Veronica, Euphemia and Elizabeth ('Betsey'). He felt love and affection for Margaret but fidelity was not in his nature. He remained true to her, as the song says, in his fashion. His pursuit of women stopped for a brief while after his marriage but then continued much as before. His work kept him in London most of the time but Margaret did not care for the life and so returned to Scotland with her growing family, leaving James to spend much of the year living a bachelor existence of theatre-going, dining out, chatting in the coffee houses and heavy drinking. There is a splendid print of him in 1769 on his way to a fancy dress party dressed as a Corsican bandit.

In 1782 Lord Auchinleck died and the estate finally passed to James. He made it his country home and moved Margaret and the children there, but it still did not meet the expenses of his lifestyle, which included keeping up a house in London and spending a good deal of his leisure time on the town. By 1789, the year of the French Revolution, he had reached as high as he was going to on the legal ladder, becoming Recorder of Carlisle, a position he achieved only by using what influence he had with a nobleman. Whatever his financial problems, however, he continued working away at what he saw as his life's work, the biography of Johnson. But he now had other problems, for Margaret was terminally ill with tuberculosis and he had a growing and expensive family. Not surprisingly, he was up to his ears in debt. His two sons were being educated in London (Boswell wanted them to go on either to Eton or Westminster) and Veronica was looking after his London house. Whatever his faults, it is clear that James loved his family dearly. He writes that some of his happiest times were spent with his children in Scotland, romping with them in the gardens, reading to them at night improving books when they were young, *Tristram Shandy* as they grew older. He was kind and tolerant, brushing off criticism from friends and acquaintances that he allowed them to be too familiar with him.

In March of 1789 he was sent urgent word that Margaret was fading fast and that he should return to Scotland. He was in despair, his position as Recorder of Carlisle required his presence on an important King's Bench case. He received a letter from Margaret herself telling him there was no need for him to leave London yet but 'my fever still continues and I waste away daily'. He eventually left in the April, blaming himself for being away so much and that through 'melancholy, I am too dissipated and drink too much wine'. He spent the next few weeks with her, passionately assuring her of his continued love and esteem and, for a little while, she seems to have rallied. So much so that he returned briefly to London where more cases awaited him.

He was never to see Margaret again for she died on 4 June. Boswell and his two sons had raced to Scotland by post-chaise, taking only 'sixty-four hours and a quarter', but it was too late. He was desolate that he had not arrived in time: 'To see my excellent wife, the mother of my children, that most sensible, lively woman, lying cold and pale and insensible was very shocking to me. I could not help doubting it was a deception. I could hardly bring myself to agree that the body should be removed, for it was still a consolation to go and kneel by it, and talk to my dear, dear Peggie.' There was nothing hypocritical in these feelings, he truly loved her, despite his inability to curb his Casanova-type excursions.

After the funeral he made arrangements for his family. Veronica would return with him to London, while Euphemia continued her education in Edinburgh. Betsey would be sent to boarding school in Ayr. He hoped he would be able to find the money, eventually, to send her to finishing school on the Continent. Alexander was due to go to Eton and James would remain at the Soho Academy in London. He himself returned to London to his work, and the completion of the *Life*.

There is another facet to Boswell's character which is missing from this brief profile. That he fawned on the aristocracy is all too evident from his journals, that he considered himself vastly superior to the commonfolk is there for all to see, but he did have a genuine hatred of what he considered to be legal injustice. On a number of occasions he had taken up free of charge the cases of people who had been sentenced to death for what he considered minor felonies, usually where need had prompted the offence. He never forgot that first execution he had witnessed. His interventions did not always prove successful, but he was at least prepared to put a good deal of time and effort into the attempt.

So let us return to him that morning as he sits reading his newspaper, a corpulent, well-dressed figure (to the end of his days Boswell liked fine clothes), his stomach full, for he has breakfasted well. He lives in an elegant house just off Oxford Street, with his two pretty, lively older daughters whom he proudly squires to one or other of the fashionable London churches on Sunday mornings. His *Life of Samuel Johnson* has received a mixed reception but is selling very well indeed and has brought him fame, and some fortune. The two boys, Jamie and Sandy, are at school, as is young Betsey, and he is managing to pay the school fees. He still drinks too much and has not entirely given up the sins of the flesh, but his adventures have become less frequent.

Having scanned the front of the *London Chronicle* he turns to an inside page and here is brought up with a start. At a time when most stories, however important, were given only a few inches he sees, to his amazement, that virtually an entire page has been devoted to a single item, the equivalent today of a multi-page spread. Nor was it the practice to give a headline to a report other than such basic information as 'London', 'The Court', 'Foreign News', but an exception had been made in this most exceptional case. The story was headed 'Escape of Convicts from Botany Bay'.

CHAPTER EIGHTEEN

The Girl from Botany Bay

THERE HAD been a brief earlier report in the preceding issue of the *London Chronicle*:

> News from Botany Bay From Her Majesty's ship the *Gorgon*.
> The infant colony is in greatest distress being in want of every
> necessity of life and by no means in that fertile state repre-
> sented, nor is there any remote possibility of it being rendered
> so . . .
>
> The following were passengers on the *Gorgon*. Major Rolls,
> Captain Campbell, Captain Meredith, Captain W. Tench,
> Lieutenants Johnstone, Kello and Dawes, Captain Edwards of
> the *Pandora*, upwards of a hundred men, women and children
> of the marine corps., ten mutineers from the *Bounty* and
> several convicts that made their escape from Jackson's Bay to
> Batavia in an open boat, tho' the distance is not less than 1000
> leagues.

The report read by Boswell on 3 July is substantially more detailed but still rather inaccurate. The boat in which they had escaped was said to have belonged to a 'Captain Smith', commander of a Dutch vessel and which 'a convict, whose name was Briant [*sic*], and who was married to the prisoner Mary Briant' had persuaded the Dutchman to part with. The provisions which the convicts had managed to take away with them were listed and there was also a brief account of the voyage to Kupang along with further particulars of 'this wonderful and hazardous escape'. The 'reporter', whoever he was, must have spoken to James Martin about their time in the open boat as the newspaper account is very similar, in its detail, to Martin's *Memorandum*. It names the prisoners concerned and tells how the

'Briants' had taken their small children along with them, then points out that all the convicts were adamant that 'terrible as these dangers were, under the circumstances they rather chose to risk their lives on the sea than drag out a miserable existence on an inhospitable shore'. The subsequent arrival at East Timor and the events leading up to their re-arrest were given prominence, followed by accounts of the deaths of William, Charlotte and Emmanuel, James Cox, Sam Bird and William Moreton.

The names, ages and past offences of the survivors were given, Mary heading the list: 'Mary Briant, about 28 years old, was capitally convicted in the name of Broad, at the Exeter Assizes six-and-a-half years ago, for a street robbery committed in Plymouth.' Here, too, are the origins of the misleading story of William's conviction: 'William Briant was convicted at the same time at Bodmin for resisting the revenue officers, who attempted to seize some smuggled property he had, and was sentenced to be transported for seven years.' As we know, William was convicted at Launceston two years before Mary, of forgery, after having been acquitted on the smuggling charge. It is possible, however, that he preferred it to be thought that he had been found guilty of the more exciting offence.

On 21 July a far more colourful report was to appear in the *Dublin Chronicle*. The unknown reporter had sought to find some local Irish interest in the story and happily this was provided by James Martin, described as 'James Martin of the County of Antrim in Ireland, thirty-two years of age, convicted at Exeter six-and-a-half years ago, of stealing some old lead and iron in the whole about 20 lbs in weight, the property of the Lord Courtenay.'

Some of the Dublin material must have come from sources other than those used by the *London Chronicle* as the Irish paper says of Mary that she was 'found guilty of stealing a cloak which, being a capital offence, she received sentence of death, but was, with the two other women who were convicted of the same offence, pardoned on condition of their going for seven years to Botany Bay.' It also gives a more dramatic account of Will Bryant's crime, in which he is pictured as attacking revenue officers and interrupting them 'in the execution of their duty'. This, one feels, owes its origin to journalistic licence and it is easy to see how the legends surrounding Will grew over the years.

There are, however, other embellishments which do not appear in any of the London accounts but which ring absolutely true.

> This escape was perhaps the most hazardous and wonderful effort ever made by nine persons (two were infants) to regain their liberty, which they declared they should not have ventured on but from the dread of starving, and the certainty that if they did survive the period for which they were transported, they should never again see their native country. They said that Governor Phillip used them very well, but that the soil did not return half the quantity of grain which had been sown on it. Their cattle had been destroyed by the natives, and a famine was the consequence. They were reduced to four ounces of flour and four of salt beef per day, half of which was cut off, if, by illness or accident, they were unable to work; they, therefore, seized the first opportunity of throwing themselves upon the mercy of the sea, rather than perish upon this inhospitable shore.

Both papers carried a statement attributed to Mary: 'I would sooner suffer death than return to Botany Bay.'

With no more ado, James Boswell sent for his hat, cloak and cane and set off for Newgate prison where, according to the papers, the returned convicts were now being held while awaiting their appearance in court. It is easy to picture him pushing his way through the busy London streets, full of the noise of carriages and carts, the cries of the street-sellers, the smell of the drains – for it was high summer – and all that busy city life which so attracted him even after thirty years in London. It was a tidy step from Great Portland Street to Newgate prison, which was next to the Old Bailey, and it would probably have taken a large, stout man, in not very good health, about an hour. Once there, he presented himself at the office of the head jailer, where he asked to see the returned transportees at once.

All five were likely to have been in the same packed room, for they had no money or goods to use as bribes for better accommodation and, anyway, the general expectation must have been that they would certainly soon be hanged, for they had not only broken their transportation orders but had also done so in the most spectacular fashion. Although it is fair to say that James was interested in the plight of them all, it is equally true that he was most interested in Mary.

EVERYTHING recounted so far about Mary is traceable in existing records which do not, apart from the mention of her watching Charlotte's burial 'dry-eyed', and the descriptions of her resourcefulness and inspiration during the escape, give any indication of her state of mind at any time during her adventures. But it is, surely, possible to conjecture what her feelings might have been at this juncture.

At first, after Charlotte's death, she must have seemed in a kind of emotional limbo, worn out by sorrow and illness, caring little whether she lived or died, numb to any feelings. Had she still been confined in the appalling conditions she had suffered on the *Rembang*, it is unlikely that she would have survived for she had reached the limits of her endurance; she had no strength or spirit left with which to fight. But gradually, given comfortable accommodation, care, even kindness, she would slowly begin to regain her old resilience. For she was, most of all, a survivor.

Her feelings towards Will during that long voyage home must have been very mixed. The choice she had made for pragmatic reasons had been amply vindicated during their time together in New South Wales. There would surely have been a certain kind of rough affection between them, not least because they had been through so much. They had worked, slaved, starved together and defended each other. He had stolen for her and been flogged for it, they had made love in their rough bed in their little hut, where she had borne him a son; and he had also proved a fair stepfather to Charlotte. By the standards of the penal colony, he had provided her with a privileged life. He was unusual, independent, highly skilled, articulate and literate and she had admired the way that, unlike the others, he had actually made friends with the aborigines, admitted their skills in fishing and navigation and been prepared to learn from them. There had been much about Will that she could like and respect.

Then he had betrayed them all, and her twice over. In Kupang he had made no secret of the fact that he was prepared to go home alone and find himself another younger, prettier woman, leaving his 'lag wife' behind to do the best she could, in spite of her proven loyalty and the part she had played in the escape. Although he had threatened at the outset of their marriage that he might do this, as time passed Mary perhaps put this to the back of her mind. Now she must have wondered if it would not have been better if he had managed to find a berth on a homegoing ship as soon as they reached Kupang. At least then there would have been a chance that all of them, including her two children, could have survived. Instead, he had spent his time drinking and bragging about his prowess, his brilliance in outwitting the Governor and the guards, and about their great escape; drunken boasting which had led to disaster and the crushing of all their hopes.

The length of the voyage to England gave Mary time to regain her physical strength and some of her emotional equilibrium. She must, during the journey, have discussed with the others what would happen next. Hanging was the penalty for breaking transportation orders, as Edwards had continually pointed out to them. In the case of those, like Mary, where a previous death sentence had been commuted to transportation, they were in double jeopardy for, by returning illegally, their original death sentences still stood. It was with astonishment that, on reaching Newgate, they discovered that they had become celebrities. Their fame had gone before them, even hardened criminals being prepared to show respect for the five people who, having been taken to the other side of the world, had actually made it home.

WE DO NOT know what Boswell expected to see when he met Mary, but she was certainly no large-bosomed, glamorous adventuress of the kind he had found so enticing as a young man. Instead he met a thin, sallow, dark-haired woman, her face marked with suffering but with large and remarkable dark eyes. What she saw was an ageing, plump, red-faced gentleman in a fancy coat and elaborate waistcoat. Already dozens of people had visited Newgate to stare at the famous prisoners. No doubt she assumed he was just another, and so took little interest when he told her he had come especially to see her. His name meant nothing to her; she was not even moved when he told her he was a lawyer. Tomorrow they were to be brought before the Stipendiary Magistrate in his Office and it was widely assumed in Newgate that this was no more than a preliminary to their being committed for trial, itself a mere formality which would lead, inexorably, to the procession to Tyburn Tree.

Undeterred, Boswell repeated that he was a well-respected lawyer. He had read the story of the escape and had been most moved by it, so much so that he had rushed down to Newgate to put his expertise in the law at her disposal.

Why? she asked. He was somewhat taken aback. Because of the dire straits she was now in. Surely she fully realized the possible outcome? That her original capital sentence still stood because she had broken her order? That she might well end up on the gallows? Memories of the long-dead Hannah Diego, dragged screaming to the rope, still haunted him as he looked at the young woman before him.

Yes, she knew all that. But what was the alternative? She had already been imprisoned in Plymouth and Exeter, on a prison hulk, on a convict transport, on a strange shore thousands of miles from home, in irons on the open deck of the *Rembang*.

She had lost her husband and both her children. If she was not hanged, then what was there to look forward to but more years in gaol?

But Boswell refused to be dissuaded from doing what he could to help her. He was nothing if not stubborn, whether seeking admission to stately homes to persuade the occupants to invite him to dine with them, pursuing young women who continually said 'no' or, as in the case of a young sheep-stealer, John Reid, fighting to save him from the gallows when all hope was at an end. He would attend the Magistrate's Office the following morning, see what the outcome was, and then visit her again. He bade her farewell before seeking out her fellow survivors to tell them that he would be looking into their affairs as well. He walked from the prison with a slower step for there was no hurry now; time for the coffee house or a visit to a friend to whom he could describe his meeting with the convicts. What the men had said of Mary stayed with him, that 'she had shown greater courage and resource than any of them'.

The next day the five prisoners were brought up before the magistrate, Nicholas Bond. Word of their appearance had spread and his Office was soon packed with spectators, including Boswell. So dense were the crowds that the gaolers bringing in the prisoners had to fight their way through.

Nicholas Bond appears to have been an urbane man and he listened attentively as he took each convict through their story, but he paid particular attention to Mary. Afterwards he was to say that he had found her response and demeanour very impressive. She answered his questions intelligently and in a clear voice, which only faltered slightly when he asked her about the fate of her family. Briefly she described the deaths of Will, then Emmanuel and, finally, Charlotte, and how she had come close to death herself. She freely admitted the leading role she had played in the escape. Bond had already heard from James Martin that it was her force of personality, will and tenacity that had seen them through the dangers of their epic voyage.

He asked her if she was sincerely repentant for the offence

which had originally brought her to court and she told him that indeed she was. There was a murmur of approval in the room. But why, he continued, had she taken such a terrible chance, not only for herself but for her children, risking all their lives in an open boat on perilous and unknown seas? Because, she repeated yet again, it was better to die than return to Botany Bay.

The public was clearly on her side. Nicholas Bond thanked her courteously and then announced that he was not yet prepared to commit the prisoners for trial. They would be returned to prison and then brought back for further examination the following Thursday.

Such was the public sympathy that there and then a collection was taken among those present to give all five some funds to cover their immediate needs. It was obvious they were destitute and it was common knowledge that in Newgate cash bought better accommodation, food, clean clothes and water. Bond allowed the collection to take place and the money to be handed to them.

The sympathy continued even into the press reports. Surely, asked the *Chronicle*, there was room for charity here? The woman had already paid sufficiently dearly for her original crime. 'His Majesty is ever willing to extend his mercy,' wrote the commentator. 'Surely never have there been objects more worthy of it.'

So, once again, Boswell was allowed in to see Mary. She had come through her first hearing triumphantly, he told her, and he had no doubt that she would do so again at the second examination. He had rarely seen such a sympathetic crowd and felt as certain as he could be, in the circumstances, that she would not be sentenced to death.

Mary's response still seems to have been less than enthusiastic. The prospect of years in Newgate until they and their adventure had been long forgotten and no public sympathy remained was not enticing. Whether Boswell's next move had been in his mind originally or whether her attitude had put it there is not known. But if, he said, as he suspected, Bond decided not to commit them for a further trial, announced that there was now no question of the implementation of the death penalty and returned them to Newgate for a further term of imprisonment, he would go for a free pardon.

Mary was no longer a naïve girl and therefore entertained little hope that such a plan would be successful. James Boswell was always a name-dropper but on this occasion what he said happened to be true. Henry Dundas, the present Home Secretary, had been his schoolfellow at the private academy in Edinburgh; moreover, they had both been at university together. The fact that they had never got on was immaterial. He would take up her case with Dundas in person.

After Boswell had gone Mary was left to ponder on his motives. Certainly he seemed genuine enough in his desire to see her freed, but what else? Whether Boswell had discussed with her even at this early stage the possibility of setting her up in lodgings on her release, he does not say. Mary had had more than enough practical experience of trading sexual favours for survival and she must have read something of Boswell's proclivities in his manner and behaviour without him needing to be explicit about it. But that was all for the future.

Following their second examination on 7 July 1792, Mary Bryant, James Martin, John Butcher, William Allen and Nathaniel Lilley were formally put to the bar of the Old Bailey and ordered 'to remain on their former sentence, until they should be discharged by due course of the law'. The government, it was said, had no desire in this case to proceed with the full rigour of the law. They were, therefore, sent back to Newgate under an indeterminate sentence, a place which, according to a further report in the *London Chronicle* dated 12 July, 'they considered a paradise compared with the dreadful sufferings they had endured on their voyage'.

It is an interesting footnote that no mention of this sensational story, featuring as it did a woman born and bred in Cornwall and sentenced in Exeter, appeared in the relevant editions of the *Western Flyer and Sherborne Mercury*, even though many lesser London court cases received a brief note.

Mary therefore returned yet again to prison, albeit with the conditions considerably alleviated by the money collected for her. Meanwhile James Boswell, the bit firmly between his teeth, set about getting her a pardon.

CHAPTER NINETEEN

A Cornish Jaunt

The opinions of men with respect to Government are changing
fast in all countries. The revolutions in America and France
have thrown a beam of light over the world, which reaches into
man.

Thomas Paine

JAMES BOSWELL could hardly have chosen a more difficult
time to plead for the release of the transportees: all the
anxieties which had been concerning the population when Mary
first took to the road back in 1786 were now even more
pronounced in the England to which she had returned.

For three years detailed reports of the upheavals in France
had been reaching the country, resulting in even more acute
paranoia, if that were possible, on the part of a government
terrified that the revolutionary virus would cross the Channel
and spread across the British Isles. Financially times were much
harder and now even the hitherto protected middle classes were
beginning to feel the pinch. Newspapers, both in London and
the provinces, began to be dominated by reports of riots and
unrest at home, as well as by the latest violent happenings in
France. The fear of new ideas was fuelled by the publication by
Thomas Paine of his *Rights of Man*. The First Part appeared in
1791, the Second in February 1792.

Paine's argument that Britain should also do away with its
monarchy, become a republic and empower its people to take
charge of their own destiny, was the stuff of nightmares to the
political establishment. His detailed exposition on the evils of a
system where corruption was endemic, where a population had
to be kept down by want and ignorance in order to maintain the

status quo, had the politicians thirsting for his blood. 'If we look back to the riots and tumults which have happened in England,' Paine wrote,

> we shall find, that they did not proceed from the want of government, but the government itself was the generating cause; instead of consolidating society it divided it; it deprived it of its natural cohesion, and engendered discontents, which otherwise would not have existed . . . excess and inequality of taxation, however disguised in their means, never fail to appear in their effects. As a great mass of the community are thrown thereby into poverty and discontent, they are constantly on the brink of commotion; and deprived, as they unfortunately are, of the means of information, are easily heated to outrage. Whatever the cause of the riots might be, the real one is always want of happiness. It shows that something is wrong in the system of Government.

In the June of 1792 Paine was charged with Seditious Libel but the case was put back until December, during which time he left the country. The 'enormous offender' was tried in his absence on the grounds that 'Tom Paine, being a wicked, seditious and ill-disposed person and being greatly disaffected to our Sovereign Lord the King and to the happy Government and Constitution of his Kingdom, published a false and scandalous libel of the said Government.' After six hours of abuse 'Mr. Attorney General was about to reply on the part of the prosecution, when the gentlemen of the jury told him there was no necessity for giving himself the trouble: and immediately found the defendant guilty.' Such is justice.

Yet the conditions which so fired Paine were clear for all to see, as was the seething discontent of the population. The 18 July 1791 edition of the *Western Flyer and Sherborne Mercury* carried a brief report of the arrival in Botany Bay of the ill-fated Second Fleet. It had taken from the June of the previous year for the report to reach Britain, communications being so slow. The penal colony, readers were told, 'was in a very distressed state, many sick and sickening for want of food of which they were in deplorable need.' At least 270 convicts had died on the passage, it concluded.

It is unlikely that the item was read with much interest as the paper was dominated by horror stories of 'Huge Mob Riots' in Birmingham. With the enclosure of land accelerating, driving workers off the land at the same time as small craftsmen were being superseded by the new manufacturers, hundreds and then thousands of people took to the streets of Birmingham, looting and smashing everything in their path. They burned down the houses of local landowners, rioted through the streets of neighbouring towns, 'the women particularly active in all depradations'. Houses, farms, shops were reduced to ashes and it took three troops of dragoons to quell the riots, leaving sixteen people dead and many more injured. Those rioters who escaped hid out in old coal pits, coming out at night to continue their activities.

The other substantial story in the paper was the description of an event which might as well have taken place on another planet – the Grand Ball given by his Royal Highness, the Prince of Wales. It was a truly splendid affair. The Prince 'wore a silk coat of a teagreen ground, closely embroidered with silver thread, spangled with diamonds'. There followed detailed descriptions of the gowns worn by the great ladies attending the function and all, continued the writer, were soon lost in amazement at the new coach which brought the Duke of Bedford to the scene, 'the coachmen in blue velvet livery, the coach itself painted with blue flowers on a white ground, picked out in gilt, the inside covered with red morocco leather'. The ladies in his party were particularly fine, the Duchess appearing in 'a dress of chocolate-coloured striped silk crêpe covered in gold gauze'. She also wore the full family set of diamonds.

While Birmingham might have captured the headlines, similar unrest was rife in Cornwall as the centralization of the mining industry continued relentlessly, with more and more people fighting for a share of the profits. While the 'capital adventurers', technicians and smelters quarrelled over who had the most profit, the badly paid, badly fed miners, underpinning the enterprises, finally reached breaking point. Instead of odd sporadic protest marches and disturbances there were now full-scale riots as hungry, desperate miners marched through the towns laying them to waste as they went. The Army had to be called in to put down a riot in Truro. The Cornish landowners were so worried that when, in 1792, the government ordered that local armed associations be set up in country areas to protect the nation against a possible invasion from the French, the local gentry objected saying they 'doubted the wisdom of arming the working classes'. One vicar warned his congregation from the pulpit against arming the 'tinners . . . who may turn their arms more against the farmers and the gentry, than against any invading French'.

As in Birmingham, Cornish women joined their men in the 'depradations', assisting them to ambush carts of grain on the roads. Corn dealers complained of being 'terrorized' by bands of men and women demanding they sell at a fair price. Matters reached such a pass that the mine-owning Mr Basset of Tehidy swore in fifty special constables which he led one night to the houses of the ringleaders. Fifty were arrested, taken to Bodmin gaol and tried at the next assizes. Three were sentenced to death, and the rest to transportation. Despite pleas for mercy, Basset was determined to hang at least one of them – which he did – vainly hoping that it would have 'the most salutary effect on the mining people, after which their manners might change from rudeness and disrespect to a proper obedience'.

It is hardly surprising therefore that the 'ten young persons' who attended a meeting to 'celebrate the French Revolution' in St Austell, the nearest sizeable town to Fowey, in the same month that Boswell was exerting himself on Mary's behalf, kept a very low profile. The event was a subdued affair which passed off 'with the utmost respectability'. Others, however, had 'felt it prudent to decline invitations to attend. Later, a crowd of about a thousand gathered on the Parade in Plymouth to see Thomas Paine burned in effigy 'amid the acclamation of those assembled on the occasion. The whole passed off without the least riot of any kind.' The government had kindly provided funds for such events to be held up and down the country.

It was against this background and to a Home Secretary who was a close confidant of Pitt the Younger and an admirer of Edmund Burke – and whose top priority was maintaining law and order at all costs – that James Boswell attempted to take his plea that five convicted criminals, all of whom had broken their transportation orders, and one of whom was a woman still under a capital sentence, should be given a free pardon.

THE LAST time Boswell had contacted Dundas was to remind him of a promise he had once made, asking that he now implement it. Dundas had replied by telling him he had a vivid imagination. So first Boswell thought it prudent to sound out Evan Nepean, the Under Secretary at the Home Office, who had had so much to do with the organization of the First Fleet and the setting up of the penal colony. Nepean replied saying that already the government had shown clemency by not proceeding against the transportees with the full rigour of the law. 'Government would not treat them with harshness, but at the same time would not do a kind thing to them, as that might give encouragement to others to escape.'

Time was becoming a problem for Boswell as he was about to go on holiday. For a long time he had promised an old friend, the Reverend William Johnstone Temple, rector of St Gluvias Church, just outside Falmouth, that he would visit him. All the preparations had been made for Boswell and his two elder daughters to make this great excursion; indeed, aristocratic owners of large estates had already been alerted to give him hospitality *en route*. Now, plans had to be changed for Boswell did not feel he could leave London until, at the very least, the question of Mary's pardon had been put in hand.

On 10 August he delivered a letter addressed to Lord Dundas asking for an appointment to see him to discuss the case of 'the five persons now in Newgate who escaped from Botany Bay'.

Even the magistrate, Nicholas Bond, was favourably disposed towards them, he added. Two days later he received a reply from Dundas fixing an appointment for the following Wednesday. This was the day after the date Boswell had proposed setting out on his holiday but he was prepared to accept the inconvenience this caused in order to put his case in person to the Home Secretary. On the morning of 15 August he duly presented himself at Dundas's office only to be kept kicking his heels for hours. Finally he was informed that Dundas would not be coming in that day.

The next morning he sat down in a rage and wrote Dundas another letter:

> Dear Sir,
> I staid in town a day longer, on purpose, to wait on you at your office yesterday *about one o'clock*, as your letter to me *appointed*; and I was there a few minutes before one, but you were not to be seen. The only *solatium* you can give me for this unpleasant disappointment, is to favour me with two lines directed *Penrhyn, Cornwall*, informing me that *nothing* harsh shall be done to the unfortunate adventurers from New South Wales, for whom I interest myself, and whose very extraordinary case surely will not found a precedent. A *negative* promise from a Secretary of State I hope will not be with-held, especially when you are the Secretary, and the request is for compassion.
> I always am,
> > Very faithfully Yours,
> > James Boswell

This time Dundas replied at once and a letter was delivered to Boswell the next day to the effect that he would 'duly consider' his plea for the 'Botany Bay prisoners'. This information was relayed to Mary and only then did Boswell finally set off on his deferred trip to Cornwall, a place now doubly interesting to him as it was the county of his new protégée.

★

BOSWELL'S 'Cornish Jaunt', as he called it, deserves accessible publication for much of it is very funny. He and his two daughters drove out of London on a fine, sunny morning and, as they passed through Oxford Street, he 'felt the love of London' very strongly. Once out of the city, they travelled by easy stages beginning with a call at Bagshot where young Betsey was staying with a schoolfriend, 'Miss Williams' and her family. There was, it seems, a slight atmosphere over supper as, when the young Miss Williams had visited Great Portland Street, James, somewhat the worse for wine, had made embarrassing advances to her . . . Next came Salisbury, where they admired the cathedral and dined with the Bishop, before being shown by Lord Pembroke the grandeurs of his great estate.

After a brief stopover with a banker friend in Exeter, the small party crossed the Tamar into Cornwall. It was raining. It would rain for the next four weeks, almost without stopping. As he jolted along the road in the downpour, Boswell notes that he did not think much of Mary Bryant's home county. 'The county from Launceston to Bodmin and onwards, until we came within view of Truro, seemed as dreary as any I have ever seen . . . It had the wilderness of our highlands without any of the charm and I wondered that my friend Temple should have so praised Cornwall.' He cheered up, however, on arrival at the St Gluvias Rectory where he was warmly greeted by Temple, his 'peevish' wife and large family of children.

Boswell's descriptions of Cornwall give a colourful picture of its appeal to a middle-class gentleman who spent most of his time in London; a Cornwall far removed from that of the Broad family of Fowey. He found Land's End impressive:

> The clustering rocks had the boldest appearance I have beheld, but the sight of the tremendous elevation above the ocean was horrid. I now at last felt the great sensation I had long imagined of being at the Land's End of England, about 600 miles from Auchinleck or Edinburgh. We returned to Penzance for dinner. I had, in the morning, eaten some fresh pilchards broiled. I liked them exceedingly. They are fatter and more savoury than

> herring. I ate two more before dinner. Fish is very cheap in
> Penzance, a large cod's head and shoulder, which we had for
> dinner, costing only ninepence with half a glass of brandy.

He thought Cornish cream disgusting, however.

He began his relentless round of visits to the owners of great
estates. 'Visited the Bassets of Tehidy and was told they had had
three granduncles killed in battle for Charles I. Tehidy has a
pretty park.' He then dined with Lord Eliot of Port Eliot: 'Had
dinner of two courses and desert and I bottle each of madeira,
hock, sherry (27 years old), port, claret and after dinner a bottle
of champagne; also canary, while cyder and beer were always
available.'

He was rowed across in a boat to visit Sir John St Aubyn in
his castle on St Michael's Mount,

> though the town built at the harbour be no doubt profitable, it
> is a disgusting nuisance to have a parcel of low, dirty people,
> collected there and a vile smell of fish and garbage lying about.
> It is now the property of Sir John St Aubyn who has fitted up
> and ornamented the rooms of the castle with taste and expense
> and would he but remove the town, might make a charming
> residence of it.

He was, he wrote, hailed everywhere as 'the great biographer', the *Life* was selling even in the farthest West. He went to
the theatre in Falmouth where 'the playhouse was very mean,
with but two rooms in a low inn'. The performance was a
benefit for a Mrs Kemp and it included three plays, *Which is the
Man?*, *The Wapping Landlady* and *The Padlock*. 'Only saw the
first Act but acted really well. Company belonged to young
Hughes, son of one of the proprietors of Sadlers Wells. My
mind *rusts* so soon in the country, especially in damp weather.'
He then described the inside of the theatre:

> I noticed in a box three foreign gentlemen and a pretty
> little French mademoiselle whom I knew for some time in

London by the name of Divry. We took no notice of our having
ever been acquainted. She has come to town with one of the
foreigners to stay until he sails.

> 'Je reconnais les atteintes,
> Qui n'ont autrefois charme . . .'

as the French song goes. But I checked such feelings remember-
ing what a mercenary and base creature she was. She . . .
[Here Boswell inked out further details of his relationship with
Mlle Divry.]

One of his last visits was to Lord Falmouth, who 'scouted
the notion of universal representation in Parliament. He said
there was one word that should be struck out of our language –
liberty. He would substitute the word protection, by which
persons and property are secured. He also wished to abolish the
word Constitution; his argument for this I do not accurately
recollect.'

Before leaving Boswell was introduced to another vicar, the
Reverend John Baron of Lostwithiel, who was a friend of
Temple. Lostwithiel is close to Fowey and it seems that Boswell
discussed Mary and what he proposed to do, with both men.

The 'jaunt' lasted a number of weeks but once back in Great
Portland Street, he made immediate enquiries at the Home
Office as to how the case for the freeing of Mary was progress-
ing. It was not. Dundas was still, he said, giving it his 'consideration'. As the months went by Mary might be forgiven for
thinking that Boswell's promise to get her out of Newgate
amounted to little but empty words. But Boswell stoutly refused
to be put off. He haunted the Home Office, continued to
importune Evan Nepean and drove a civil servant, by the name
of Mr Pollock, nearly to distraction. A steady stream of letters
reached Henry Dundas with every week that passed. James
Boswell could not, and would not, give up.

CHAPTER TWENTY

A Handful of Dried Leaves

H OME SECRETARY Henry Dundas did not end his considerations until the following year and it was not until 2 May
1793 that Mary finally received her free pardon:

Mary Bryant, Alias Broad

WHEREAS Mary. Bryant alias Broad, now a prisoner in Newgate,
stands charged with escaping from the persons having legal
custody of her before the expiration of the term for which she
had been ordered to be transported AND WHEREAS some favourable circumstances have been humbly presented unto us on her
behalf, inducing us to extend our Grace and Mercy unto her
and to grant her our free pardon for her said crime, OUR Will
and Pleasure therefore is that you cause the said Mary Bryant
alias Broad to be forthwith discharged out of Custody and that
she be incerted for her said crime in our first and next
general pardon that shall come out for the poor convicts in
Newgate without any condition whatsoever; and for so doing
this shall be your warrant, GIVEN at our Court of Saint James's
the Second Day of May 1793 in the Thirty-Third year of our
reign.

By His Majesty's Command,
Henry Dundas.

It was seven years and six weeks since Mary had received her
original sentence and, since her arrest on the Plymouth highway
in January 1786, she had spent seven years and four months in
captivity, barring her brief period of liberty. Her late teenage
years and young womanhood had all been lost in gaols, prison
ships and the penal colony at the other end of the world. Before

taking Mary out of Newgate, Boswell visited the four men who were still imprisoned there, promising them that he would continue his efforts to have them released as well. Twelve days later, on 14 May, he tried a new approach, writing to the Home Secretary's wife, Lady Hope Dundas (whom he had met as a young bride) pleading her to use her influence to persuade her husband to allow the four men to go free immediately. Lady Hope responded by return of post, informing him, sharply, that she made it a rule never to discuss any such affairs with her husband.

Boswell had already made plans for Mary. He had raised a certain amount of money among his friends, even going so far as to turn up, uninvited, at the breakfast table of the then Lord Chancellor, Lord Thurlow, asking him if he would also subscribe to the fund. 'I asked him', he writes, 'to give something to Mary Broad. He exclaimed, 'Damn her blood, let her go to a day's work.' But when I described her hardships and heroism, he owned I was a good advocate for her, and said he would give something if I desired it.'

Boswell had found lodgings for her in Little Titchfield Street, rooms to which he took her straightaway; he kept account of what he received in funds towards her upkeep on a piece of paper headed 'Mary's Money'. It shows that she was bought gowns, a bonnet, a shawl, some shoes and a prayer book when she came out of Newgate.

He also wrote to his friend William Temple at his vicarage, asking if he could raise some funds towards Mary's keep while she recovered from her ordeal. According to Frederick Pottle, Temple replied saying that he would do so, but then, on 18 July, wrote to say that he had been discouraged in his collection by the allegation that Mary's family were 'eminent for sheep stealing'. This is, to put it mildly, extremely unlikely. Cornwall was not a county for sheep and even had it been so, there was nowhere they could have been kept in any numbers anywhere within easy reach of the Fowey estuary; nor is there any reason to believe that a respectable family of mariners, carpenters and other small craftsmen would stoop to such a thing. One explanation might be that there was gossip about someone called Broad who had been sent to Botany Bay and the received wisdom was that it was a man and sheep-stealing his offence.

Throughout their short relationship Boswell always referred to Mary as Mary Broad not Bryant. Whether this was at her request, he does not say. He described her to his friends as a widow, so he acknowledged that she had indeed been married, but in other ways he seems to have preferred to ignore the past existence of Will. How intimate their relationship was is not known. Frederick Pottle concludes that 'there is the clearest evidence that his benevolence was disinterested. Boswell's life was irregular, but the *Journal* (which is usually very frank in such matters) hints at no improper connection with Mary Bryant. On the day of her departure from London he took his favourite son, James (then aged fifteen), with him when he went to her lodging. If she had been his mistress, he would never have allowed James to meet her.' None of this seems sufficient evidence to make out a case, but it is one view.

His close friends had others. News that 'the girl from Botany Bay' had been released from prison on a free pardon, obtained by James Boswell, caused something of a storm. Fully aware of his well-known sexual proclivities, especially for working girls, they could hardly contain themselves. One intimate, William Parsons, wrote a widely circulated poem called 'The Heroic Epistle from Mary Broad in Cornwall to James Boswell, Esquire in London'. A remarkably tasteless piece of doggerel, it tells how Mary has returned to Cornwall and is now pining away for love of her portly James, 'the Apollo of Auchinleck'.

> Was it for this I braved the ocean's roar,
> And plied those thousand leagues the lab'ring oar?
> Oh, rather had I stayed the willing prey
> Of grief and famine in that direful bay!
> Or perished, overwhelmed in the Atlantic tide!
> Or home returned, in air suspended, died.

He goes on to imagine a scene on the scaffold where both die for love of each other:

> Great in our lives, and in our deaths as great,
> Embracing and embraced, we meet our fate:
> A happy pair, whome in supreme delight
> One love, one cord, one joy, one death unite!
> Let crowds behold with tender sympathy
> Love's true sublime in our last agony!
> First let our weight the trembling scaffold bear
> Till we consummate the last bliss in air.

What the exact relationship between Boswell and Mary was remains, in the words of the Scottish verdict, non proven. What is clear from Boswell's *Journal* is that he had a profound admiration for Mary, for her resilience, strength of mind and adventurous spirit, and that there was a very real affection and a true friendship between them.

For Mary, the transformation in her life on her release from Newgate must have been almost more than she could cope with. The nearest analogy today would be that of a hostage freed from a Beirut cellar, for she, too, had to come to terms with freedom, of being released from years of appalling conditions and uncertainty; and with the return of feeling came the knowledge, reinforced, that she had to face her new life without her children. Presumably there was a kind landlady to look after her needs in Little Titchfield Street. Now she had a pleasant place to live, pretty clothes to wear, good food, a comfortable bed, a kind friend and, above all, freedom. Freedom to walk in the parks, to go out into the streets and admire the shops, to see the sights, such as St Paul's Cathedral and the Tower of London. After seven long years, she could come and go as she pleased. One source suggests she might have found employment but this is unlikely. Boswell never suggests she did so and the skills she had learned for survival in a penal colony would hardly have fitted her for respectable employment in London.

'The Girl from Botany Bay' spawned a host of legends.

One, which lasted for a long time, was carried in – where else?
– the *Dublin Chronicle* of 4 June 1793:

> A gentleman of high rank in the Army visited her at Newgate,
> heard the detail of her life and for that time departed.
>
> The next day he returned and told the old gentleman who
> keeps the prison that he had procured her pardon, which he
> showed him, at the same time requesting that she should not be
> appraised of the circumstance.
>
> The next day he returned with his carriage and took off the
> poor young woman, who almost expired with the excess of
> gratitude.

There is no basis of fact whatsoever in this.

However, a mention of Mary in the Annual Register of
Events for 1792, which was published in the year of her release,
does ring true. Following a rather inaccurate account of the
escape and subsequent tribulations of the five transportees, it
concludes that there are hopes of a pardon for the 'Girl from
Botany Bay' and notes:

> The resolution displayed by the woman is hardly to be paral-
> leled. At one time their anchor broke, and the surf was so great
> that the men laid down their oars in a state of despair, and
> gave themselves up as lost; but this Amazon, taking one of their
> hats, cried out 'Never fear!' and immediately began to exert
> herself in clearing the boat of water. Her example was followed
> by her companions and by great labour the boat was prevented
> from sinking until they got into smoother sea.

Whether Boswell and Mary were lovers or not, he certainly
visited her frequently and at all hours and it was on his way
home from Little Titchfield Street late one night, rather drunk,
that he was attacked in the street. What we now call mugging
was very prevalent in the London of the day and such assaults
were widely reported in the press. The *London Chronicle* for 8–11
June notes that 'Mr. James Boswell was knocked down, robbed

and left lying in the street, stunned. He was found by a passing gentleman who called the Watch. He suffered a severe cut to the back of the head and a contusion on both his arms.' The injuries caused him to suffer 'severe pain and fever', but at least he survived the ordeal: the same issue of the paper carried the story of a similar attack on an Italian gentleman in Berwick Street, Soho, who suffered a 'severe skull fracture', from which he died three nights later.

Boswell and Mary appear to have seen each other regularly again, once he had recovered. She told him more of her life both before her arrest and afterwards, speculating on whether or not her parents were still alive, uneasy about trying to find out, fearing that if she did they might prefer to disown her. There is no doubt that during that summer of 1793 she was happy where she was, living a life very different to that of most women of her background. Ironically, if she had gone straight home to Fowey she might well have done so only to die, for it is evident from the parish records that some virulent epidemic swept the town between July and September of that year and that no less than thirty-eight people died in the space of those few weeks, twenty-one of them babies and infants.

Then, on Sunday 18 August, the two worlds, the past and present, collided without warning. A respectably dressed gentleman called on Boswell at Great Portland Street.

This morning there called on me a Mr. Castel of No. 12 Cross Street, Carnaby Market, a glazier by trade, who told me that he was a native of Fowey and knew all the relations of Mary Broad very well and that he had received a letter from one of them directing him to me; that he wished to inform them about her and also to introduce her sister Dolly to her, who was in service in London. He then mentioned that a large sum of money had been left to Mary Broad's father.

I had a suspicion that he might well be an impostor. However I carried him off to see her and from his conversation it appeared that he really did know her relations. She did not recollect him but he described how he had seen her in her younger days. I was pleased with her good sense in being shy to him.

Boswell had tried to persuade Castel to leave the telling of any other news until he himself had had a chance to check it out, but Castel would not be silenced. He told Mary almost immediately that her family had come into a fortune and, then, if anything further were needed to turn the scene into a good imitation of the last act of a popular melodrama, he gave her the final piece of news – that Dolly was in London too; not only that but actually living close by. It seems that Mary herself thought this all too good to be true for she firmly refused, says Boswell, to be in any way 'elated'.

Without more ado, Castel said he would bring Dolly to meet Mary that very evening. 'I walked with him nearly to Oxford Street,' says Boswell, 'then returned to Mary and cautioned her not to put trust in anything he said until I brought her sister myself.' He was uneasy and 'sauntered restlessly, calling on Mary again on the way home only to find that Castel had already brought her sister Dolly to her, a fine girl of twenty or so, who had been in great concern about her and showed the most tender affection.' Dolly, of course, was not twenty; she was two years older than Mary, but no doubt looked younger as she had not had to undergo the hardships and stresses which had aged her sister.

The meeting of the two women was an overwhelming emotional experience for them and both were reduced to tears. At first, Dolly could only clutch Mary's hand and sob. They had seven missing years to catch up, a lifetime of experience in Mary's case. Their parents, Dolly told Mary, *were* alive and still living in Fowey, and, yes, her father had been left some money which had improved their circumstances considerably. As for herself, she was now cook to a grand household.

Boswell found Dolly 'a very fine and sensible young woman'. She was pretty and obviously appealed to his roving eye for, a few days later, he called on her at her place of work, the house of a Mrs Morgan in Charlotte Street, off Bedford Square.

'She expressed herself grateful to me and said if she ever got money she would give me £1000. Poor girl, her behaviour pleased me much. She gave me on my inquiry her whole history since she came to London, from which it appeared that she had most meritoriously supported herself by good service . . . but the work was much too hard for her, a young and slender girl. I resolved to exert myself to get her a place more fit for her.'

Then, only a few days later, Boswell received a letter from Fowey, which he describes as coming from a Mrs Edward Puckey, another 'sister' of Mary. In this he was incorrect for, as we know, she had no other sisters, but it is fair to assume that 'Mrs Edward Puckey' was the cousin who had married Ned Puckey at that happy wedding all those years before. She told Boswell that Mary should now come home to Fowey where she would be 'kindly received', and her communication was soon followed by a letter from her husband Ned, confirming the story of the 'fortune'. Boswell notes it as being of some £300,000 but this is frankly impossible; that kind of money, in today's terms, would have made the Broads the equivalent of multi-millionaires and there is no record in the wills registered in the record office in Truro of *anyone* leaving such a vast amount of money anywhere in Cornwall during the relevant period. The most likely source of the inheritance is a Peter Broad, possibly an uncle, a childless widower, described as a master mariner, who had died during the time Mary was abroad and who left £2000–£3000 to be divided between a number of relatives. By the standard of the times this *was* a fortune.

If this was indeed the case then it is by no means certain whether any of it ever came to Mary, for later Ned Puckey wrote again asking Boswell for legal advice as how best to ensure a share for her. There is no record of any reply.

Meanwhile Mary hesitated, unsure what to do next. She was torn between continuing her comfortable life in London and returning home to see her family. Dolly felt that she should go, that their mother and father would want to see her more than anything else. But Mary was restless and doubtful as to whether she would ever be able to settle down to a quiet and unadventurous life. Elizabeth Puckey wrote yet again saying that the whole family now knew of her survival and that Mary would be 'warmly welcomed'. But still she could not come to a decision.

Boswell also seems to have been in two minds as to what Mary should do for the best. If she left London he would miss her, yet he agreed that it was her duty to go home to Fowey. Finally he replied to Ned Puckey on her behalf, saying that 'she would be happy to go'. It would be nice to think that he taught her to read and write but it seems he did not for she was still illiterate when, in the October, she eventually decided to return to Cornwall.

Boswell made all the arrangements for her. They decided that the easiest way to make the journey was by boat (no fear of highway robbers that way!) and so, 'I fixed that Mary should sail to Fowey in the *Anne and Elizabeth*, the Master being Job Moyse. It was necessary she should be on board that night (12 October) as the vessel was to be afloat the next morning. Having all along taken a very attentive charge of her, I engaged to see her on board.' In fact he turned down two tempting dinner engagements to do so. Then comes the most tantalizing piece of information of all. 'In the forenoon I went and wrote two sheets of paper of her strange escape.' They have never been found.

After dining Boswell went to her rooms in Little Titchfield Street in a carriage and took Mary and a box containing her possessions to the boat. 'My son, James, accompanied me and was to wait at Mr. Dilly's 'til I returned from Beal's Wharf, Southwark, where she was to embark.'

The unlikely pair, whom fate had thrown together, spent their last hours in each other's company, first in the warm kitchen of the tavern on Beal's Wharf, where they dined, then later in the public bar where they drank a bowl of punch, inviting the landlord and the captain of the vessel to join them.

As the time came for her departure Mary began to have doubts regarding the course she was about to take. She realized that she could not have stayed in London indefinitely but was now suffering very real apprehension about what might await her in Fowey. She would be a nine days' wonder, the girl from the village who had run away to be a highway robber and had been transported to Botany Bay, the girl who had twice escaped hanging. Pretty clothes and an attractive manner would not carry much weight with those who had known her from childhood. She mused out loud to Boswell as to what might happen if her relatives did not treat her well. Even if it proved to be true that they had been left some money and were now comfortably off they might not feel inclined to look after her. At the last moment she told Boswell her 'spirits were low'.

He replied that she could set her mind at rest, for 'I had assured her an Annuity of £10 yearly so long as she behaved well and that, therefore, being independent, she might quit her relations whenever she pleased!' He taught her to sign her name, 'so I would recognize it on receipt of the money'. The annuity was to be paid half-yearly and, to this end, Boswell told her, he had contacted the Reverend John Baron of Lostwithiel so that it could be sent to him (in case of problems in Fowey) to pay to Mary each time it became due. It was a most generous gift for it gave her what she valued most, independence.

They parted as affectionate friends. Boswell saw her safely into her cabin, paid the captain for her passage and handed her an allowance to cover her immediate needs, plus five pounds: the first part of the annuity.

She gave him her most precious, indeed her only, souvenir of the last seven years: a handful of dried sarsparilla leaves, the 'sweet tea' she had pulled from the bush by her cabin the night of her escape, over two years ago, when she had crept out into the darkness carrying the sleeping Emmanuel in her arms. Like her, the leaves had survived everything that had followed.

Boswell went home alone, for young James had become tired of waiting for him at 'Dilly's' and so had gone back to Great Portland Street. The lawyer, biographer of Johnson, man-about-town and lover of women then sat and drank his usual nightcap before going to bed. By the time the *Anne and Elizabeth* slipped down the Thames in the grey light of dawn, on her way to Fowey Haven, he was fast asleep.

It was the first time in all her long voyaging that Mary Bryant had set sail a free woman.

Epilogue

MARY RETURNED safely to Fowey. Boswell had impressed upon her that not only should she put her signature to receipts for the half-yearly annuity, but that she should also keep him informed as to how she was and what was happening to her. If she could not write and tell him herself, then she must ask the Reverend John Baron or some member of her family who could write to do it for her.

The first news Boswell had was in a letter from Edward Puckey, dated 16 February 1794, expressing Mary's grateful thanks for all his kindness to her, which she signed 'M.B.'. A second letter from the Reverend John Baron, forwarded by William Temple, enclosed a receipt for five pounds, also signed by Mary. A note from Baron recorded her good conduct since her return to Fowey. On 13 October 1794 Boswell, writing to his brother David on the subject of his finances, asked him to pay five pounds into the account of 'the Reverend John Baron of Lostwithiel, Cornwall, as he takes charge of paying the gratuity to Mary Broad'. Again he received a receipt, this time dated 1 November of that year. On that occasion, the receipt was sent direct from Lostwithiel and again it bears Mary's own 'M.B.'.

Boswell died soon afterwards and his family swiftly cancelled the annuity. The receipt of 1 November is the last certain record we have of Mary's existence.

What happened next is conjecture. Within two or three years of her return, there is no trace of her living in Fowey, nor of William and Grace. They disappear from the town records and none of them is buried in the parish. The Puckeys, however, continued to live there and flourish.

It is unlikely that Mary would have been treated then as she might have been now, when, no doubt, she would be the local celebrity. She would have found it hard to gain any acceptance from such a small community, in a county itself isolated from the rest of England. Fingers would have been pointed, there would have been endless gossip. Any man who showed an interest in her, supposing she wished to marry again, would soon have been fully informed of her past, if he did not know it already.

It seems possible, if the Broads really did come into some money, that they took the opportunity to move elsewhere. It might be that William, Grace and Mary bought a small property between them, or that Mary went off on her own and made a home for herself, although there is no record to this effect. Just as there is no trace of them in Fowey, there is none in any of the surrounding parishes within a wide radius.

However, a number of researchers have pointed to a Mary Bryant who appears in the register of the parish of Breage, near Helston, forty miles further south along the coast. All the researchers tend to dismiss her as not being the same Mary Bryant on the grounds that she would then have been forty-two. However, in the records it is noted that on 9, 16 and 23 August 1807 banns of marriage were published between Richard Thomas 'of this parish' and Mary Bryant 'also of this parish'. What makes the entry slightly unusual is that most women – but not all – are described either as 'spinsters' or 'widows'. Mary Bryant is not described as either. Was this because, if this was our Mary, no one knew for certain if her Australian marriage was valid and so did not know how to describe her?

The marriage entry is dated 13 October 1807 and the register is signed, in the presence of the curate Mr Herring, by Richard Thomas and Mary Bryant, with her mark. This Mary Bryant also could not write.

For someone who wanted to remain in her home county, the southern end of Cornwall was a fair choice. Forty miles along bad roads made Mount's Bay and the Lizard peninsula almost another country. She could quite well have lived there without anyone knowing anything at all about her past, especially if she had some money of her own.

A search in the register of baptisms produced nothing for several years, which is odd, if Richard and Mary Thomas were an ordinary young couple and were still living in Breage parish. But then, on 7 April 1811, there is an entry for the baptism of a child, Mary Anne, daughter of Richard and Mary Thomas of Breage. Past researchers never got as far as looking under 'births'; again, presumably, because of Mary's age. If this was, indeed, our Mary Bryant, she would have been forty-six and at the edge of her childbearing years, but it is not all that uncommon for women, then or now, to give birth to a perfectly healthy child at that age and we know that her physical constitution must have been extremely robust. In July 1812 there is another baptism entry for a daughter, Elizabeth, but she must have died immediately since she appears straightaway in the deaths register, where her age is given as '00 years', which suggests either a stillbirth or a perinatal death.

Drawing on obstetric knowledge, rather than academic, it might well mean that this was an older woman who might not have conceived for some time but then had what would have been called in Cornwall then, and much later, 'a change baby', that is, a baby conceived on the menopause when there is an upswing in hormonal changes. This would also account for there being no other traceable child born to Richard and Mary Thomas.

For at least the next fifteen years the Thomases appear to have lived in the same area – and survived – as did Mary Anne. She must have lived at least to the age of fifteen, possibly for a normal lifespan.

I would like to think that this is, indeed, our own Mary Bryant, and that she finally lived out her life in a good relationship, in this most beautiful part of her home county, and with a surviving child to compensate, in part, for the deaths of Charlotte and Emmanuel. But I emphasize, there is no proof. Professor Pottle hoped that somehow or other she had emigrated to America as she would have made a splendid pioneer.

★

BOSWELL WAS as good as his word in continuing to press for the release of the other escaped convicts who were confined in Newgate. Nine days after the mugging which had caused him such serious injury, he wrote again to Evan Nepean, from his bed, begging that nothing be done with these 'unfortunate men' until he could talk again both with him and with Governor Phillip, who had arrived in England some three weeks earlier and had immediately been pounced on by Boswell, asking for clemency.

On 17 August 1793 he visited the men in Newgate 'to assure them personally that I was doing all in my power for them'. He never let up and finally, on 2 November, all four were released. The first thing they did was walk to Great Portland Street to thank Boswell for all he had done for them.

Boswell never fully recovered from the attack made on him and this, coupled with the way he had abused his own health, particularly with heavy drinking, brought about a severe decline. He was far from well throughout the summer of 1794, on some occasions only dragging himself out of his home to attend the trial of Warren Hastings, as an observer, a trial which he considered to be a miscarriage of justice.

He then seems to have regained his health a little, for early in 1795 he resumed his social round but on 13 April, while visiting the Literary Club, he collapsed and had to be carried home as he was unable to walk. He never went out again. He recovered sufficiently to write to members of his family and to his great friend, William Temple (himself recovering from a riding accident), warning them that his end was near. His doctor diagnosed 'a swelling on his bladder, which had mortified'. He was in great pain. He died on 19 May 1795 attended at his bedside by his brother David, his sons Alexander and James, and his daughters Veronica and Euphemia. Veronica had acted as his devoted nurse.

THE LIFE of Watkin Tench, now a Captain, continues to read like something from a swashbuckling novel. On his return from

New South Wales, he was posted to the Channel Fleet. In the June of 1793 there occurred what the French rightly describe as 'le désastre de Quiberon'. Only the office-bound military could have conceived of such a scheme. The Bretons, increasingly disaffected with the way the Revolution was proceeding, were encouraged to rise and throw off their Paris yoke and the English government agreed to back a band of some five thousand French émigrés who wished to join them. The insane choice of a landing place was Quiberon, on the tip of a peninsula some eleven kilometres long and less than half a kilometre across at its widest point; at its narrowest, it is only the width of a road. The French force was backed up by the English warships of the Channel Fleet.

The result was inevitable. The émigrés marched up the peninsula like lambs to the slaughter, and slaughtered they were, along with thousands of 'Chouans' (members of the Breton resistance) who had joined them. They walked straight into the arms of thousands of crack French troops, the 'Blues', under the command of General Hoche, many of whom were based at Fort Penthievre, about halfway up the Quiberon peninsula, and which has total control over the peninsula in both directions. Those that did not die in battle were taken prisoner, some 6200 in all. Many of these were lined up and shot, either in the town of Auray or in the surrounding villages. The youngest was a boy of fourteen, the oldest a man of eighty. (Following the enormous storm which hit the western coast of France in 1989, the skeleton of a young woman was found on the beach near Quiberon. She had died from a musket wound and had either joined the men in the uprising or had been executed afterwards.)

It is a pity Watkin Tench did not leave his views on this débâcle, which he must have observed at close hand. He was soon to have the opportunity of seeing even more of France.

After the Quiberon uprising, the government decided there should be a continuing British naval presence off the coast of Brittany. Tench was now serving on the HMS *Alexander*, a ship of the line carrying seventy-four guns. The weather was bad and she had become separated from the rest of the Channel Fleet when she found herself attacked by three French 'seventy-fours'. For several hours the men on the *Alexander* succeeded in beating off two of the enemy vessels, but on sighting the arrival of an entire French squadron she 'struck her colours' to the third ship. By this time, according to naval reports, 'she had lost her main yard, spanker boom, and all three top gallant yards' and had sustained multiple damage elsewhere. Forty members of the crew were either dead or dying.

The survivors were taken off by the French and put into a prisoner-of-war camp in Brittany, possibly that in Audierne. One source says that Tench made a daring escape across Brittany to Roscoff, stole a boat and sailed home. Another, that he was so well regarded by his captors that he was given parole until he was exchanged in May 1795. During his imprisonment he kept a diary, extracts from which were published in 1796. He then continued serving with the Channel Fleet until 1802.

He retired, a Major-General, in 1816, but three years later was restored to the active list as Commandant of the Plymouth Division where he stayed until his final retirement in 1827.

After his imprisonment in France he married Anna Maria, daughter of a naval surgeon, Robert Sargent of Devonport. They had no children of their own but in 1821 they adopted the four children of his sister-in-law, when her husband, a naval captain, died in the West Indies. He lived until 7 May 1833, his wife surviving him some fourteen years. Apart from his journals and his naval record, we know nothing else about him.

His capture in France resulted in his second term of imprisonment as a prisoner-of-war. He must have thought of Mary Bryant while he was there. Perhaps, following her example, he did at least make an attempt at escape.

A lover of liberty and a believer in the rights of man, I can best end by repeating his own words on the escaped convicts: 'I confess that I never looked at these people without pity and astonishment. They had miscarried in a heroic struggle for liberty; after having combated every hardship and conquered every difficulty.'

OF THE FOUR convicts imprisoned in Newgate with Mary, John Butcher, alias Samuel Broom, had made his own efforts to obtain his freedom. He wrote to Dundas on 23 January 1793 saying that he was willing to return to Botany Bay 'on proper terms'. He pointed out that as he had been brought up 'in the thorough knowledge of all kinds of land and capable of bringing indifferent lands to perfection,' he should be given the opportunity of proving this, and of his worth to the new colony, by providing them with food. Even on his release, the government did not take up his offer so he enlisted as a private in the New South Wales Corps, returned to New South Wales, and was eventually granted twenty-five acres in the district of Petersham Hill in 1795.

It is not known what happened to the other three, apart from the fact that James Martin gave his *Memorandum* to Jeremy Bentham. One imagines him returning to Ireland and dining out on his experiences for the rest of his life.

The neurotic Lieutenant Ralph Clark returned home to his beloved and perfect Betsey Alicia. She must have had a lot to live up to. Whether he ever told her of his fall from grace with Mary Branham or that he had left behind a daughter, named after her, is unknown. He never referred to either in his diaries.

On his return, Clark was posted to Chatham, then to the West Indies where he joined HMS *Sceptre*, along with his son, 'Ralphie'. The boy, listed as a midshipman, was only eleven years old. Both saw action at sea, on one occasion resulting in the capture of several French ships. Clark wrote to Betsey Alicia that there would be prize money, even little Ralph being likely to receive forty pounds. However, Clark contracted dysentery while on shore leave, then, while being sent to accept the surrender of a French outpost, he was shot and wounded by a sniper. He was taken back on board the *Sceptre*, where young

Ralph was already in the sickbay suffering from yellow fever; both died on the same day. Even more bizarre, neither could have known that Betsey Alicia had died of puerperal fever in the Marine Hospital in Chatham, on or about the same day, following a stillbirth. Clark may, however, have descendants in Australia. Mary Branham eventually received her freedom and disappeared with her daughter, Alicia, into the unknown.

Bibliography

ABBREVIATIONS:

BL   British Library
DL   Dixon Library, Sydney, Australia
ML   Mitchell Library, Sydney, Australia
PRO   Public Record Office

MANUSCRIPT SOURCES

Journals, Diaries, Accounts and Correspondence

Bligh, Captain William, *Unpublished Journals*. ML

Bowes-Smyth, Arthur, *Journal of a Voyage to N.S. Wales in the 'Lady Penrhyn' 1786–89*. ML Safe 1/15 Sydney

Bradley, William R. N., *Journal 1786–1792* ML Safe 1/4 Sydney

Easty, John, *A Memorandum of a Voyage from England to Botany Bay in the 'Scarborough' Transport. 1986–1793*. DL

Gardner, Lieut. John, *Account of the Voyage of HMS Gorgon from England to Australia and return to England, 1791–1792*. BL

King, Philip Gidley, *Journal, Norfolk Island (1791–1794)*. MS1687. ML

Martin, James, *Memorandums*, London University Library. Bentham 16. ff.11719–204.

Southwell, Daniel, *Journal and Seven Letters*. BL

GENERAL PAPERS CONSULTED

Annual Register of Events, 1786 Vol. 28; 1792 Vol. 34

Bentham Papers, London University Library

Bonwick Transcripts, ML

Burney Collection, BL

Colonial Archives, Algemeen Rijksarchief, The Hague. Letters, Nos. 3831. pp. 8, 9, 32.33.

Historical Records of New South Wales Part II Vol. 1. ML

Macarthur Papers ML
New South Wales Entry Books, CO202, CO360, CO369. ML
Newgate Calendar (ed. J. Robins). Vol. 3 1825
Public Record Office: Assizes 5/144. Gaol Book 23/8 for Western
    Circuit; Assizes 24/26 Transportation Orders

FIRST SOURCE MATERIAL

Contemporary books, and/or books giving details of their authors'
personal experiences of the period, pamphlets and newspaper articles.

Boswell, James, *Papers, Journal 18* (ed. Professor F. Pottle). London,
    1934
    Letters of James Boswell (ed. J. Tinker). Oxford, 1924
Clark, Lieut. Ralph, *Journals and Letters 1787–1791*. Sydney, 1981
Collins, Captain David, *An Account of the English Colony in New South
    Wales*, 2 Vols. London, 1798 and 1802
    Dublin Chronicle, 21 July 1792
Edwards, Captain Edward, *Voyage of the HMS Pandora* (ed. Basil
    Thomson). London, 1915
    Papers PRO XC/B 3561 ADM 1/1763
    Gaol Book 23/8 Western Circuit ASSI 23/8 William Bryant
    ASSI 24/26 Mary Broad
Hamilton, George, *A Voyage Around the World*. London, 1793
    London Chronicle, 3 July 1792
    Pardon of Mary Bryant Correspondence and Warrants Entry
    Book. NO 13/9 f.221 PRO.
    Newgate Register H.O. 25/26 p.57
    Parish records of Boconnoc, Fowey, Lostwithiel, Breage. Corn-
    wall County Record Office
Phillip, Arthur, *Voyage to Botany Bay*. London, 1789
    Sherborne Mercury, 20 March 1984, 3 April 1786, 18 July 1791, 17
    December 1792, 4 June 1793, 4 July 1793
Tench, Watkin, *Narrative of the Expedition to Botany Bay*. London, 1789
    Complete Account of the Settlement at Port Jackson in New South Wales.
    London, 1793
    Sydney's First Four Years. Sydney, 1961

White, Surgeon-General James, *Journal of a Voyage to N.S. Wales.* London, 1793

SECOND SOURCE

Alford, Katrina, *Production of Reproduction? An Economic History of Women in Australia 1788–1850.* Melbourne, 1984

Bateson, Charles, *The Convict Ships.* Sydney, 1974

Beddoes, Deirdre, *Welsh Convict Women.* Barry, Wales. 1979

Clark, C. M H., *A History of Australia*, four volumes, Melbourne, 1962–1978

    (ed.) *Sources of Australian History.* London, 1957

    (ed.) *Select Documents in Australian History 1787–1850.* Sydney, 1977

    The Origins of the Convicts Transported to Eastern Australia 1787–1852. HS vol 7, nos 26–27 May–June 1965

Cobley, John *Sydney Cove 1788.* London, 1962

    Sydney Cove 1789–1790. Sydney, 1963

    Sydney Cove 1791–1792. Sydney, 1965

    The Crimes of the First Fleet Convicts. Sydney, 1970

Currey, C. H., *Transportation, Escape and Pardoning of Mary Bryant.* Sydney, 1963

Dixson, Miriam, *The Real Matilda.* Sydney, 1976

Donkin, Nancy, *The Women Were There.* Blackburn (Victoria), 1988

Forsyth, W. D., *Governor Arthur's Convict System* , London, 1935

Hughes, Robert, *The Fatal Shore.* London, 1987

Ingleton, Geoff, *True Patriots All.* Sydney, 1952

Inglis, Brian, *Poverty and the Industrial Revolution.* London, 1971

Jenkins, A. K. Hamilton, *Cornwall and Its People.* London, 1945

Johnson, W. B., *English Prison Hulks.* London, 1957

Pottle, Professor Frederick, *Boswell and the Girl from Botany Bay,* Address to Elizabethan Club. Yale, 1932

Ragvenes, Y., *La Chouannerie Bretonne, Les Emigrés et l'affaire de Quiberon.* 1989

Rawson, Geoffrey, *Strange Case of Mary Bryant* (semi-fiction). Sydney, 1938

Robson, L., *Convict Settlers of Australia.* Melbourne, 1981

Rowe, John, *Cornwall in the Age of the Industrial Revolution.* Liverpool University, 1953

Rumsey, H. J., *Pioneers of Sydney Cove*. Sydney, 1937

Shaw A. G. L. *Convicts and the Colonies: A Study of Penal Transportation*. London, 1966

Summers, Anne, *Damned Whores and God's Police*. London, 1975

Thomson, E. P., *Making of the English Working Class*. London, 1963

Williams, Raymond, *The Country and the City*. London, 1985
   Culture and Society 1780–1950. London, 1958

Index